AND LINCOLNSHIRE As Surveyed Delineated and Humbly

d Surveyor and teacher of the Mathematicks &css The Explanation of the Map or Plan Fo

Scale numbred 55 110 160 & shews you the distance in yards from one part of the Town to any part of the same. For if you fix your Eyes upon any
...es in Yards. But if you have a mind to be yet more curious you may take the distance of any two Places with a pair of Compasses and
...and to know the distance in Feet **Multiply** the number of Chains (contained betwixed the said distances) by 66 (the feet in one chaine) and the
...account for the parts of Squares that are in the same, how many whole Squares they make then add them to the number of whol
...from is the Area of the same. Note each Square that is formed by the Parallel Lines all over the Map **contains two Ro**
...Francis Duke of Buccleuchs. All other things relating to the Said Plan are explained & entertained within the Same   Ano Domini 173
...mbers and Patron of the Gentlemens Society there

THE North East View of the Conventual Church Built about the year of our Lord 1050

THE South West View of the Town Hall and Record Room Built about the Year of our Lord 1620

A View of Some Remains of the Priors Prison Now called the Oven Built about the Year of our Lord 1230

THE North East Prospect of Some Remains of the Priory Built in the year 1300

AYSCOUGH FEE HALL Built by Sʳ Richard Aldwyn Merchᵗ of the Staple About 1420

THE High Bridge Formerly of three Stone Arches with a View of the Old Oratory and Societys Museum

---

LINAE   GYRVIORUM

Peterb SPALDINGLÆ Spaldinge Spaldynge Spalding by Ingulphus, Petr Bles & Others Continuers of his History SPALDYNG & SPALDING by Camden, Dugdale, Spelman,
...ung from Thence, as author of Amity, Pleasure Peace & Plenty, having ye same day weekly devoted to Her by ye Pagan Saxons & Romans, as by the Arabians, Indians & other Eastern Nations
...ylonda enclosed round about with Riverlets & Draines a Fairer Town (says Dʳ Holland in his Transl of Cam Brit) than a Man would look to find in this Isl'd &c. According
...ng in ye Mercian Kingdom & ye Estate of Thorold of Bokenhale Lievtenant of Lincolnshᵉ he founded a cell here; Upon the Norman Conquest ye King gave it with ye Remaines of ye Mercian
...f Quality & distinction) interr'd near the High Alter of the Conventual Church greatly Augmenting ye Number of Monks & their Revenue, Subjecting the to his Abbey of St Nicholas at
...ᵈ to Parlam 49 H3 was a Justice in Eyre for Essex &c rebuilt the Great Gate Porta Maxima Prioratus, & Porters Lodge at ye End of ye Granaries (Dugd Clavicularium) Wᵐ Lytelyart Lᵈ Prior wᵗʰ
...rch of ye Staple & Ladys Chapell now ye Free Grammar School abᵗ 1315 in wᶜʰ year 24 Octᵇ the 1ᵗ P. received & entertained H 9 & 2ᵈ At his Court in a Splendid manner at his Priory here
...here, now commonly called the Oven, from its form in ye Flons Conded Sentenced here were kept till their Execution abᵗ which ye famous ordinance was made in the Priorat of John IV 1405 Who
...dings Castells were bestowed on Cha Brandon Duke of Suffolk of whom ye Townsmen & others purchased them Spalding is a Creek to the Port of Boston, accordᵍ to ye Book of Rates & Molloy
...site is an Handsom Town Hall & Record Room built abᵗ 1620 by Jn Hobson Esq at his own expence, wherein the Sessions of Sewers & of ye Peace, & ye Lords Courts are held & ye Town business is done

ASPECTS of SPALDING

Front cover: Photograph c. 1900, looking south over "High Bridge" and the River Welland.

Back cover: Emily Kate Parkinson at the wheel of her Benz motor car 24th February 1901.

Front endpaper: John Grundy's Map of 1732.
Rear endpaper: "Environs of Spalding" c.1890.

ASPECTS of SPALDING

LIMITED FIRST EDITION (1986).

ASPECTS
of
SPALDING
1790 - 1930

in words and photographs by
NORMAN LEVERITT & MICHAEL J. ELSDEN

CHAMELEON INTERNATIONAL

SPALDING   LINCOLNSHIRE   ENGLAND

MCMLXXXVI

Dedications

To Rosemary for all her encouragement and help in pursuance of my interests.

Michael J. Elsden

To the memory of my parents - William and Elsie Leveritt.

Norman Leveritt

Published by
Chameleon International,
Spalding, Lincolnshire, England.

Designed and Typeset by
Speedprint Design,
The Crescent, Spalding, Lincolnshire.

Bound by
Woolnough Bookbinding,
Irthlingborough, Northamptonshire.

© Copyright N. Leveritt, M. J. Elsden and Chameleon International.

All right reserved. No part of this book may be reproduced, stored in a retrieval system or transmitted in any form or by any means, electronic, electrostatic, magnetic tape, mechanical, photocopying, recording or otherwise, without permission from the publisher.

ISBN 1 870149 00 9   (Limited First Edition)

ISBN 1 870149 01 7   (Special Edition)

Contents

DEDICATIONS	6
ACKNOWLEDGEMENTS	9
FOREWORD	11
PREFACE	13
SETTING THE SCENE	15
THE LIVING VEIN	19
RIVERSIDE MEANDER	35
TOWNSCAPE - SHEEPMARKET	59
HALL PLACE	67
MARKET PLACE	75
CATTLE MARKET	83
HORSE FAIR	87
TRADE AND COMMERCE	89
CHURCH AND CHAPEL	113
HIGH DAYS AND HOLIDAYS	155
IN THE PUBLIC EYE	163
TRANSPORT, RAIL & ROAD	181
EPILOGUE	189
BIBLIOGRAPHY	190
INDEX	191

"When found, make a note of".

Captain Cuttle.
(Dombey & Son. by Charles Dickens.)

Acknowledgments

The authors wish to thank the Council of the Spalding Gentlemen's Society who by allowing them unrestricted access to the archives in the possession of the Society enabled this volume to be produced.

They must also express their gratitude to successive editors of the Lincolnshire Free Press and Spalding Guardian who have allowed them to make extensive use of the files of these newspapers, a facility which has proved invaluable.

They also wish to thank Mr. J. T. Brindley, the Chief Executive of the South Holland District Council, who gave them permission to make extracts from the records of the former Spalding Improvement Commissioners and Spalding Urban District Council; Mr. J. S. Fordham, Headmaster of the Spalding Grammar School, for the use of material from "The Bentleian"; Mr. J. W. George, who generously made available his unpublished "History of the Spalding United Reformed Church"; the Rev. J. C. Moon, Vicar of St. John Baptist, Spalding, for information taken from the church guide book; the Rev. John W. Smith, Superintendent Minister of the Spalding Methodist Circuit, for the opportunity to use the extensive Methodist archives, now in the custody of the Spalding Gentlemen's Society; Mr. R. H. Lake and Mr. E. Whittaker, for details concerning the early years of the Spalding Christadelphian ecclesia; Mrs. J. Martin, for information regarding St. Norbert's Roman Catholic Church; the members of the Spalding Gentlemen's Society who have helped in all manner of ways, and finally to Mr. R. N. Whiston, President of The Spalding Gentlemen's Society, who kindly provided the introduction.

For all statements of fact, and expressions of opinion in the following pages the authors are alone responsible.

"You will find it a very good practice always to verify your references, sir!"

Dr. Routh (1755-1854).

Foreword

As President of the Spalding Gentlemen's Society I was delighted and honoured to be asked to write a foreword for this publication.

It enables me to pay a well earned tribute to the dedication of two of our most enthusiastic members, Norman Leveritt and Michael Elsden for their search into the many details of the Spalding scene which they have now captured, by photograph and description to form a valuable permanent record.

It is strange that buildings, when once demolished, seem to fade quickly from memory. I have often wondered why old Holyrood House, with its pleasant Georgian elevation and which figures on quite a number of paintings and drawings, is our only recollection of this building. We know from the demolition records that basically this was originally a half-timbered Jacobean house with a characteristic "jetty", or over-hanging first floor. We also know that it was altered to its final form about 1780 by Fairfax Johnson, Maurice Johnson's grandson. It is our loss that there does not appear to have been any drawing, painting or illustration recording for posterity the original design of the house.

It is therefore fortunate that by the publication of this work such omissions cannot happen again. Here we have a full representation of the Spalding scene with its interesting buildings, not all of them architectural gems, but each playing its part in the life of the town.

This is a valuable collection and we must be grateful to the authors for the care they have shown and the time and labour they have spent in providing us with such a splendid permanent visual and graphic description of the Spalding environment both past and present.

I wish them every success with this Publication.

R. N. Whiston

"Knowledge advances by steps, and not by leaps".

Lord Macaulay.

Preface

In 1940, Harry Gooch, published "A History of Spalding", which contained the result of much research, and which has been and still is very frequently consulted by all who are interested in the history of the town and district. At the time of publication the author realised how much more information still remained to be discovered, and some time later thought of issuing a revised edition. Unfortunately he was unable to accomplish this task.

Since then a number of publications dealing with different aspects of the history of the town have appeared. Among them "Spalding An Industrial History", by Neil Wright, "700 years in the life of Spalding Parish Church", edited by Marion Brassington, and "Bulbs in Britain. A Century of Growing", by Reg Dobbs.

The present volume broadly covers the period from the 1790's to the 1930's. In it the authors have tried to convey, by word and illustration, something of the atmosphere of the life of the town and its people in a totally different era, to record something of its history, and to revive the memory of some of its bygone worthies.

Forty-six years ago Harry Gooch wrote that the collection of material of interest appertaining to his native town had been a 'pleasing hobby'. The present authors can make the same claim, and in this book endeavour to share some of their discoveries with a wider public.

They are conscious of how much more remains to be discovered - of how much more research remains to be done. In this connection they would appeal to all who are interested in the history of the town to make every effort to collect and preserve written, documentary and photographic material relating to its past, for in the course of their work they have become sadly aware of how much of importance has been lost or destroyed.

Spalding,
August, 1986.

Norman Leveritt
Michael J. Elsden

Setting the Scene

The reminiscences of Mrs. Smalley - from an interview with the "Free Press", about 1940.

Spalding's Sea-Faring Days

It is not many, if any, local residents who can claim to have an old sea-faring captain buried in their garden but this can be made by Mrs. J.B. Smalley, of Albion Street, Spalding, who celebrated her 94th birthday recently.

Mrs. Smalley is remarkably alert and in spite of her great age is still able to fulfil the majority of normal household duties. In addition she knits at least two pairs of socks each week and the afternoon following her birthday saw her helping at a local jumble sale.

Eldest daughter of the late Mr. and Mrs. Ellis Pannell, of the Shipyard, Marsh Road, Spalding, Mrs. Smalley has lived for a good deal of her life by the side of the River Welland and can tell a wonderful story of the flourishing old river trade carried on at one time.

Days of Big Ships

She tells of the days when Albion Street was overhung with glorious old elm trees and formed a rope walk, and the bigger vessels turned round opposite the Vine Inn, in fact the more widely excavated river at this point is still visible. The biggest ship she could remember was the schooner W.S. Howard, and in addition to other schooners, lighters, sailing vessels and billyboys plied to and fro.

She remembers the cobbled fish market at the foot of High Bridge and that over 60 years ago, the most convenient manner for the majority of Crowland residents to come to Spalding market was on a barge which discharged its passengers at the steps still visible at the top of Vine Street. (below)

Many Large Cranes

There were several big cranes along by the river and large boats came right up to the High Bridge. Numerous vessels unloaded near where Messrs. Groom's woodyards is. There was an exceptionally big crane on the river bank opposite "The Limes", in Double Street and, said Mrs. Smalley, Herring Lane became so named because of the large amount of fish which were sold along there. There were towing paths on each side of the river all the way to Fosdyke and horses could pull lighters and barges right down to the sea.

She was married in 1870 by the Rev. J. C. Jones, Baptist Minister, and recalls that on the morning of the wedding there were nineteen vessels moored between their house and High Bridge and to celebrate the event her father was called upon to supply half a gallon of ale to each vessel.

The town in those days, she said, was full of inns and public houses especially along by the river where nearly every house was inhabited by either a ships captain or a member of the crew of a ship.

Water's Purity

The only drinking water available at the Albion Street end of the town then was from a pit in Spalding Marsh or out of the river after the tide had gone down. All such water had, of course, to be filtered. The first tap to be put in that part of the town was outside the residence of Mr. Maples (Willesby House), and this was later moved across the road and for several years stood on the river bank, under an elm tree.

Mrs. Smalley well remembers how the Chain Bridge was at one time just a set of chains across the river over which people could walk if they so desired. The present bridge was put there as the result of some children getting drowned whilst trying to cross the river.

Evolution of Transport

The evolution of transport has come well within the life of Mrs. Smalley. From the river traffic she went on to recall other means of getting about in the good old days. There was no road from Spalding to Deeping; it was necessary to go on the Crowland Bank. Motor cars were non-existent. The early railways had just been completed, at least the Peterborough to Boston via Spalding section. She recalled that when she went from Spalding to Boston by train she had to travel in an open truck, with seats around the side, not as good as a modern cattle truck. The old station at Spalding was a very little place, she added.

The London coach, drawn by two grey horses, used to arrive in the Market Place and the time they departed to and from Wisbech each day - 8.30 a.m. and 1.30 p.m. - served as a clock for residents en route.

Mrs. Smalley has a wonderful retentive memory and could talk for several hours upon various aspects of old Spalding.

New Cattle Market Agitation

Among the many other things she recalled was a move about seventy years ago, to have Spalding cattle market, in the exact spot where it is situated today, which was defeated after the town had been canvassed as the result of agitation by the late Mr. Major Shadford. It was maintained that to take the cattle market from the streets would result in a great loss of trade to the shops.

There was hardly a shop in the whole of the town then, said Mrs. Smalley, where the proprietor did not live over the premises. Bridge Street was even narrower than it is today. In Hall Place there stood the old Town Hall with accommodation underneath for old market stalls etc. It was demolished about 1852. (1854 sic).

About 1880 there was only one house in Pennygate and if one stood where Halfords is now situated, (corner of Swan Street), apart from two thatched cottages on the site now occupied by Mr. C. Wheatman's house, there was a clear view to far beyond what is now Hawthorn Bank. The town in those days consisted of the Cowbit and London Roads, High Street, Commercial Road, Marsh Rails Road, Westlode Street, Pinchbeck Street, Hall Place, Market Place and Bridge Street.

The Quakers

A great religious body in the town in her early days were the Quakers, who also owned a considerable amount of property. The Quaker women wore long grey cloaks, grey poke bonnets and white frills, and the men large Quaker hats. They had an unusual meeting place, in addition to the present Quaker Chapel, it was in Marsh Rails Road, and known as the Folly. There was a large orchard and in the middle of it a mound completely surrounded by water, with a special meeting place on the top of the mound, with large church shaped windows.(1)

There were no boots and shoes bought ready made. "I was like many others", she said, "made my own boot tops from felt, or soft leather if it could be got. These were then taken to a shoemaker who fitted soles".

Then there was the old gosherd, who went about buying geese and used to drive them all the way to Ipswich market along the roads. He performed this task each week.

No Cemetery

There was no cemetery, where it is today. Funerals still took place in Spalding Parish Churchyard, where her eldest sister is buried. People were also buried in later years in the grounds of the Baptist and Congregational Chapels. There were then no hearses for funerals. The coffin was carried by professional bearers who wore black habits with hoods on their heads for grown-ups and white gloves and hoods for children. There would be relays of three teams if the coffin had to be carried a considerable distance.

Buried in Garden

This led Mrs. Smalley to recall that the former occupant of her own house, a Captain Stanley Jackson, was buried in the garden. The stone slab which bore date of death, 1842, and inscription, is still in the garden, although now reversed. He directed that unless his wife agreed to his being buried in the garden she should be left penniless. The house later was let free, but to be kept in repair by the master of the old Free School at Spalding and for many years after Mrs. Smalley lived in the house, the old schoolroom, attended by some present Spalding residents, was at the end of the garden. This interview with Mrs. Smalley would not be complete without reference to the remarkable amount of knitting she has completed in her time. In the last war she worked magnificently for the soldiers, and is doing her share in this war. In addition she has completed a considerable amount of work for various bazaars from time to time organised by the Spalding Division of the St. John Ambulance Brigade and the Congregational Chapel.

(1). *There was no Quaker meeting house in Marsh Rails Road. These were the pleasure grounds of William Massey (1763-1846). They covered about 2 acres and were laid out in the early 19th century. They were known as the 'Islands'. A small cottage with castellated battlements and Gothic windows was erected on the estate. In later years the place was known as "Mr. Massey's folly", and the cottage as "The Folley". William Massey, was a very prominent member of the Society of Friends, and noted for his extensive charity. He spent much time in these grounds, and this doubtless gave rise to the mistaken idea that it was a place of worship.*

Page 15: Photograph from 1900, looking south towards "High Bridge".
Note the steps down to the water at the end of Vine Street.

Overleaf: North towards "High Bridge". From an engraving by Hilkiah Burgess, published in 1823.

To the Inhabitants of Spalding in the County of Lincoln this View of
SPALDING HIGH-BRIDGE &c.
Is most respectfully inscribed by their much obliged & humble Servant Millicent Burgess.

Drawn & Engraved by H.Burgess.

The Living Vein

High Bridge

"A bridge at Spalding has existed for a very long period. It is stated that the Romans built a bridge here to carry their main road across the Welland.

In the reign of Richard I, in an order made as to disafforesting the marshes, they are described as extending to the 'great bridge of Spalding'. In a Commission sent by the King in 1324 to make enquiry and to view the banks and sewers in Holland, it was presented 'that the great bridge, called Spalding brigge, was then broken and ought to be repaired at the charges of the whole town'. At the Survey of the Fens made by order of King James (1605), the bridge over the Welland at Spalding is mentioned. In 1642, the bridge is described as being of great antiquity, and as 'twelve foote in the waterway and five foote deepe', and 'the stone pillar or pier in the midst thereof which supported the two arches', as having been 'lately removed by the drainers of Deeping Fen, when they widened the river'. In the Deeping Fen Act of 1661, the Adventurers are required forthwith to build 'the great bridge over Spalding River, commonly called the High Bridge, of lime and stone".

W.H. Wheeler, "A History of the Fens of South Lincolnshire &c. &c.". 2nd. edition. Boston. 1896. pages 448 - 449.

Above: The River Welland, Spalding, 1827. From a watercolour by Hilkiah Burgess (1775 - 1868), Spalding Gentlemen's Society's collection.

This shows the warehouses at the southern end of Double Street near High Bridge. On the right the "Ship" warehouse.

Two photographs about 1900 showing timber being delivered to George Burdett, timber merchant, High Street. On the right in the lower picture, the "Ship", warehouse, (Double Street), of Hallam & Blackbourn, grocers, Market Place.

The well known engraving by Hilkiah Burgess, dated 1823, (page 18) depicts a wooden bridge. By 1837 this was in a very dangerous state, and it was decided by the Adventurers of Deeping Fen to erect a new stone bridge.

The foundation stone was laid on 28th June, 1838, the day of Queen Victoria's coronation.

"The Lincolnshire Chronicle", of 6th July, 1838, reported -

'The first stone of the new bridge at Spalding was laid on the coronation day by Mr. Langworth, the architect, but the attention of the people was so occupied by the processions of the Sunday Schools, that the ceremony passed almost unnoticed, except by the workmen engaged at the bridge'.

On the 19th October the same paper noted that -

'The contractors for the new stone bridge at Spalding, Messrs. Woodston & Collins, are indefatigable in their exertions in forwarding the works, which are in rapid progress: the arch will be turned in a few days'.

The stone used is said to have been salvaged from the sunken churches along the Yorkshire coast between Spurn Head and Hornsea.

When the bridge was opened, by Theophilus Fairfax Johnson, it was named 'Coronation Bridge', but the name never seems to have gained general acceptance, and it has always been known as 'High Bridge'.

Albion Brewery

The brewery which was built in 1824, was the property of John Richard Carter (1790 - 1864), of Spalding, solicitor and brewer, who sold it in 1846 to Henry Bugg the Younger and William Henry Bugg, of Spalding, brewers.

Later the premises were used as a guano store, and in 1890 were purchased by Lee & Green, mineral water manufacturers.

Below: From a watercolour of 1827 by Hilkiah Burgess. Showing the brewery and "Chain Bridge".

Chain Bridge. 1827.

A footbridge, named Chain Bridge, is marked on John Grundy's 1732 Map of Spalding. In 1844 "after successive conflicts with vessel masts, (it was finally worsted in the struggle" (1), and replaced by a swing footbridge, named Albert Bridge, built by John Capps at a cost of about £300. This too has now gone, and been replaced by a single-span concrete bridge.

Below: From a watercolour by Hilkiah Burgess (1775-1868). Spalding Gentlemen's Society's collection.

Chain Bridge crossed the river at the bottom of High Street. It had a double drawbridge swung on chains. The illustration shows the drawbridge raised to allow a barge to pass through.

(1). *"Spalding Sixty Years Ago". A Reminiscence. by G.F. Barrell. 1897.*

Pannell's Boat Yard

In 1822, John Pannell, was landlord of the 'Jolly Crispin' Inn, which was near Chain Bridge, and it was there he commenced the boat building and carpentry business which was carried on by his family for 120 years.

In the pre-railway days there was a flourishing trade on the River Welland and it was not considered unusual for as many as forty small vessels - sloops, ketches, schooners, brigs and lighters - to be counted on the river at one time between Fosdyke and Spalding High Bridge.

There was evidently a lack of provision for the proper repair of such craft, and on 17th April, 1837, the owners and captains of vessels trading up the River Welland sent a petition to the trustees of the Outfall of the River Welland asking them to allow John Pannell to lay down a slip in the River Welland bank for hauling up vessels for the purposes of repair. Permission was granted and the slip duly laid down.

At times the yards of Messrs. Pannell and Smith Dring (the latter owned an adjoining yard), were hives of industry and gave regular work to a number of men. On occasions there were vessels waiting their turn for repairs, and small boats were put together on the upper floor of the shed.

Spalding enjoyed an extensive carrying and coasting trade in corn, wool, coal, timber &c., until the opening of the Great Northern Railway, in 1848, which eventually absorbed a great portion of the river traffic. The need to maintain the river for drainage purposes enabled the river trade to continue to some extent, and in 1896 the river was still navigable for vessels of 120 tons, and some trade in coal, oil-cake and timber carried on.

John Pannell, who died in 1843, was succeeded in the business by his son, Ellis Pannell. He died in 1877, and was followed by his son, John Ellis Pannell, who died in 1888, aged 39. His brother, Joseph Ellis 'Joe' Pannell then took over the family business. He died in 1942, aged 78.

The River Welland - A Winter Scene looking towards Chain Bridge.

"Stayed on the homeward voyage", a photograph by Frank Parkinson taken during 1903.
A view from High Street.

Curiosity

'American' or 'Colonial' houses on Commercial Road by the side of the river. The same building can be seen in the lower photograph of the previous page.

Steamer Aground 1908

The SS Mistley of Harwich, a large iron steamer, aground near to the spot where the West Elloe Bridge now crosses the river. In the background can be seen Pannell's boatyard.

The vessel was proceeding up the river to discharge a cargo when she was stranded by the receding tide. The Mistley was much larger than any vessel that had previously navigated the Welland, and at the spot where it stranded, the current, being impeded, rushed with great force on either side of the steamer, considerably undermining the banks, large portions of which were carried away. A large hole was also made in the bed of the river. To assist the Mistley to refloat a quantity of the cargo was unloaded and carted to Spalding by means of waggons. The incident attracted many visitors from the town to see the unusual sight.

Gas Works

The Spalding Gas Works were erected in Albion Street by George Malam in 1832, the foundation stone being laid by Theophilus Fairfax Johnson (1790 - 1853), on the 8th of June in that year. In 1841 George Malam became bankrupt, and the undertaking was purchased by Messrs. Ashley Maples of Spalding, and William Crosskill, of Beverley. In 1856 they were supplying consumers at the rate of 6s. 3d. per 1000 cubic feet. In 1862 the works were purchased by the Spalding Improvement Commissioners from the proprietors for £13,700. The Emgas yard occupies the same site today. (Next to Willesby House.)

Above: The new large Retort House was opened in 1898 and the photograph is thought to record the official opening. Prominent local personalities on the platform are thought to include - from left to right:-

2.	George Hall, auctioneer and valuer;
3.	Major Shadford, chemist;
4.	G.F. Birch, corn merchant;
5.	E.I.R. Stapleton, builder;
7.	J.T. White, bulb grower;
9.	J.T. Atton, stonemason;
13.	Fred Sly, farmer;
14.	Martin Taylor, market gardener;
15.	Andrew Aitken, farmer.

Opposite above: Coal being unloaded at the Gas Works about 1900. The timber wharf behind the barge can still be seen today.
Below: An engraving showing the Gas Works, the large Retort House being apparent on the right. In front of it, along the riverside, can be seen the ropewalk of William Hames (1819 - 1907).

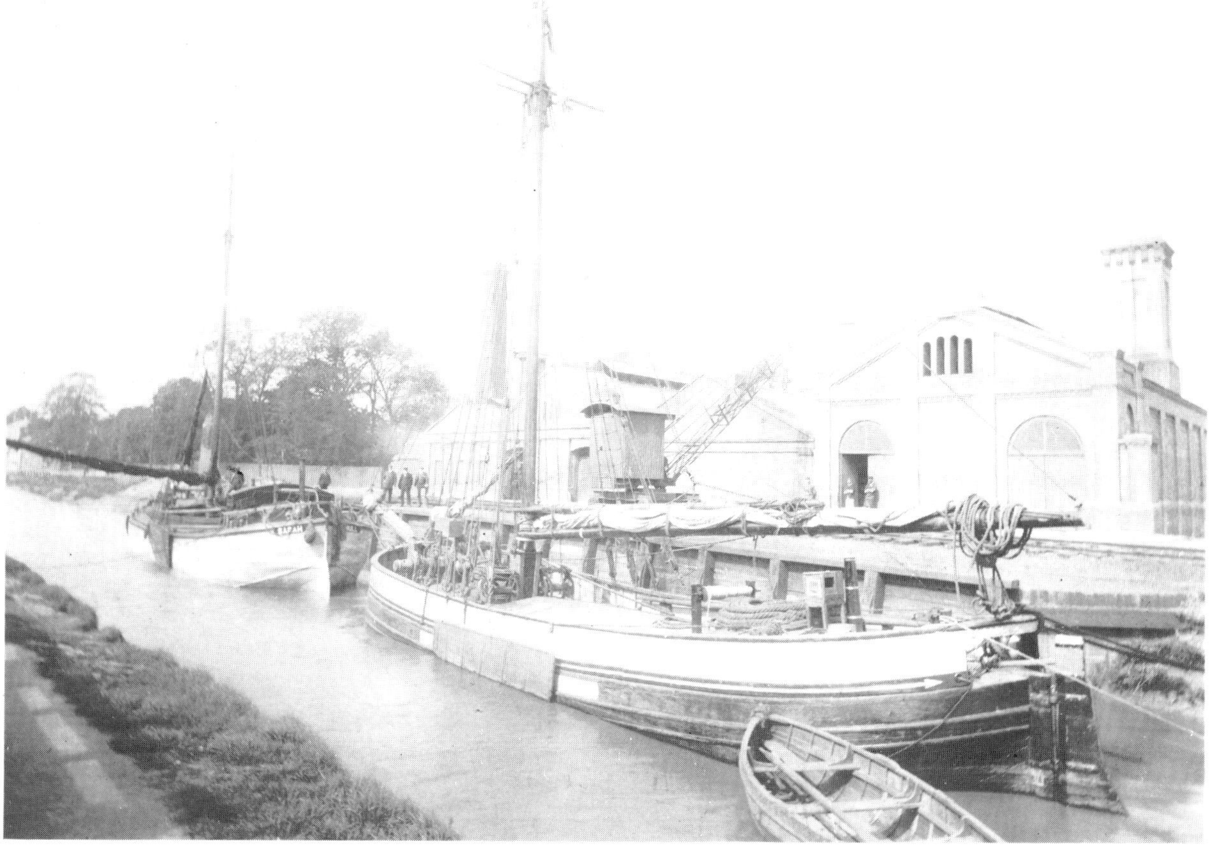

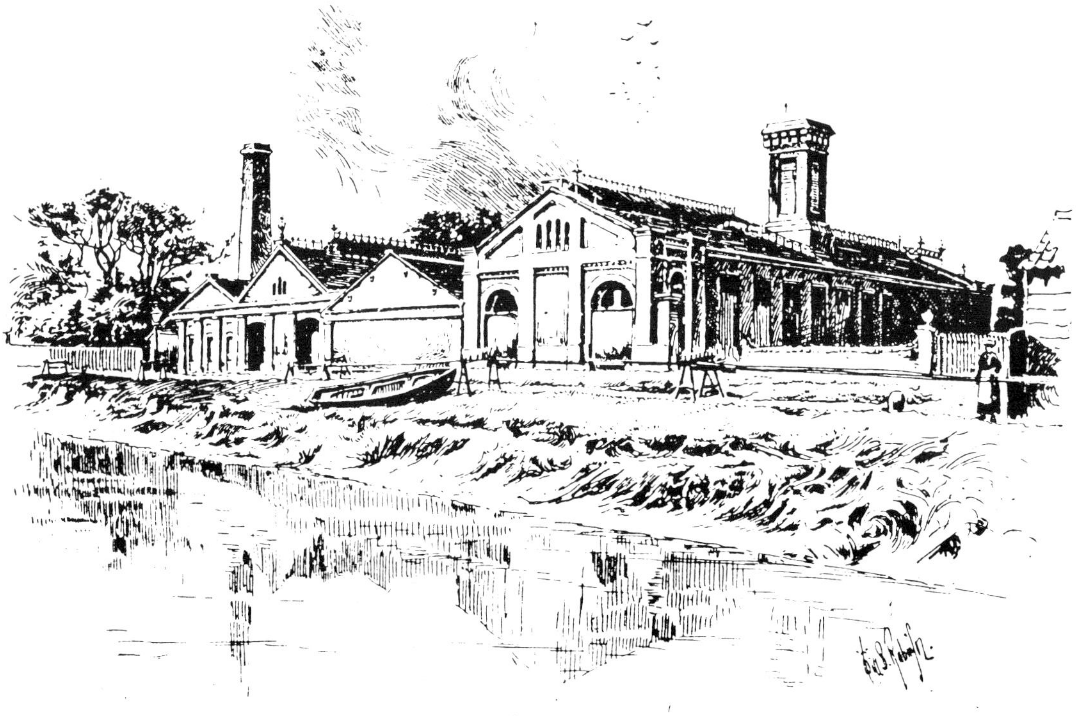

Little London Bridge

The bridge itself had previously served to carry the railway line over the Welland, on to Holbeach. It was replaced in the 1890's when it became necessary to carry a double line of track. At the request of the Spalding Improvement Commissioners the old bridge was removed and re-erected as a road bridge near to Lock's Mill, being a gift to the parish by the Midland and Great Northern Railway Company. Up to this time, with the exception of footbridges, High Bridge had been the only other bridge over the river at Spalding.

The work was carried out under the direction of Mr. Cave, manager for the engineeers, Handysides, of Derby. It was reported that not a single hitch had occured during the course of erection.

It was damaged during the severe floods of 1947, and subsequently replaced by the present structure.

This page and next four photographs:- Erection of Little London or Locks Mill Bridge, 1895.

The Opening of Little London Bridge

The opening of the new bridge over the Welland near Little London, Spalding, on Wednesday evening last (July 3rd, 1895), excited a good deal of interest. Although the weather was dull and rain fell during the ceremony, there were at least five hundred persons present. The bridge had been appropriately decorated with bunting by the road surveyor and his men under the superintendence of Councillors Atton and Enderby.

Five pair-horse carriages conveyed the following gentlemen to the scene:

> Mr. S. Kingston (Chairman of the Council);
> Mr. W. H. Mills J.P. (Vice Chairman);
> Mr. M. Shadford (Chairman of the expired Improvement Board);
> Mr. H.H. Harvey (Clerk to these bodies);
> Messrs. G. Hall, G.F. Birch, W.B. Lowden, J.T. Atton,
> W. Jepson, E.W. Gooch, A. Aitken, G. Sly, F. Sly,
> H. L. Enderby, S. R. Harper, J. Wilson & M. Taylor (Urban
> Councillors); and Messrs. H.M. Proctor and
> R. Hockney (late Improvement Commissioners).

The bridge was reached shortly about 6.30, and the first carriage was drawn in the centre, punctually to time, amid the hearty cheers of the assembled concourse and to the accompaniment of the raindrops.

There was peculiar appropriateness about the selection of Mr. Samuel Kingston to declare the new Lock's Mill Bridge open. All his business life has been spent in Spalding; for twenty years he was a member of the extinct Improvement Board which carried out the negotiations for the new bridge, he was one of the deputation which waited upon the Railway Company and urged the granting of the boon, and he is the first Chairman of the new Urban Council which now takes over the bridge.

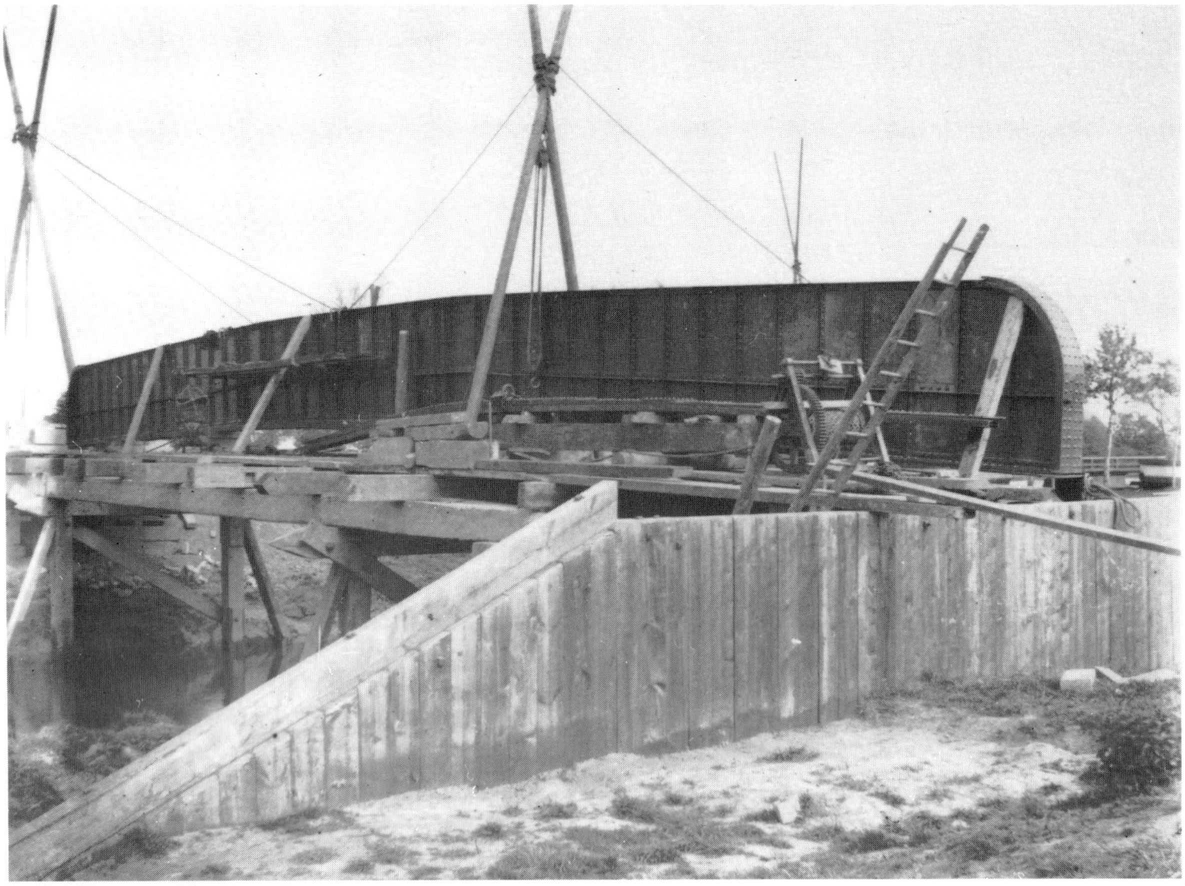

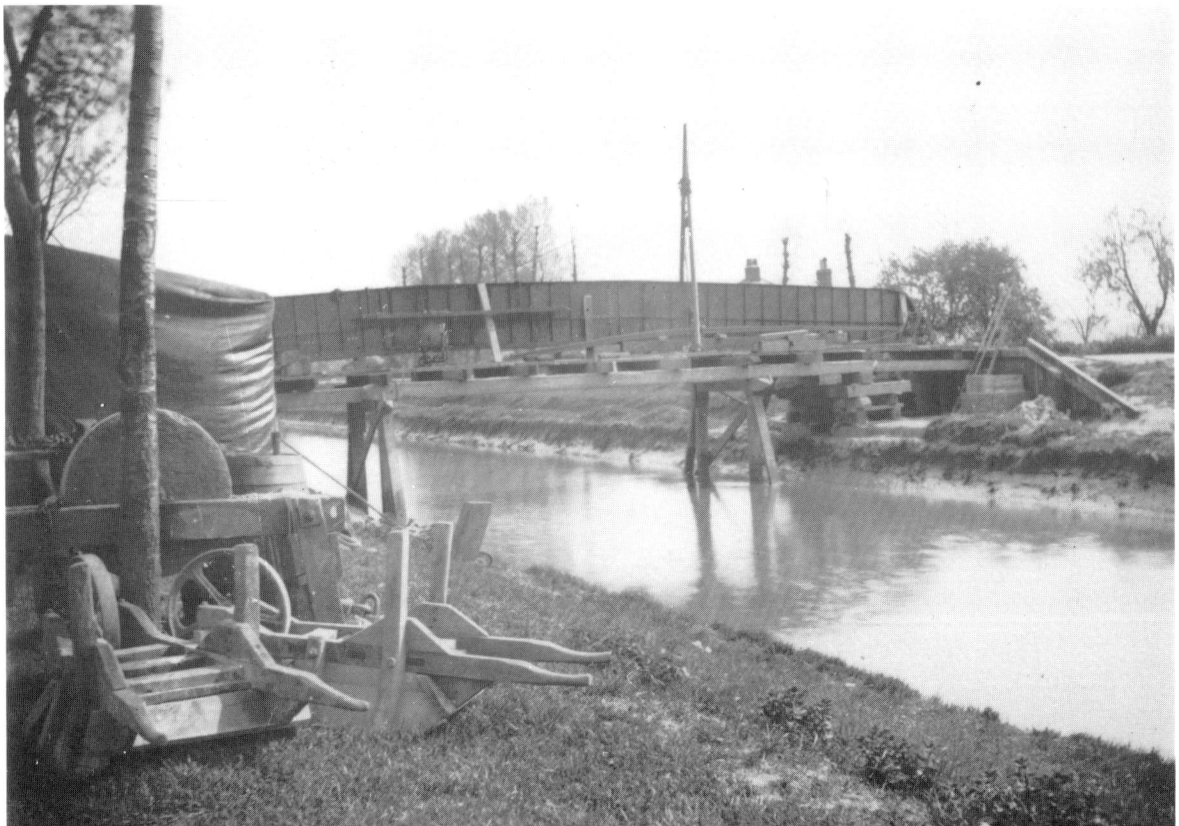

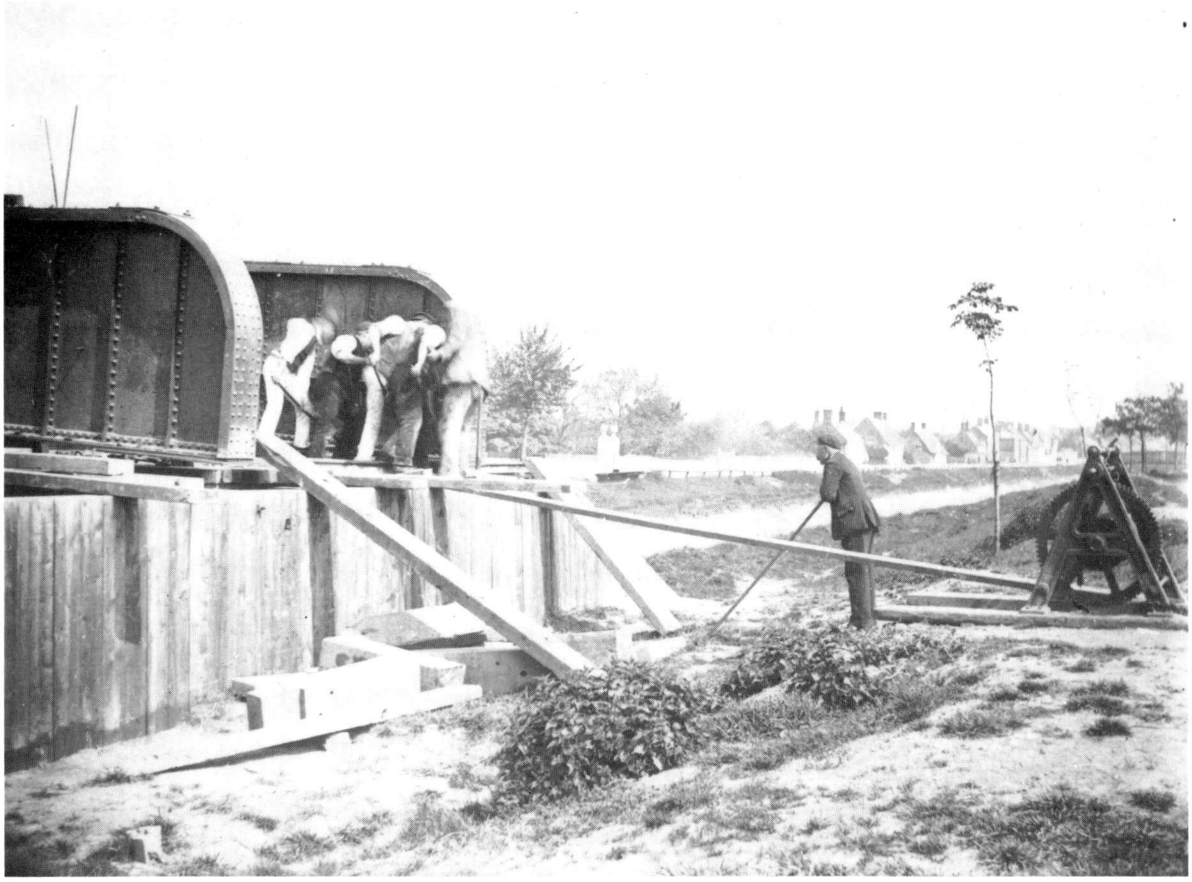

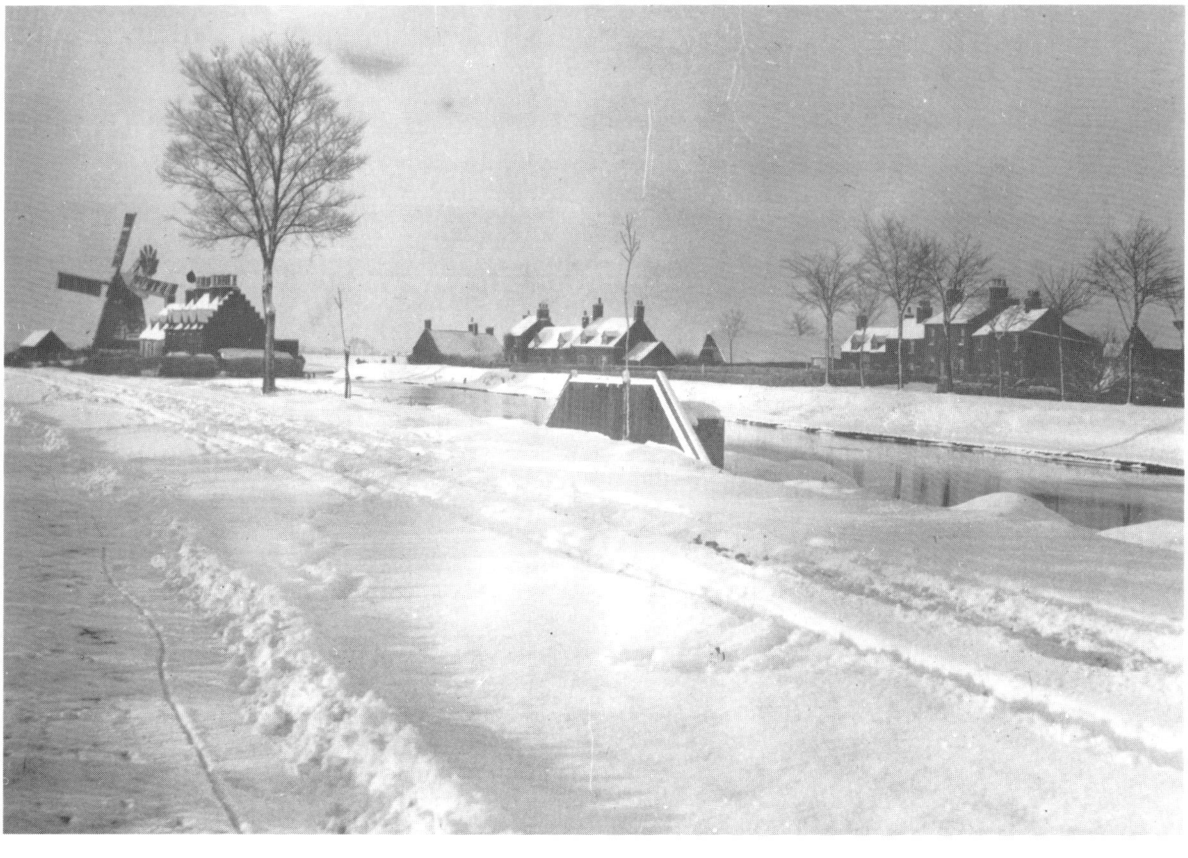

Lock's Mill, on St. Catherine's Island, Cowbit Road

Canon Moore in a lecture entitled "The History and Recollections of Spalding" (1885) stated that the Mill was so called because 'at this spot on the river were constructed, by Captain Perry in 1726, pointing doors and a lock for navigation purposes, as well as for protecting the river from being silted up and destroying the drainage'. Captain John Perry had been extensively employed by Csar Peter the Great of Russia as Comptroller of the Maritime Works in that country until 1710. In 1716 he published 'An account of Russia', and in it referred to his friend, Mr. Goodfellow, English Consul at Moscow in 1706. Canon Moore suggested that Mr. Goodfellow may have been associated with Captain Perry in reclaiming the Fens, his name being perpetuated in the Goodfellow's School in Spalding Common, which was erected in 1871, at a cost of £1,600.

The Mill was not a very powerful one, but worked two pairs of stones, and it was at times kept going night and day in order to cope with the brisk business which then prevailed. The largest quantity of flour ground at Lock's Mill in any one year is recorded at 800 quarters, and this was only accomplished by the mill being worked days and nights, and on Sundays whenever there was wind. It was a favourite subject for artists and photographers. It was demolished in 1899, being then described as the oldest mill in this district. The materials and fittings when disposed of realised about £19.

Previous page: A winterly scene thought to be during the severe winter of 1895. Part of the construction for the base of the new bridge can be seen in the foreground.

Below: Spalding Locks and Cowbit Wash in the distance. From a watercolour by Hilkiah Burgess, 1827. Spalding Gentlemen's Society's collection.

More than forty years later (April, 1869) it was reported that 'Cowbit and Crowland Washes have been flooded for a longer period this winter than for many years past, being at this time covered with water nearly to the Lock's Mill' (South Holland Magazine. April, 1869).

Opposite top: The Mill and cottages taken from the water's edge on St. Catherine's Island.

Opposite below: A similar photograph taken from the opposite direction about 1899.

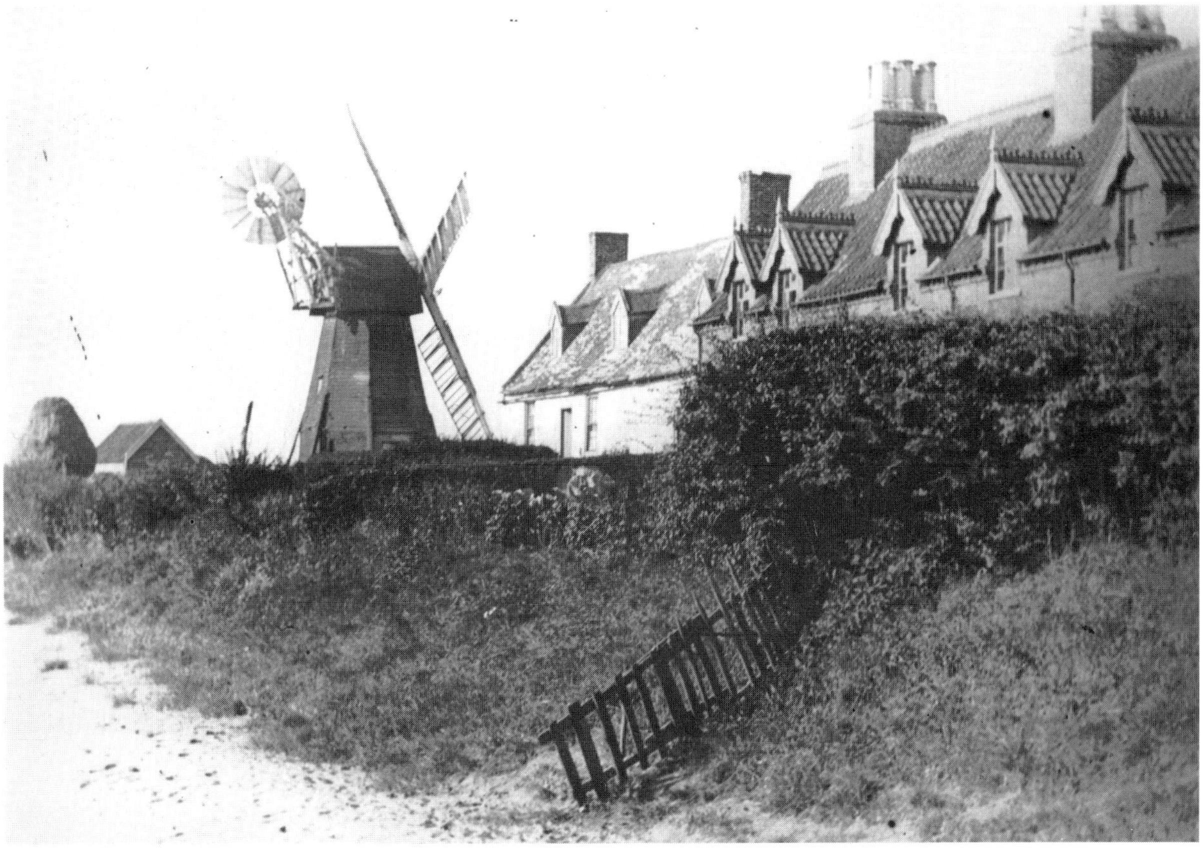

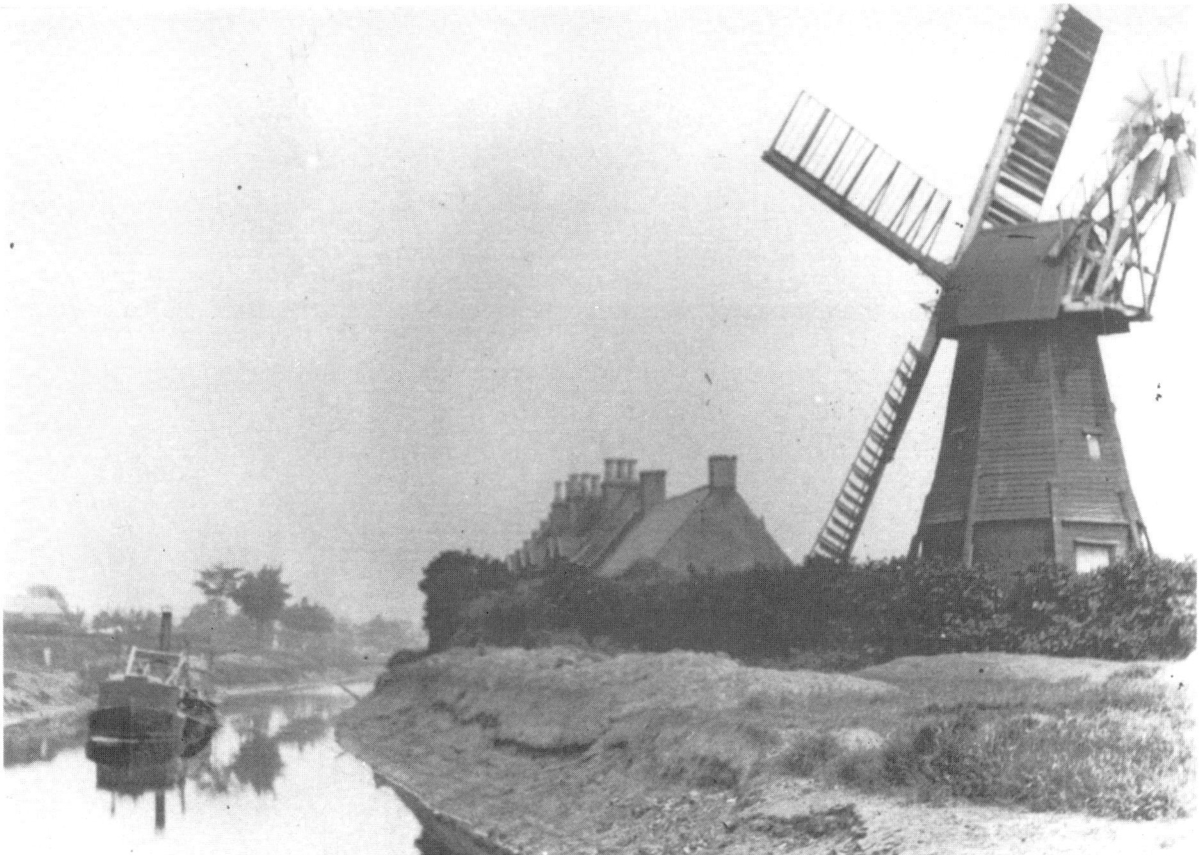

Victoria Bridge

John Grundy's map of Spalding (1732 - see endpaper), shows a footbridge in existence at this point over the river. It is thought to have been erected by public subscription, towards which Dr. Dinham was the principal contributor. It is believed that the bridge was at that time built more immediately for his private accommodation and that of patients visiting him, than for the use of the public at large, it having been erected just opposite his house, and always known as Dinham's Bridge.

In 1809 being in a 'ruinous and dangerous state', it was repaired at the expense of the Vestry. It again became very dilapidated, and on 9th July, 1835, the Surveyors of the Highways were instructed to stop it up altogether. It was rebuilt in 1837, and then called Victoria Bridge - that being the year the Queen came to the throne. 'Old Robin' Harmstone records that "In the year 1837, a fine showy and commodious suspension bridge of cast iron, cast by Tuxford and Sons, Boston, by subscription at a cost of about £300, was erected on the site of the old wooden Dr. Dinham's bridge; it fell on Sunday night January 26th, 1845, about eight o'clock, with a tremendous crash, being very windy and a large tide, and an unusual quantity of boats on the river, which it was expected, ran against the bridge and broke the stays; a new bridge has been built in its place by Mr. John Capps, at a cost of about £100".(1) The present footbridge was constructed in 1868.

(1). *"Notices of Remarkable Events and Curious Facts, with various and interesting scraps connected with The History and Antiquities of Spalding, in the County of Lincoln, and the places adjacent. Collected and Treasured in Memory by "Old Robin Harmstone". Spalding. Printed by Joseph Ashwell, Bridge Street. 1848.*

Riverside Meander

Ayscoughfee Hall

Ayscoughfee Hall, Spalding. 1818. From a watercolour by Hilkiah Burgess (1775-1868). Spalding Gentlemen's Society's collection.

The home of the Revd. Dr. Maurice Johnson, J.P., (1756 - 1834), Vicar of Spalding 1782 - 1825, and of Moulton from 1780. He was also a Deputy-Lieutenant of Lincolnshire, Chairman of the South Holland Quarter Sessions, and President of Spalding Gentlemen's Society. He married, at Spalding, in 1779, Ann Elizabeth Buckworth (1752 - 1827), daughter of Theophilus Buckworth, High Sheriff of Lincolnshire, 1787. In 1807, their only daughter, Anne Elizabeth Johnson, was married at Spalding to William Moore (1784 - 1866). In 1811, the Revd. William Moore became Curate at Spalding, and ultimately succeeded his father-in-law as Vicar at Spalding in 1825 and at Moulton in 1834. He, too was Chairman of the South Holland Quarter Sessions, and President of the Spalding Gentlemen's Society.

January, 1868: Advertisement.

AYSCOUGHFEE HALL, SPALDING

To be LET on Lease,

THAT picturesque FAMILY MANSION known as Ayscoughfee Hall, SPALDING together with the Pleasure Ground, Garden, Green-house, Forcing-house, Pits, Ice-house, Stables, &c. The House contains dining, drawing, breakfast and billiard rooms, library, 6 best-bedrooms, 5 dressing-rooms, and 5 servants' bed-rooms, and suitable offices. In the Yard are Two Coach-houses, Stabling for 6 horses, Cow-houses, Piggery, and Dog Kennel. The House will be partially Furnished, and considering its character and the excellent condition in which it is, at a very reasonable Rent. About 32 Acres of fine Grass LAND may be taken with the House and the Right of Shooting over 1500 acres.

The House may be viewed on obtaining a written order from

J. and R. SWAN and BOURNE,
Solicitors, Lincoln.

The Owl Tower and Lake, Ayscoughfee Gardens

In 1848 'Old Robin' Harmstone, wrote 'The present owner and occupier, Maurice Johnson, Esquire, has built a very handsome tower at the head of the fish-pond, on four pillars, which is 50 feet high . . . . .'. In 1912 it consisted of a smoke-room, with a staircase leading to the owl-chamber, which was 'the resort of these birds at the present time'.

In 1918, Mrs. Barbara McLaren, widow of the Hon. F. W. S. McLaren, M.P., selected this site for the erection of the town's War Memorial.

In 1921 the tower was taken down, after an unsuccessful attempt to save it from demolition had been made by a number of prominent residents, including Councillors E. I. R. Stapleton, C. A. Banks, E. H. Gooch, and Dr. E. P. Farrow.

It was replaced by the present War Memorial, built to a design of Sir Edwin Lutyens, the famous architect, who designed the Cenotaph in Whitehall. The War Memorial was unveiled by General Sir Ian Hamilton on 7th June. 1922.

Ayscoughfee Hall and Gardens

In 1851 Maurice Johnson (1815 - 64), left his mansion of Ayscoughfee Hall, in which his family had resided for nearly 200 years, to live at Hotham Hall, near Hull. He later removed to Redgrave Hall and then to Benacre Hall in Suffolk. From thence he removed to Blundeston House, near Lowestoft, where he died in 1864, aged 49. Twice married, he was survived by his widow, Isabella Mary (Swan) Johnson (1826 - 1905), and four daughters. Although the Johnson family continued to own the property, they never again took up residence, and the Hall was let. The last tenant, from 1874 to 1896, was Charles Foster Bonner (1814 - 96), of Spalding, solicitor, for many years Chairman of the Spalding Improvement Commissioners.

In 1897 a proposal to acquire the Hall and Gardens as a permanent memorial of the Jubilee of Queen Victoria was brought forward. The inception of the scheme was due to the initiative of Samuel Kingston (1829 - 1905), of Spalding, auctioneer and valuer, the first Chairman of the Spalding Urban District Council. The proposal to purchase the estate was laid before a public meeting called to consider the scheme in May 1897. It was well received. Over £1,000 were raised as a result of a public subscription, and the remainder of the purchase money, which with legal costs, amounted to £1,100, was borrowed upon the personal security of a number of residents. Every effort was made to clear off the outstanding debt. This was finally achieved in time for the Trustees to hand over the property to the town free of debt on Coronation Day (August 9th, 1902). "It was an historic occasion, and Mr. S. Kingston, who handed over the keys to Mr. G. Hall, as the Chairman of the Urban Council for the year, was cordially thanked for the ability and success with which, despite unexpected difficulties he had piloted through the undertaking". (1)

The purchase money (£2,000) was by no means considered as representing the value of the estate, consideration having been paid to the fact that the Hall & gardens were being purchased for the benefit of the town. Amongst generous subscribers to the scheme were Samuel Kingston, W. S. Royce, E. W. Gooch, G. F. Birch, J. T. White, and many others. The original Trustees of the property were Messrs. S. Kingston, G. F. Birch, H. L. Enderby, E. W. Gooch, M. Taylor, and J. T. White; whilst the Committee of Management consisted of S. Kingston, Chairman; W. A. Southwell, Vice-Chairman; Messrs. J. T. Atton, G. F. Birch, H. L. Enderby, W. Fletcher, G. W. Ham, G. Hopper, M. Taylor, J. T. White, J. Wilson, E. T. Waring, T. C. Stubbs, H. White, W. White, G. Birch, H. Birch, A. V. Seymour, E. A. P. Seymour, with A. L. Seymour as Hon. Secretary.

'In the year 1904 it was proposed to convert Ayscoughfee Hall into a Free Library, and the expense of adapting the building for the purpose was offered to be defrayed by Mr. Andrew Carnegie, who promised a sum of £800 for that object, whilst there were also other generous offers in support of the project. Unfortunately, however, an objection was taken to the necessary rate for Free Library purposes - though it would not have exceeded 1d - and upon an informal poll of the parish in December, 1904, the proposal was negatived.' (2)

(1) & (2). *"Ayscoughfee and its History"*. Spalding Free Press Printing and Publishing Co. Ltd. 1912. pages 2 and 5.

The result of the Free Library Poll was as under:

Against the Library	773
For the Library	337
Majority against the Library	436

The poll was about fifty per cent of the total voters = the number of votes recorded being 1,110 out of 2,240.

"Spalding Free Press", of 6th December, 1904.

Right: The plaque commemorating the acquisition of Ayscoughfee Hall and Gardens for the use of the town.

Above: The Hall at the beginning of the Twentieth Century.

Below: As it is today. Note the tall chimneys have gone and the Magnolia grown considerably.

Holyrood House, Churchgate

Holyrood House was demolished in 1959, after being in existence for at least 450 years. During that time it has been the home of some of the town's most prominent inhabitants, and was from 1743 to 1755 the meeting place of the Spalding Gentlemen's Society.

It consisted of a main rectangular portion facing the river, with two wings - the so-called "Guildhall", at the north end, and an 18th century addition with staircase at the south.

The late T. W. (Bill) Townsend, of Spalding, a recognised authority on local history, who made a special study of the house, reached the conclusion that the house had been built about 1500, more probably a few years after the turn of the century than before. It was originally known as "Gayton House".

Sir William Rigdon (1558 - 1610), of Dowsby, built additional stone buildings and offices to the house, using timber and stone which belonged to the house of the Warden or Master of the Guild of the Blessed Virgin Mary and St. Thomas, which stood in the churchyard. It is more than probable that, when the "Guildhall", was added to the house, it was intended to be used as the kitchen and servants' quarters.

Gayton House - Fairfax House - Holyrood House. A magnificent façade covering earlier origins. Referred to by the President of the Gentlemen's Society in his Foreword.

In the 17th century the house was occupied by the Hobsons, a family who were great benefactors to the town. The estate then passed to Colonel Hales, and in 1684 it was purchased from him by William Ambler (1663 - 1727). William Ambler was an influential figure, being a magistrate and also deputy-lieutenant of the County. He was a feoffee of the Spalding Living, a Commissioner of the Court of Sewers, a Governor of the Spalding Grammar School and the Willesby School, and the first President of the Spalding Gentlemen's Society.

The house ultimately came into the possession of the Johnson family, by the marriage, in 1709, of Maurice Johnson 'the Antiquary', with Elizabeth, the daughter of William Ambler, who then resided in the house as owner. From 1743 to 1755 part of the house was used by the Spalding Gentlemen's Society as a meeting room and museum, for which they paid Maurice Johnson, the Secretary of the Society, and the owner of the premises, a rent of four pounds per annum.

Walter Johnson (1720 - 79), barrister-at-law, son of Maurice and Elizabeth (Ambler) Johnson, was the next to live at the house. He married Mary, daughter of Thomas Fairfax, of Fleet, and they had one son, Fairfax Johnson, (1753 - 1818). It was in Fairfax Johnson's time, about 1785, that the central

Venetian window was inserted, and the porch added. Fairfax Johnson left the house, and other estates, to his cousin and brother-in-law, the Revd. Walter Maurice Johnson (1757 - 1832), Vicar of Weston and Master of the Free Grammar School at Spalding who re-named the house 'Fairfax House'. For many years it was occupied by Miss Elizabeth Ann and Miss Mary Ann Johnson, daughters of the Revd. W. M. Johnson. They left by will, funds for the building and partial endowment of the Johnson Hospital. Miss E. A. Johnson died in 1872, and her sister in 1878. The house was purchased in 1878, by Fitzalan Howard (1844 - 1930), of Long Sutton, but then residing at Osborne House, Wisbech, for £2,200. He changed the name to 'Holyrood House'. The Howard family were the last resident owners. The house was demolished in 1959, and the Town Hall occupies the site today.

Haverfield House, London Road

Haverfield House, a white brick and stone house was built in the late 1870s for Alfred Hobson (1830 - 1905), of the firm of Hobson & Co., drapers. The architect was William Henry Mills (1838 - 1930), and the builder Stephen Dawson, both of Spalding. The laying out of the estate proved a costly affair, as several houses were bought and pulled down, and the public footpath known as Elm (or Vise's) Walk, close to the house, was closed, Alfred Hobson considerably widening and improving Haverfield Road as compensation. Altogether the place was estimated to have cost him £12,000.

It was Alfred Hobson's grandfather, William Hobson, who in 1790 founded the large drapery establishment in the Market Place. Alfred Hobson became a partner in the firm when about 22 years of age, and like his father and grandfather possessed a keen business instinct, and under his control the business undertaking developed considerably. The Hobson family were amongst those who were

Haverfield House in the late 1870s.

mainly instrumental in founding the Congregational (now the United Reformed) Church at Spalding about 1818, and were always closely associated with the cause, giving it consistent and generous support. Alfred Hobson was for many years a director of the Spalding Water Works Company, and at the time of his death was a Grammar School governor, a member of the Spalding Town Husbands, a Deacon of the Spalding Congregational Church, of which he had been a member for 56 years, and the only Nonconformist serving on the governing body of the Johnson Hospital. In politics he was a Liberal, but took no active part in political life. He several times declined a seat on the magisterial bench.

In 1907 the property was purchased by Edward Milne, of Rochdale, for £3,600. Edward Milne was the principal partner in the firm (Milne & Co.) which owned the Spalding pea factory. He resided at Haverfield for some years and made extensive improvements. He was succeeded by John Henry Bunting (1850 - 1933), a farmer and landowner, who played a prominent part in the public life of the town and district. He was thought to have purchased the property for about £7,000. The house was unoccupied following his death.

Haverfield being demolished in 1936.

In 1934 - 35 the Spalding Club Company considered the possibility of purchasing Haverfield, but at an extraordinary general meeting held in August 1935, the members decided against the proposal.

Haverfield was demolished in 1936, and the Odeon Theatre was erected on the site. The cinema was opened on 28th February, 1938, the opening ceremony being performed by Councillor J. H. Longstaff, J.P., then Chairman of the Spalding Urban District Council, who was supported by the Rev. Canon Basil G. Nicholas, M.A., Vicar of Spalding. There was a musical interlude given by the band of the 1st Battalion The Queen's Own Cameron Highlanders. The programme on the opening night consisted of:

                  Universal Talking News;
                  Mickey Mouse Cartoon 'Clock Cleaners'; and
                  'A Star is Born', with Frederic March and Janet Gaynor.

The cinema subsequently renamed the 'Classic', and the 'Gemini', is at the time of writing disused.

Above, below and opposite: Various views of the "White Horse", taken around the turn of the century.

The White Horse Inn

Built out of the materials of the former Benedictine Priory this is one of the oldest buildings in Spalding, and was known as Berguery House in the 17th century when it was occupied by William Willesby (1576 - 1631). It was William Willesby's son, Thomas Willesby (1618-82), who was the founder of the Petit or Willesby School at Spalding.

In 1732 it was known as "The George". In 1792 John Sills was the Landlord of the "White Horse". Succeeding Landlords whose names are known include John Turner, 1822, John Randall, 1826, Ann Wright, 1842 and 1846, Jeremiah Hardmeat, 1849, Christopher Coward, 1856, Charlotte Coward 1861 and 1863, and Edmund Dawson, 1868. At the end of the 19th century Thomas Drury was Licensee. He was a prominent official of the Spalding Licenced Victuallers Association, and also Surveyor of Highways for the Moulton and Weston district to the Spalding Rural District Council. He died in 1903, after being Landlord for ten years.

Welland Hall and Belvedere

Very little is known of the early history of Welland Hall. This fine Georgian mansion was, according to 'Old Robin' Harmstone, built by William Bailey, a Deeping Fen Farmer. It is thought the house was built, at least, in two stages, parts of the back being older than the front.

Documentary evidence, from the title deeds, prove that in 1836, the property had passed into the hands of Henry Hawkes (1779-1842).

The Hawkes family came from Norfolk during the second half of the 18th century, and eventually became the owners of considerable property in the town and district. William Hawkes (1719-86), was treasurer to the Adventurers of Deeping Fen, a post subsequently held by his nephew, Thomas Hawkes (1750-1800), who was also the first agent in Spalding for Garfit & Claypon's Bank of Boston.

During the 18th and early 19th century the Hawkes family were members of the Society of Friends (Quakers), and numerous references to them occur in the minutes of the Spalding and Wainfleet Monthly Meeting of the Society of Friends. Anne Hawkes (1719 - 1806), the wife of Thomas Hawkes (1710 - 84), came to Spalding from Norwich in 1783. She was a Quaker Minister, and is remembered as "a striking example of commendable zeal", in her attendance of meetings for worship and business.

In 1851 Henry Hawkes sold the hall, and what is now part of the Grammar School playing field to the "Eastern Counties Wisbech and Spalding Railway", for £8,000, also receiving £5,000 compensation "for the personal annoyance and inconvenience of compulsory eviction from his said Residence", sums which he was paid only after he had taken the Railway to the High Court of Chancery and won his case.

In 1872 it was in the occupation of Miss Sarah Ann Phillips, who had a Ladies' Day and Boarding School. For the first time the house was described as Welland Hall. In 1874 she purchased the property from the Railway Company, and remained in possession until 1899, having married Captain William Sanders Walter in 1876. In 1901 it was purchased by a Boston corn merchant, William Cooper, but remained a private school for girls until 1920. At Welland Hall in 1919 there were 80 girls, and of these

---

Welland Hall School for Girls,
SPALDING.

Principal - - - - **MISS PAGE, B.A. (London).**

*Lately Head Mistress of Dewsbury High School for Girls,
and formerly Mistress in Cheltenham Ladies' College and
Worcester High School for Girls.*

MISS PAGE is assisted by a highly efficient staff of trained and certificated resident mistresses and visiting teachers. Pupils are prepared for Cambridge Higher, Senior and Junior Local Examinations, R.A.M. and R.C.M., Local Centre and School Examinations, and Examinations of the Royal Drawing Society.

WELLAND HALL is a large country house specially adapted for a School, with large garden, playing field and gymnasium. Bursaries, value £15 and £3, are offered for competition at intervals to Girls under 13.

Full Particulars can be obtained from the Principal.

20 were boarders, but during that December the private school was to terminate its career, and the Principal, Miss Page, was to leave for New Zealand. In 1919 the Spalding Grammar School and the Holland County Council negotiated for the purchase of the hall so that the girls' school "could be continued there on higher and broader lines". In 1920 the house was sold to the Governors of the Grammar School, and later that year changed hands once more when the Governors of the Grammar School sold it to the Holland County Council. Since 1920 it has been the Spalding High School for Girls until 1984 when the remaining junior department finally joined the senior school at the Stonegate site.

Belvedere was built for J.T. White, by John Peake, of Spalding, and completed in 1900. John Thomas White was born at Yeovil, Somerset, on 27th September, 1847, the son of John White, contractor and drainage surveyor, who moved to Parson Drove. He was educated at Wisbech, and assisted his father in various river and railway contracts. In 1873 he purchased a fancy goods and marine store business in the Sheep Market at Spalding.

He was one of the pioneers of the bulb industry in Lincolnshire in the early 1880s, and no history of the small beginning of the industry at Spalding and its development would be complete without reference to the part he played in the making of it. Although engaged in an entirely different line of business his foresight led him to the belief that the soil of the Spalding district was peculiarly adapted to bulb-growing to supply the increasing cut flower demand, and as one of the pioneers he embarked in the culture of snowdrops, narcissi, daffodils and tulips, and the building of greenhouses to force them into bloom. Eventually the business of J.T. White & Son became one of the largest in the Spalding district. He was the largest bloom grower in the kingdom. About 1925 he retired from active participation in this business. In 1927 he was awarded the Victoria Medal of Honour by the Royal Horticultural Society - a fitting recognition of his pioneer work.

He was a member of the Spalding Urban District Council from 1896 to 1919, representing the West Ward, and served as Chairman from 1906 to 1908. He was also, for many years, a member of the Spalding Town Husbands, but declined to serve as a magistrate owing to partial deafness. In politics he was a Liberal, and was a deacon of the Spalding Baptist Church for about forty years. A total abstainer. He died, at Belvedere, on 21st May, 1930, aged 82.

The Royal Oak Inn

The "Royal Oak", is listed in White's Directory of Lincolnshire for 1826. Samuel Carey was then the Landlord. Other landlords have included Jas. Collins, 1842; Samuel Ogden, 1856; J. Vamplew, 1868; George Wright, 1876; Arthur Borrell, 1885; William Earl, 1905; and Walter Scampion, 1912.

The photograph taken in 1936 on Cowbit Road, shows the building prior to its demolition. The present public house being then in the course of erection can be seen in the background.

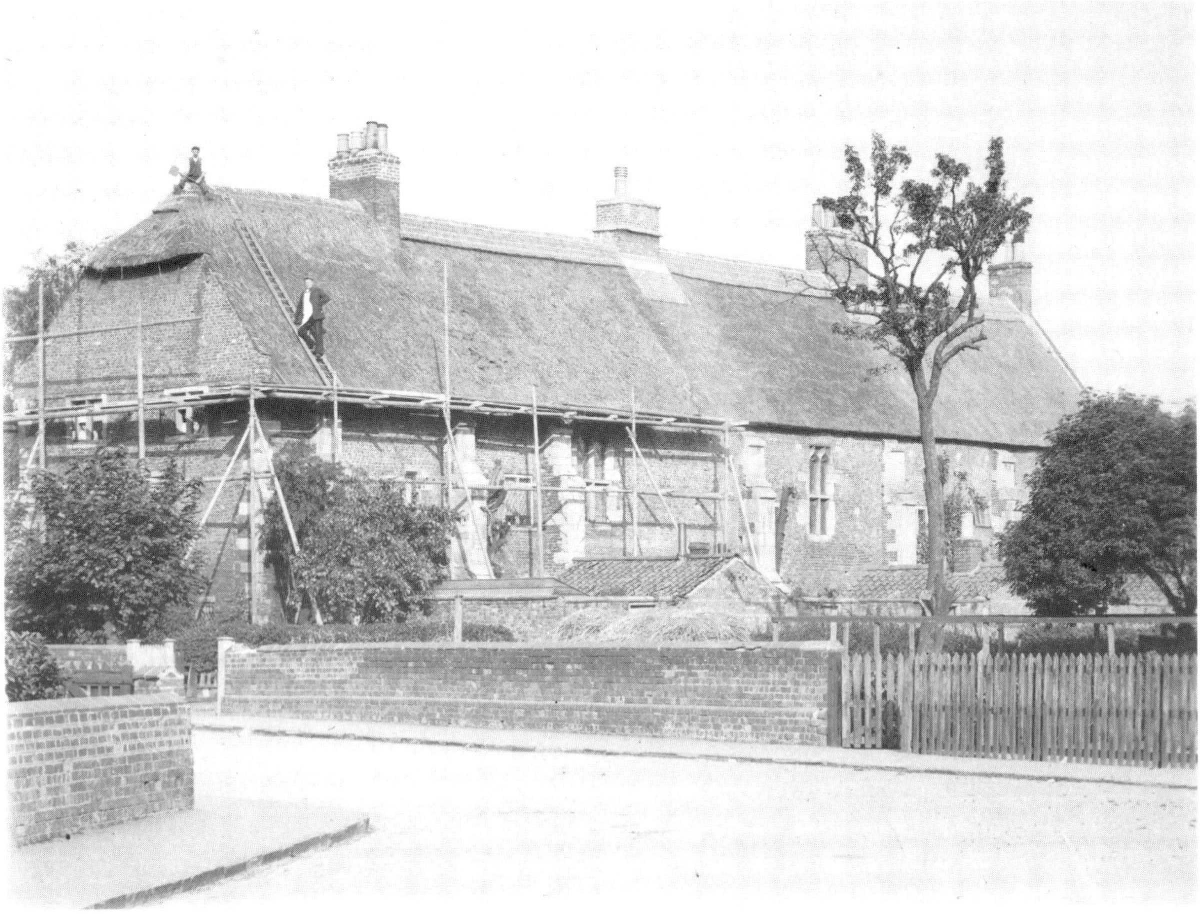

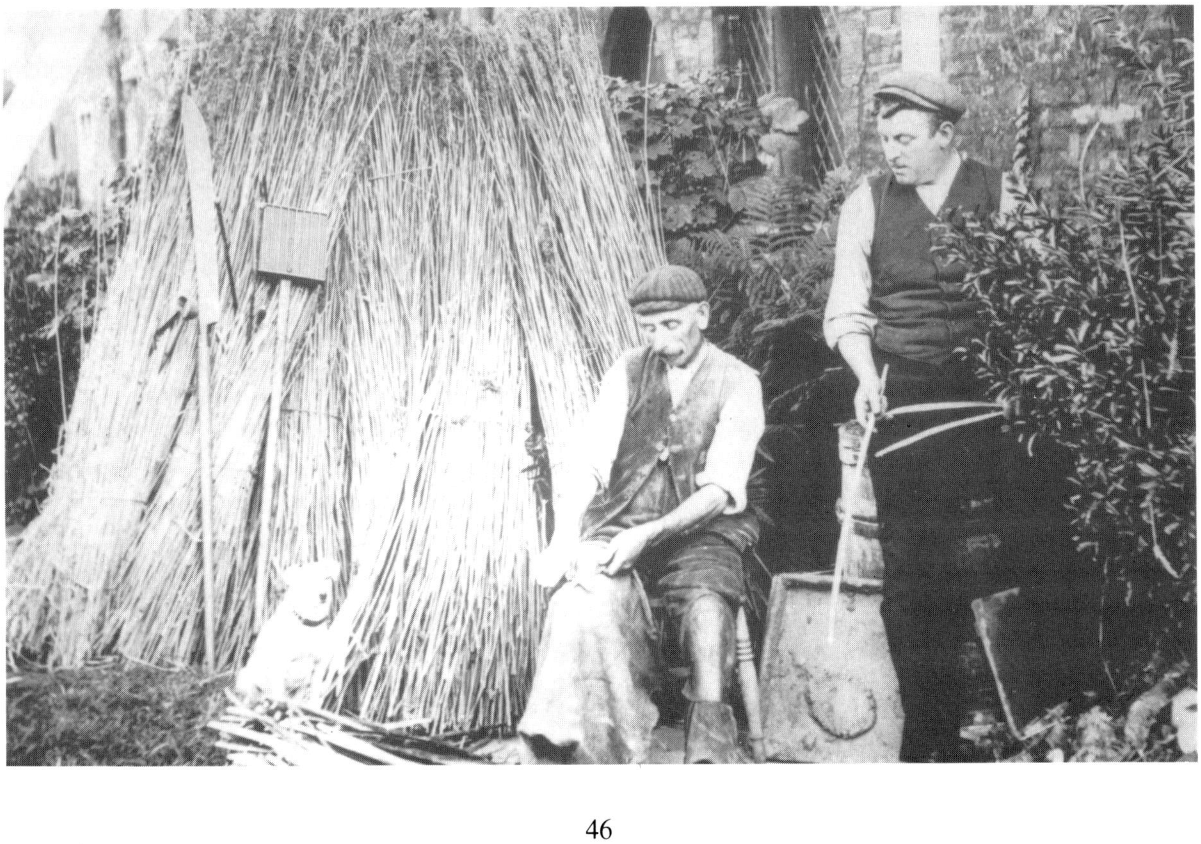

Thatching the Abbey Buildings 1908

Left above: John Scotney and his mate thatching the Abbey Buildings. The roof was said to be one of the largest thatched surfaces in the country, covering 5,000 square feet. The existing thatch, which was between 100 and 200 years old, was 16 inches thick, and all composed of reeds. 1,000 bundles of reeds, and 5,000 strips of willow were used.

The Abbey Buildings originally consisted of one large room, but were converted into separate dwellings about 1870. Previously it had been occupied by a market gardener who cultivated the land surrounding it.

On 13th June, 1873, the Spalding Improvement Commissioners 'Ordered that the Cottages in the Abbey Yard and belonging to the Revd. L. R. Ayre be designated by the name of The Old Priory and that they be numbered as a separate row'.

Opposite below: John Scotney and his mate preparing the willow strips used to fasten the reeds on the roof. When the strips were ready for use they were called "broaches". A photograph taken at the Abbey Buildings in 1908. With John Scotney is his little terrier which accompanied him wherever he went.

Reed thatching was a professional craft, and John Scotney, of Spalding, whose family had been thatchers for many generations, also carried out the Earl of Yarborough's thatching in the north of Lincolnshire.

John Scotney claimed that reeds were invaluable for thatching, lasting six times longer than straw, being far from inflammable - which was one of the chief arguments against thatching - and warmer than any other material.

Left: John Scotney cutting fenland reeds.
The "tools of the trade", can clearly be seen against the bundles of reeds in the background.

Star Public House, Cowbit Road

Below: The Star Public House, 1848. From a watercolour by Hilkiah Burgess (1775 - 1868).

This stood on Cowbit Road, next to Westbourne House (now No. 3 Cowbit Road), the residence of Joseph Henry Bugg, brewer and spirit merchant. (1) In 1842 John Pike was the landlord. In a lecture given in 1885, Canon Moore referred to it as a 'picturesque feature' which had been 'obliterated within the last five years'. He described it as 'a long low thatched house, with porch and gabled chamber over it' and that 'the entrance to the porch consisted of a semicircular moulded brick archway of chevron pattern, which had the appearance of considerable antiquity. It had evidently been added to the house, and doubtless had been in work in some other place previously'. When J. H. Bugg acquired the property he pulled the house down but 'had the old archway carefully taken down and reset in his garden wall, nearly upon the spot where it formerly stood'. According to Canon Moore the old house was for many years 'neither more nor less than a beggars' opera, the dilapidated exterior typifying the condition of the interior and its occupants'. By his Will, dated 19th October, 1719, William Atkinson, of Spalding, gentleman, left the property to the governors of the Grammar School 'in trust for the master of the school'. They came into possession in 1751. In 1835 for the public house and premises (1a. 2r. 32p.) the governors received a yearly rent of £31. 10s. 0d. In 1876 J. H. Bugg acquired the property in exchange for two acres of land in Priory Road on which the Grammar School and Master's House were built, by subscription, in 1880-81.

(1). *The name was changed to Burg in 1877. See 'An Index to Changes of Name 1760 - 1901' by Phillimore and Fry, 1905.*

Right: The archway on Cowbit Road today.
Opposite top: No.3 Cowbit Road, formerly Westbourne House.

Roadmen.

The men are working in St. Thomas' Road around the turn of the century, near the junction with Priory Road. The field is now the Grammar School tennis court. In the background are the houses in Priory Road.

Grammar School

For a time, at the opening of the 19th century, there was only one pupil at the school. Later, as Dr. Thomas Cammack, J.P. (1792 - 1872), he was to become a prominent figure in the public and professional life of the town and district. Canon Moore wrote - "He was educated under the Revd. Walter Maurice Johnson as Master, and the Revd. Henry Spooner as Usher in the Royal Free Grammar School at Spalding. He was a great favourite with his Masters. Encouraged by their kindness, his application and talent made him at one time the head boy of the School. For some time he was the only boy in the School". (1)

At this time the school was held in the parish church, where it remained until 1881. Dr. S.H. Perry, who was a pupil there, described the school-room as "a little barn-like structure on the top of what is now St. Thomas à Becket's Chapel on the south side of the church. They went up a flight of stone steps to the top of the Chapel. It had a sort of concrete floor, and was quite a simple affair...." (2).

Above: The chapel of St. Thomas à Becket, or the Lady Chapel, on the south side of the Parish Church. The Grammar School was held here until 1881. The arches leading into the South Transept were walled up, and a floor inserted across the chapel which formed an upper room. The schoolroom was entered by a door on the west side reached by a flight of steps from the outside. (see plan on page 116)

The Revd. Edward Moore was headmaster from 1835 to 1866. The Schools Inquiry Commission, which reported in 1866, stated "..... The school has increased slowly since the year 1837, when it contained two boys. There are now 20 in attendance. It is not, however, popular. Boys have been sent to Moulton, 4 miles distant, and to other schools in preference. At the time of my visit the school was in a fairly satisfactory state for its size. Until about a year and a half ago it was taught almost entirely by the second master, who is from St. Bees. He is chaplain of the Union, and holds a curacy (3). Recently, however, he has been assisted by his son and by a third master, who was a senior optime, and formerly master of a private school. He leaves at midsummer (1866). It is said that before he came the discipline was very lax; but since his appointment there seems to have been no ground of complaint. The highest boy (aged 13), has been well grounded in the classics. He was third for the open scholarship at Uppingham. The next 6 or 7 were doing easy Latin construing, and elementary Greek in two classes; they had some notion of construing, but were inaccurate in grammar. The same may be said of their French. The dictation, geography, and history were very fair; the arithmetic only moderate. . . . there is a general wish for new buildings, but no money to erect them. . . .

. . . Total income £206.17s.6d. gross. £192. 14s. 5d. net. Head Master receives whole, and pays all outgoings, including salaries to three masters.

. . . . . . No residence for master, but a house in Church Street now vested in Town husbands has been claimed for this purpose. Property managed by Head Master. School kept in part of Parish Church. Site most objectionable, there being no access to it except through the church-yard. . . . . Government and Masters. - Four Governors, self electing, incorporated; majority appoint and dismiss Head Master; make ordinances. If they do not appoint a master within 40 days after a vacancy, St. John's College, Cambridge, may do so. Practice is to appoint a clergyman to be headmaster. No restriction on other employment".

In the 1870's the number of pupils again fell, and the Revd. D. L. Scott, Headmaster from 1874 to 1876 used to say he had at one time four scholars, whom he divided into six classes; when asked how this was done, he would explain, with a smile, that the same boy could be in more than one class.

Above: October 1877. The Headmaster, the Revd. Alfred Harre, assistant masters and scholars outside the Parish Church. The square or college caps were introduced in 1870.

In 1877, the Revd. Alfred Harre succeeded the Revd. J. A. Kershaw as Head Master. It was during his term of office that the school was transferred to Priory Road. In 1879 the Charity Commission established a Scheme for the administration of the School under which the number of governors was increased to 14. Of these, four were appointed by the Spalding Improvement Commissioners, two by the Justices of the Peace for the Parts of Holland, two by the Board of Guardians for the Spalding Poor Law Union, and two by the Subscribers to the Willesby School of the Foundation. There were also four co-optative Governors "appointed to office each for the term of his life", they were Theophilus Maurice Stephen Johnson, the "Squire", of Spalding; Canon Moore; Charles Foster Bonner, solicitor, and Dr. Marten Perry. Future co-optative Governors were to be appointed for the term of eight years. The Revd. Alfred Harre left in 1883 to become Headmaster of

(1). *The minutes of the Spalding Gentlemen's Society. Vol. VI. fols. 89 - 90.*

(2). *"The Bentleian". Easter, 1926. Vol. V. No. 2. page 414.*

(3). *The Revd. Michael Sisson. He was Chaplain to the Spalding Workhouse, and Perpetual Curate of Moulton Chapel. He was granted the annual pension or allowance of £30 by Order of the Charity Commissioners dated 18th May, 1877. He died in 1885.*

Steyning Grammar School, and was followed by the Revd. O. D. Inskip from 1883 to 1886, during which time the number of scholars increased from less than thirty to seventy. He resigned in December, 1886, on becoming Head Master of Framlingham College. There were 83 candidates for the vacant post, which carried a salary of £150 per annum, with house, and a capitation fee of £2 per scholar per year. The Revd. Thomasin Albert Stoodley was the successful applicant. He held the post from 1887 to 1894 when he became Rector of Folkingham, and was succeeded by the Revd. Edward Martin Tweed, M.A. who was the last clergyman headmaster. He remained until 1909 when he was appointed Rector of Burton-Le-Coggles, near Grantham.

School and School House

"Things were put upon a more satisfactory basis with the erection of the present Grammar School building in 1880. After much agitation, influential Spaldonians got together, a local commitee was formed, a new scheme formulated, and subscriptions to a building fund obtained. Five hundred guineas was cleared by a big Fancy Fair held in the Corn Exchange in the autumn of 1880. The present school building was formally opened on August 8th, 1881." (From "The Bentleian". Vol. I. page 7. 1922.) It provided accommodation for twenty boarders.

Opposite top: Early 1890's The Headmaster, the Revd. T. A. Stoodley, M.A., assistant masters and pupils. The square caps are no longer worn.

Front row:	Sindall, Dring, H. Newton, unknown, unknown.
Second row:	Fletcher, G. Bailey, unknown, Britton, Cross, C. Skinner, unknown, Cyril Harvey, Hack, S. Grounds.
Third row:	Loughton, C. Mills, Robinson, assistant master, the Revd. T.A. Stoodley, M.A., Headmaster (1887 - 94), assistant master, C. Bemrose, T. Palin, T. Reeks.
Fourth row:	T. Marshall, unknown, Dawkes, Davy, Aitken, Webster, J. Kinder, Davy, E. Smith, North, L. Massey.
Back row:	W. Harvey, Plowright, H. Luck, A. Proctor, G. Phillips, Sisson, C. Harvey, F. Enderby, G. Gibson, W. Button.

Above: A photograph at the Unveiling and Dedication of the School War Memorial, 25th July, 1923.

Back row: J. R. Green, H. J. Dash, B.A., Haydn Chester, M.C., A.R.C.O., R. E. Richardson, M.C., B.A., B. C. Atkin, H. Y. Green, S. Brice.

Third row: R. W. B. Gleed, B.A., L Beeken, R. T. Proctor, E. W. Bell, Councillor F. Sly, Rev. F. H. Adames, J. F. Alexander, Rev. G. T. Turberfield, J. Goode, M.A.

Second row: J. B. Smeathers, E. V. Spicer, L.C.P., F.S.A.M., Councillor H. G. Frost, Councillor R. S. Donington, F. White, A. Lount, Rev. L. Smith, M.A., Rev. S. Yates, Rev. H. Burn, Rev. F. L. Buxton, Alderman J.H. Bunting, Mrs. C. Banks, M. Caiger, M.A., L.C.P., W.F. Howard.

Front row: Dr. A. J. Stiles, M.D., J.P., Rev. E. M. Tweed, M.A., Councillor J. T. Brown, Councillor J. T. Atton, J.P., Alderman F. Howard, J.P., the Right Rev. the Lord Bishop of Lincoln, Lieutenant-Colonel G. J. Barrell, T.D., Rev. B.G. Nicholas, M.A., L. J. Driver, M.A., Councillor J. W. Gleed, M.A., J.P.

PRICE TWOPENCE.

Grammar School, Spalding.

The ANNUAL Athletic Sports

Will be held in the SCHOOL FIELD, on

Thursday, May 20th, 1915,

AT 2 P.M.

PRESIDENT and TREASURER:
Dr. E. C. CHAPPELL

Judges—Rev. E. L. MARSDEN, Rev. T. H. TARDREW, and Mr. DRIVER.

Timekeeper—Mr. SPICER.

Starter—Mr. BELL.

Starting Judges—Mr. R. S. DONINGTON and Mr. H. C. REEKS.

COMMITTEE—
BUTTERY II., GREEN, PAGE I., NEAL, ROBINSON, GIRDLESTONE, OVERTON, and BRICE.

RULES.

1.—No boy will be allowed to take more than Three Prizes of any kind whatever, though should he win more than three he may choose which he will take. The Championship Medal counts as a prize.

2.—A Second Prize will not be awarded unless five boys compete in the event, and a Third Prize unless Eight compete.

3.—None but Officials and Reporters will be allowed to stand INSIDE the Ring.

"FREE PRESS" CO., LTD., PRINTERS, SPALDING.

1—Bowling at Wickets (Girls over 15).
Prizes:—1st, Case of Scissors; 2nd, Silver Set; 3rd, Hatpin.
1st   2nd   3rd

Bowling at Wickets (Girls under 15).
Prizes:—1st, Handbag; 2nd, Serviette Ring; 3rd, Hatpin.
1st   2nd   3rd

2—Bowling at Wickets (Boys over 14).
Prizes:—1st, Watch; 2nd, Cycle Bell; 3rd, Pencil Case.
1st   2nd   3rd

3—Bowling at Wickets (Boys under 14).
Prizes:—1st, Camp Brushes; 2nd, Cycle Bell; 3rd, Watch Strap.
1st   2nd   3rd

4—100 Yards Handicap (under 18).
Prizes:—1st, Camp Brushes; 2nd, Cycle Bell; 3rd, Pencil Case.

FIRST HEAT.
2.—Benner .... scr.
49.—English .... scr.
82.—Whitewick ...... scr.
33.—Martin .... scr.
5.—Graham .... 8 yds.
74.—Pick .... 8 yds.
1st   2nd

SECOND HEAT.
29.—Guy .... scr.
19.—White, L. .... scr.
32.—Humphries .... 4 yds.
43.—Barker .... 4 yds.
41.—Jepson .... 6 yds.
39.—Waltham .... 6 yds.
1st   2nd

THIRD HEAT.
84.—Wright .... scr.
26.—Burrell .... scr.
59.—Tointon .... 4 yds.
28.—Edgley .... 4 yds.
15.—Parkinson .... 4 yds.
57.—Sellers II. .... 8 yds.
17.—Sellers II. .... 8 yds.
1st   2nd

5—100 Yards Handicap (18—15).
Prizes:—1st, Camera (Presented by Messrs. Bell & Osborn); 2nd, Cycle Bell; 3rd, Pencil Case.

The first two in each Heat to run in Final.

FIRST HEAT.
50.—Fidler .... 4 yds.
46.—Brotherton .... 4 yds.
81.—Walmsley .... 8 yds.
3.—Burgess .... 8 yds.
8.—Bates .... 10 yds.
7.—Holmes .... 10 yds.
65.—Collin .... 10 yds.
37.—Skinner .... 12 yds.
1st   2nd

SECOND HEAT.
73.—Patterson .... 4 yds.
10.—Marshall .... 4 yds.
31.—Hubbard .... 8 yds.
69.—Hardy II. .... 9 yds.
4.—Murrell .... 10 yds.
56.—Radford .... 10 yds.
44.—Blackbourn ...... 12 yds.
25.—Brown .... 12 yds.
1st   2nd

THIRD HEAT.
27.—Dicker .... scr.
77.—Ridlington .... 6 yds.
52.—Money .... 6 yds.
80.—White, R. .... 7 yds.
22.—Bartley .... 8 yds.
80.—Turner .... 10 yds.
38.—Walden .... 12 yds.
1st   2nd

FOURTH HEAT.
62.—Bailey .... 6 yds.
40.—Ward .... 9 yds.
79.—Sales .... 10 yds.
36.—Sellars I. .... 12 yds.
76.—Reeks I. .... 12 yds.
42.—Aitkin .... 12 yds.
55.—Preston .... 12 yds.
1st   2nd

6—100 Yards Handicap (over 15).
Prizes:—1st, Watch and Chain (Presented by Mr. Louth); 2nd, Clock; 3rd, Belt.

The first two in each Heat to run in Final.

FIRST HEAT.
68.—Girdlestone ...... 4 yds.
45.—Cole .... 4 yds.
41.—Brooks .... 5 yds.
67.—Woolcock .... 6 yds.
21.—Frost .... 8 yds.
51.—Armstrong .... 8 yds.
1st   2nd

SECOND HEAT.
4.—Green .... scr.
72.—Jakes .... 3 yds.
13.—Overton .... 5 yds.
53.—Neal .... 6 yds.
24.—Brice .... 6 yds.
51.—King .... 6 yds.
1st   2nd

THIRD HEAT.
14.—Page .... scr.
35.—Palfreyman ...... 8 yds.
64.—Chilvers .... 3 yds.
70.—Jackson I. .... 10 yds.
78.—Robinson .... 7 yds.
1st   2nd

7—100 Yards (under 18) Final.
1st   2nd   3rd   Time

8—100 Yards (18—15) Final.
1st   2nd   3rd   Time

9—100 Yards (over 15) Final.
1st   2nd   3rd   Time

30—Hockey Dribbling.
Prizes:—1st, Handbag; 2nd, Writing Case (Presented by Mr. Porter); 3rd, Silver Pencil.

The first two in each Heat to run in Final.

FIRST HEAT.
D. Scott .... scr.
E. Alves .... scr.
F. Seymour .... scr.
W. White .... scr.
K. Swallow .... 6 yds.
J. Thorpe .... 7 yds.
1st   2nd

SECOND HEAT.
Doris English .... scr.
D. Jepson .... 3 yds.
C. Mouncy .... 4 yds.
K. Sisson .... 4 yds.
D. Burgess .... 9 yds.
B. Hayman .... 9 yds.
M. Pocklington .... 15 yds.
1st   2nd

THIRD HEAT.
G. Thornton .... 4 yds.
M. Clifton .... 4 yds.
E. Clinnenson ..... 8 yds.
G. Chappell .... 15 yds.
G. Rumsey .... 8 yds.
E. Taylor .... 15 yds.
1st   2nd

31—Parents' Race.
1st, Clock; 2nd, Compass.
1st   2nd   3rd

32—Hockey Dribbling—Final.
1st   2nd   3rd

SCHOOL MARCH PAST.

THE BRIGGS CUP.

Will be held for one year by the boy securing most points; the winner will, in addition receive a medal. Points are reckoned—5 for a First, 3 for a Second, and 1 for a Third, save in Events Nos. 17 and 20, where the points are respectively, 7, 4, 1.

Winners—1910, H. E. Dennis; 1911, H. E. Dennis; 1912, G. White; 1913, J. N. M. Losh; 1914, M. S. Page.

THE HOUSE CUP.

Will be presented to the House winning most points for School work and Athletic Events.
Winner—1914, Bentley.

The Prizes will be presented by Mrs. GLEED, about 5 p.m.

REFRESHMENTS provided by Mr. Barker, may be had at Reasonable Charges during the Afternoon.

List of Subscribers, 1914.

	£	s.	d.
Hon. Mrs. F. S. McLaren	1	1	0
Mr. and Mrs. Chester		10	6
W. F. Howard, Esq.		10	6
Fitzalan Howard, Esq.		10	6
H. Chester, Esq.		4	6
Major G. J. Barrell		2	6

The following gave prizes:—Mrs. F. Howard, Mr. and Mrs. Beales, Mr. and Mrs. S. U. Green, Messrs. J. B. Allenson & Sons, C. M. Allenson, Bell & Osborn, H. L. Enderby, J. C. Harris & Son, W. Louth, A. Preston, J. T. White & Son, Wilkinson & Co.

The Committee desire to thank the above for their generosity.

SPALDING TOWN PRIZE SILVER BAND

(Conductor, Mr. F. GOLLIN)

Will perform the following Programme:—

MARCH	"Defenders"
SELECTION	"Zampa"
VALSE	"Il Bacio"
SELECTION	"England"
SELECTION	"Joan of Arc"
SELECTION	"Pirates of Penzance"
SELECTION	"Harlington"
MARCH	"University"
SELECTION	"Classic Gems"
SELECTION	"Sunny Memories"
VALSE	"Will o' the Wisp"
SELECTION	"Echoes of England"
GAVOTTE	"Menia Bells"
SELECTION	"Song Echoes"
MARCH	"Tregarthen"

GOD SAVE THE KING.

10—Three Legged Race.

Prizes:—1st, Attaché Cases; 2nd, Cycle Pumps; 3rd, Pencil Case.

The first two in each Heat to run in Final.

First Heat.	Second Heat.
A { 7.—Holmes / 41.—Woolcock	L { 77.—Ridlington / 83.—Martin
B { 80.—Turner / 49.—English II.	M { 3.—Burgess / 25.—Brown
C { 13.—Overton / 21.—Armstrong	N { 27.—Dicker / 81.—Walmsley
D { 69.—Hardy II. / 50.—Fidler	O { 28.—Edgley / 57.—Reeks II.
E { 16.—Porter / 24.—Brice	P { 84.—Wright / 76.—Reeks I.
F { 65.—Collin / 45.—Brooks	Q { 32.—Humphries / 53.—Neal
G { 18.—Stevens / 23.—Bates	R { 39.—Waltham / 70.—Jackson I.
H { 78.—Robinson / 54.—North	S { 43.—Barker / 40.—Ward
I { 19.—White, L. / 33.—Jennings	T { 36.—Sellars I. / 42.—Atkin
J { 82.—Whitewick / 52.—Money	U { 35.—Palfreyman / 44.—Blackbourn
K { 8.—Jepson / 31.—Hubbard	V { 37.—Skinner / 51.—King
	W { 30.—Barley / 72.—Hardy I.

1st Pair   2nd Pair   1st Pair   2nd Pair

11—220 Yards Handicap (over 14).

Prizes:—1st, Clock; 2nd, Cake Knife (Presented by Messrs. Bradley & Son); 3rd, Pencil Case.

The first two in each Heat to run in Final.

First Heat.		Second Heat.	
72.—Jakes	3 yds.	6.—Green	scr.
64.—Chilvers	5 yds.	27.—Dicker	4 yds.
4.—Cole	7 yds.	68.—Girdlestone	5 yds.
13.—Overton	9 yds.	45.—Brooks	9 yds.
41.—Woolcock	10 yds.	20.—White, R.	10 yds.
77.—Ridlington	10 yds.	30.—Hardy	14 yds.
24.—Brice	10 yds.	67.—Frost	14 yds.
53.—Neal	10 yds.	35.—Palfreyman	15 yds.
21.—Armstrong	12 yds.	70.—Jackson	15 yds.
16.—Porter	12 yds.	37.—Skinner	20 yds.
51.—King	15 yds.	25.—Brown	20 yds.
46.—Brotherton	15 yds.	83.—Martin	20 yds.
81.—Walmsley	18 yds.	36.—Sellars	24 yds.

1st   2nd   1st   2nd

12—220 Yards Handicap (under 14).

Prizes:—1st, Clock; 2nd, Serviette Ring; 3rd, Pencil Case.

The first two in each Heat to run in Final.

First Heat.		Second Heat.	
50.—Fidler	scr.	10.—Marshall	scr.
52.—Money	1 yd.	31.—Hubbard	4 yds.
62.—Bailey	5 yds.	65.—Collin	10 yds.
7.—Holmes	5 yds.	11.—Morgan	10 yds.
83.—Martin	10 yds.	80.—Turner	10 yds.
3.—Burgess	16 yds.	33.—Jennings	10 yds.
29.—Whitewick	18 yds.	38.—Walden	14 yds.
82.—Whitewick	18 yds.	58.—Bright	14 yds.
5.—Graham	25 yds.	43.—Barker	25 yds.
74.—Pick	25 yds.	19.—White (L.)	25 yds.
32.—Humphries	25 yds.		

1st   2nd   1st   2nd

13—High Jump.

	Height
4.—Cole	
13.—Overton	
14.—Page	
45.—Brooks	

1st   2nd   3rd

14—Bicycle Obstacle Race.

Prizes:—1st, Lamp (Presented by Mr. E. Blackburn); 2nd, Pocket Knife; 3rd, Pencil Case.

The first two in each Heat to run in Final.

First Heat.	Second Heat.
69.—Hardy II.	13.—Overton
21.—Armstrong	54.—North
11.—Morgan	79.—Stiles
47.—Buttery	59.—Tointon
49.—English II.	42.—Atkin
12.—Murrell	31.—Dicker
58.—Thorpe	78.—Robinson
67.—Frost	51.—King

1st   2nd   1st   2nd

15—Sack Race.

First Heat.	Third Heat.
24.—Brice	84.—Wright
33.—Bates	83.—Martin
49.—English II.	19.—White (L.)
3.—Burgess	29.—Guy
50.—Fidler	62.—Bailey
7.—Holmes	56.—Radford
33.—Jennings	32.—Humphries
82.—Whitewick	22.—White (R.)
45.—Brooks	68.—Girdlestone
78.—Overton	44.—Blackbourn
53.—Neal	8.—Jepson

Second Heat.	Fourth Heat.
31.—Hubbard	39.—Waltham
72.—Jakes	79.—Stiles
58.—Thorpe	42.—Atkin
16.—Porter	26.—Burrell
25.—Brown	43.—Barker
78.—Robinson	76.—Reeks
54.—North	73.—Patterson
18.—Stevens	57.—Reeks II.
28.—Edgley	64.—Chilvers
80.—Turner	59.—Tointon
52.—Money	71.—Jackson
17.—Sellars	4.—Cole
	85.—Oldershaw

1st   2nd   1st   2nd

16—440 Yards (under 14).

Prizes:—1st, Fretwork Set (Presented by Messrs. Wilkinson & Co.); 2nd, Pocket Knife; 3rd, Pencil Case.

The first two in each Heat to run in Final.

31.—Hubbard	scr.
52.—Money	scr.
65.—Collin	15 yds.
80.—Turner	15 yds.
29.—Guy	15 yds.
82.—Whitewick	20 yds.

1st   2nd   Time

17—440 Yards (over 14) Scratch.

Prizes:—1st, HARRIS CUP and Medal; 2nd, (Presented by Friend); 3rd, Belt.

The first two in each Heat to run in Final.

4.—Cole	72.—Jakes
13.—Overton	68.—Girdlestone
14.—Page	77.—Ridlington
6.—Green	64.—Chilvers
24.—Brice	81.—Walmsley
27.—Dicker	45.—Brooks
	46.—Brotherton

1st   2nd   3rd   Time

18—Slow Bicycle Race.

Prizes:—1st, Lamp (Presented by Mr. Beales); 2nd, Compass; 3rd, Belt (Presented by Mr. A. Turner).

The first two in each Heat to run in Final.

First Heat.	Third Heat.
1.—Ashwell	12.—Murrell
47.—Buttery	83.—Martin
78.—Robinson	68.—Girdlestone
24.—Brice	13.—Overton
4.—Cole	67.—Frost
69.—Hardy II.	14.—Page
31.—Hubbard	59.—Tointon
	81.—Walmsley

Second Heat.
9.—Losh
58.—Thorpe
64.—Chilvers
26.—Burrell
11.—Morgan
54.—North
77.—Ridlington
30.—Hardy I.

1st   2nd

19—One Kilometre Scratch Race.

Prizes:—1st, Dress Case; 2nd, Fishing Rod; 3rd, Belt.

The first two in each Heat to run in Final.

4.—Cole	72.—Jakes
13.—Overton	68.—Girdlestone
14.—Page	64.—Chilvers
16.—Porter	24.—Brice
	27.—Dicker

1st   2nd   3rd   Time

20—Wheelbarrow Race.

Prizes:—1st, Cricket Balls (Presented by Mr. H. L. Enderby); 2nd, Cycle Pumps.

The first two in each Heat to run in Final.

First Heat.	Second Heat.
A { 3.—Burgess / 7.—Holmes	J { 77.—Ridlington / 62.—Bailey
B { 72.—Jakes / 82.—Whitewick	K { 69.—Hardy / 68.—Girdlestone
C { 65.—Collin / 76.—Reeks I.	L { 81.—Walmsley / 79.—Stiles
D { 20.—White (R.) / 13.—Overton	M { 24.—Brice / 41.—Woolcock
E { 51.—King / 45.—Brooks	N { 31.—Hubbard / 25.—Brown
F { 54.—North / 52.—Money	O { 28.—Edgley / 29.—Guy
G { 4.—Cole / 44.—Martin	P { 32.—Humphries / 35.—Sellars
H {	Q { 22.—Barley

1st   2nd

21—Wheelbarrow Race—Final.

1st   2nd   3rd

22—Sack Race—Final.

1st Pair   2nd Pair

23—Three-legged Race—Final.

1st   2nd   3rd

24—220 Yards Handicap (over 14) Final.

1st   2nd   3rd

25—Slow Bicycle Race—Final.

1st   2nd   3rd

26—Bicycle Obstacle Race—Final.

1st   2nd   3rd

27—Tug of War.

HOBSON.—Woolcock, Armstrong, Brice, Hubbard, Hardy I., Dicker.
WELLAND.—Brooks, Buttery, English, Neal, Brotherton, Preston.
WYKEHAM.—Jakes, Girdlestone, Burchnall, Jackson I., Robinson.
BENTLEY.—Green, Cole, Losh, Page, White (R.), Porter.

28—Consolation Race (over 14).

Prizes:—1st, Tennis Shirts (Presented by Messrs. J. B. Allenson & Son); 2nd, Reel (Presented by Mr. S. Green); 3rd, Pencil Case.

1st   2nd   3rd

29—Consolation Race (under 14).

Prizes:—1st, Tennis Shirt (Presented by Mr. C. M. Allenson); 2nd, Belt and Tie (Presented by Mr. A. B. Turner); 3rd, Pencil Case.

1st   2nd   3rd

Previous page: The programme of events of Thursday, May 20th, 1915.

Above and below: Photographs of the school in the early 1920's.

Willesby School

The Petit, or Willesby's School was founded by Thomas Willesby (1618-82). By his Will, dated 24th June, 1682, he devised 50 acres and 3 roods of land in Tydd St. Mary, Moulton and Spalding, to seven trustees to "erect a convenient house in Spalding aforesaid, and therein to place a man of sober and virtuous life, who should be well able to teach the reading of the English Tongue, and to write, and also to instruct the children committed to his charge in the principles of the Christian and reformed religion, as a Schoolmaster, who should have for his pains (so long as the said trustees shall like and approve of him),£15 yearly, out of the rents of the said land, as his yearly stipend, for his teaching freely such poor children, whose parents inhabit within the parish of Spalding". (1)

The original building, purchased in 1685, and the school house, stood in Broad Street, on the site of the present car park, opposite the Spalding Club. The house was rebuilt in 1826, and in 1872 was described as "a good residence". In 1836 the trustees were the Rev. William Moore, D.D. the Vicar of Spalding, Charles Martin Dinham Green, Thomas Pulvertoft, John Richard Carter, Theophilus Johnson and Charles Bonner. At that date there were 68 boys at the school.

In 1845 the school was moved to Winsover Road. A meeting house, built for the use of the "Particular Baptists of Strict Communion Order", was bought for £320. Burials having taken place within the walls, few cared to deal with the property. It was however purchased by the Willesby School Trustees, who had the bodies removed to the churchyard, and converted the building into a school. (2)

In 1872, the original endowment, had by allotments at the enclosures, increased to 93 acres. It was let for about £200 per annum. The master still lived at Broad Street (No.14), and for a salary of £80 a year taught 60 boys "who are provided with books, stationery, &c. by the trustees, and out of the surplus income, each receives a cap, or some article of clothing yearly. Mr. William Sleight is the master". (3) In 1892 the Headmaster (Henry John White) received a salary of £110 a year, and with an assistant master, conducted the school for 140 boys as a Government Elementary School. (4) In 1896 there was accommodation for 156 boys and an average attendance of 148. (5)

Below: The school operating in the converted chapel.

Above: The School Football Team of 1920-21.

A pupil who entered the school in 1880 remembered when Spalding prison was next door, and recalled seeing prisoners repairing the school yard. In 1914 Arthur Mulley succeeded H. J. White as headmaster, at a commencing salary of £120 per annum. In 1937, his wife, Mrs Kate Clara Mulley, became the first lady to be elected a member of the former Spalding Urban District Council. In that year the school had 129 pupils. In 1926 Mr. J.H. Worley commenced his long association with the school as assistant master, and latterly as the (last) headmaster. The school closed in 1960, and was demolished six years later. British Telecom occupies the site today.

Right: The School c.1930.

(1). "*The History of Lincolnshire &c.*" by W. Marrat. 1814. Vol.1. pages 288 - 289.
(2). "*The History and Recollections of Spalding*," by Canon Moore. 1885.
(3). *White's Directory of Lincolnshire.* 1872. page 758.
(4). *White's Directory of Lincolnshire.* 1892. page 789.
(5). *Kelly's Directory of Lincolnshire.* 1896. page 481.

Townscape - Sheepmarket

The Prison

In 1619, the County Magistrates obtained premises in Broad Street for use as a prison. These were purchased from William Hobson, of Spalding, gent, for £64. This House of Correction was to serve the town of Spalding and "...all the other Townes Villages and Hamletts within the precincts of the severall Wapentakes of Ellowe and Kirton...". It was to be "used and ymploied as a house of Correction for the keepinge Correctinge and Settinge to Worke of Rogues Vagabonds Sturdie beggers and other vagrant Idle and disordelie persons..." (1). It was rebuilt in 1765. When a new prison was erected in the Sheep Market in 1824 - 5, the "site of the late House of Correction in Spalding aforesaid and of the Buildings and premises lately thereto belonging..", described as "fronting upon the public street called Broad Street East and another Public Street North the Punch-bowl Public House West and the Estate of Theophilus Russell Buckworth Esquire South.." was sold, in 1827, to Farmery Epworth Cunnington, of Spalding, Builder, for £910. (2). (The present Broad Street Methodist Church and Schoolroom are erected on part of the site of the former prison).

Above: The Prison in the Sheep Market, 1847. From a watercolour by Hilkiah Burgess (1775-1868). Spalding Gentlemen's Society collection.

The new prison, in the Sheep Market, was completed in 1826, at a cost of nearly £15,000. "The premises include a chapel, a treadmill, seven airing courts, divided into classes, sixteen day-rooms also divided into classes, and forty-eight sleeping cells. Excepting as regards the mill, the system of classification of prisoners is carried into full effect. There are two wheels to the mill. The chapel is divided into eight portions, radiating from the centre, so that the prisoners in any one division are unable to see those of any other. The gaol includes prisoners for all offences except capital ones. The average number of prisoners for 1835 was 39". (3)

The prison was enlarged in 1851 - 2. An official report for 1879 stated that the daily average of prisoners was 59 males and 13 females. Punishments consisted of flogging, being put in handcuffs, punishment cells, reduced dietary, &c. "Hard labour (the report stated) is enforced by the treadmill, which accommodates 34, and grinds flour and cereals generally. Other labour consists in wood-chopping, pea-picking, and oakum picking". The treadmill was said to grind sufficient corn at Spalding to bring a profit of £100 annually to the authorities. For the year ended 31st March, 1881, the average cost per head for each prisoner was £30. 17s.

The prison was closed on 31st March, 1884. The property was purchased by John Longstaff for £1,800, who sold part of the site for a Drill Hall (later replaced by the Regent Cinema, and afterwards by the Trustee Savings Bank and County Library), part (91 square yards for £200), for widening the very narrow Station Street, and on the rest built houses and shops (Station Street and Victoria Street). Station Street was then a very narrow thoroughfare, for the high prison wall ran along at what is now the edge of the pavement on the right hand side coming from the Railway Station. Some of the houses in Station Street were built of materials from the prison.

Above: The Prison in the early 1880's.

(1). *Indenture, dated 13th July, 1619, William Hobson, of Spalding, in the County of Lincoln, gent, conveyed to feoffees, for the purposes of a House of Correction -*
'One Messuage Two Cottages one Orchard and one Garden....lyeinge and beeinge in Spaldinge aforesaid betweene the Lands late the Heires of John Atkinson and a Commonwaye there called Crackepoole lane on the East and the Landes of our Sovraigne Lord the Kinge on the West and abutts upon a Common Sewer called the Westlode towards the North and upon the Lands late the said Heires of John Atkinson towards the South....'
(2). *Indenture, dated 12th June, 1827, the premises in Spalding lately used as a House of Correction were conveyed by the Clerk of the Peace for the Division of Holland in the County of Lincoln to Farmery Epworth Cunnington, of Spalding, builder, for the sum of £910.*
(3). *"Lincolnshire in 1836", pp. 120 - 121.*

H. Leverton & Co. Motor Engineers

Originally erected as a Drill Hall, and opened in 1890. It was then described as 'a red brick building with stone facings, standing on ground 125 feet by 48 feet; it consists of a large hall about 75 by 45 feet, with a fixed stage, armoury, orderly and other rooms; the hall is also let for concerts, dramatic and other entertainments, for which it is well adapted',(Kelly's Directory of Lincolnshire, 1896. page 482).

For a long time the necessity of a permanent headquarters for the F (Spalding) Co. of the 2nd. Lincs. Volunteer Battalion had been felt, and also the need for an alternative to the Corn Exchange for public gatherings. Eventually, while Captain Cuthbert Williams was the Commander of the Corps, definite steps were taken, and subscriptions solicited. The site was purchased for £625, and the contract for the erection of a Drill Hall awarded to James Leafe, builder, of Boston, for £1,250, the architect being J. R. Withers, of Shrewsbury, whose father had been the architect of St. John Baptist Church, Hawthorn Bank. The foundation stone was laid by Col. R. G. Ellison, of Boultham Hall, Lincoln, on 22nd November, 1889. At the dinner in the Masonic Hall which followed there were present, among others, Capt. Williams (in the chair), Col. Ellison, Capt. Lloyd, Capt. Price, Capt. Kingston, Lieut. Bonner, Lieut. Brogden, Lieut. Stack, Lieut. Cochrane, Surgeon England, the Rev. M. H. Marsden, the Rev. F. F. Wayet, Major Moore, Capt. Hilliam, Mr. G. F. Barrell, Dr. Morris, Dr. A. J. Stiles, Dr. Barritt, Messrs. F. Howard, T. H. Nicholls, G. E. Abbott, W. Newton, Augustus Maples, Henry Watkinson, W. W. Copeland, and Dr. King. At that time the Spalding Corps numbered 86 members. It was the hope of Capt. Williams that the Drill Hall might in future years be still further developed, so as to provide a Volunteer Club, reading room and library. The hall was formally opened on October 24, 1890, by Earl Brownlow, Under Secretary for War and Lord - Lieutenant of Lincolnshire. It was then stated that the total cost of the land and premises amounted to about £2,500, including £200 additional for an extra room in front, the expenses of furnishing &c. To meet this amount, subscriptions and donations had been received, though with few exceptions not to large amounts, and the officers of the Company (Capt. Williams and Lieuts. Bonner and Brogden),had made themselves responsible for the

A view of the interior taken on the afternoon of Tuesday, 12th October, 1909, when 24 cars were accommodated.
Inset are: Fred Myers (left) and H. Leverton, the proprietors of the business. (from "The Spalding Free Press", of 19th October, 1909).

£1,600 which still remained to be raised, and had been advanced. In 1906, little if any of this amount had been liquidated, and in that year the executors of the principal mortgagee (Mrs. Johnson), gave instructions for the sale of the premises.

Messrs. H. Leverton & Co. whose first garage was in High Street, acquired the property in 1909. The photograph shows the premises when adapted as a garage, cars being seen along the street at the side where two entrances were situated. This in turn was replaced by the Regent Cinema which was opened in 1927.

Herbert Leverton, belonged to a Surfleet family well known in connection with steam engines and threshing machines. It was claimed that his grandfather introduced the first steam threshing outfit into the district. Herbert Leverton was himself engaged in this business at Surfleet, and he was also for a number of years with Clayton & Shuttleworth, of Lincoln. While employed by that firm he on two occasions erected engines in Spain and Portugal. The connection with the motor industry dated from the time when, about 1901, he bought a second-hand car, which proved so troublesome, that before he was done with it he had to take it to pieces several times. This gave him an insight into motor mechanism which enabled him to be of assistance to other local motorists, and as time went on he gained increased experience, and his services became so much in requisition that he decided to devote his whole time to the work.

In 1904 he was joined in partnership by J. Fred Myers, and in 1907 a motor garage was opened in High Street. On 30th June, 1909, they acquired the former Drill Hall in the Sheep Market. In 1912 Herbert Leverton emigrated to Tasmania, selling his shares to his partner, but making a condition that the Company would always carry the Leverton name.

THE SPALDING CINEMAS
Telephone 98.

The Regent — Open Weekdays 6.10 and 8.20.

MATINEES TUESDAYS & SATURDAYS at 2.15 p.m.

Cafe Open from 3 p.m.

Regent Cinema

Built on the site of the Drill Hall, which was later used as a garage by Levertons, the Regent Cinema was opened by the Spalding Picture House Co. Ltd., 20th June, 1927. The architects were P.L. Brown & Son, of Newcastle-on-Tyne; the builder, John Peake, of Spalding. It provided seating accommodation for 850 persons, and was described as a 'first-class house of entertainment, complete with café, where patrons can enjoy a refreshing cup of tea, or a cooling ice cream, amid pleasant surroundings'. In 1927 two performances were given every evening, Mondays to Saturdays, at 6.10 and 8.20, with a matinee on Tuesday afternoons at 2.15. Prices: balcony, 1/6d; upper balcony, 1/3d; back stalls, 9d; stalls, 9d; children under twelve 6d.

The first film presented was "Mademoiselle from Armentières", with Estelle Body. It was here that Spalding had its introduction to sound films in January, 1930.

On the evening of 20th March, 1929, David Lloyd-George, addressed a large crowd, assembled in the Sheep Market, from the balcony of the cinema. He was supporting James Blindell, the Liberal candidate for the Holland-with-Boston parliamentary constituency. A By-Election had been caused by the death of A.W. Dean (Conservative), who had been M.P. for the division since 1924.

The Regent was closed 2nd February, 1959, and subsequently demolished. The Trustee Savings Bank occupies the site today.

Above: The Sheep Market was paved with asphalte and the permanent iron pens erected in 1876. A carriage works stood on the site now occupied by the Post Office.

The Sheep Market

On 19th January, 1876, the 'Fairs and Markets, Market Places, Market Tolls, Duties and Rights and other premises part of the Manor of Spalding in the County of Lincoln', were conveyed by the Lady and Lords of the Manor of Spalding (Mrs. Isabella Mary Johnson, of Blundeston, Suffolk; John Swan, of Lincoln, Gentleman; the Reverend Edward Moore, of Spalding, Clerk in Holy Orders and Charles Foster Bonner, of Spalding, Gentleman) to the Spalding Improvement Commissioners (who were the predecessors of the former Spalding Urban District Council and the present South Holland District Council) for the sum of £4,000.

The Sheep Market described 23 years later by J. H. Diggle.

'The sheep are snugly penned in the triangular space skirted on one side by the Sessions House and the new Drill Hall (which stood on the site of the present Trustee Savings Bank), a site conveniently near the railway station. The toll is 1d. per sheep, with slight variations, 2s. being charged for the accommodation of a ram "in August". There is space for 1,300 sheep, but rarely are the pens quite full. The total number of sheep penned during the past year (1899) has approximately been 26,000, an average of 500 per week. The sale of fat sheep has greatly declined, partly owing to the ploughing up of a large acreage of pasture land, and partly owing to the stock auctions now conducted at Holbeach, Bourne, Donington, Long Sutton, Sleaford &c. The principal buyers of fat sheep are Alderman Redhead and Messrs. Stanley Brothers of Peterborough; James Freeman & Sons of St. Ives and Mr. Philip J. White, a large wholesale and retail butcher, resident at Long Sutton. The store sheep are chiefly supplied by neighbouring farmers; comparatively few only are brought by dealers. The principal farmers who at present use the sheep market are: Messrs. Thos. Atkinson & Sons, Messrs. H. Clark, A.H. Clark and H. Clark, jnr., Green Waltham and Joseph Waltham, S. Frier and G. Frier, H.M. Proctor and E.B. Proctor, J.W. Rowland, S. Kingston, J.H. Grundy, the Messrs. Casswell and others. Sales are affected personally by the graziers, the commission agent having largely lost his hold on transactions with sheep.'

Sessions House

The Sessions House was built in 1842 - 43. The architect was Charles Kirk, of Sleaford. The contractors Booth & Walker, of Bramley, near Leeds. White's Directory described it as 'a large and handsome building, erected out of the County rates, in 1843. In the Tudor style, at a cost of more than £6,000' (1). Materials used in the construction included 800,000 bricks, 12,000 cubic feet of stone, 350 chaldrons of lime, 8,000 tons of sand, 4,500 cubic feet of timber, 5,000 tons of shingle, 500 bundles of lath, 12 tons of slates, 2 feet 6 inches x 3 feet, 3 tons of iron hooping, 20 tons of iron and iron beams, 10 tons of sheet lead, 100 barrels of cement, and about 1,000 feet of superior glass (partly plate glass).

It was opened at the midsummer Quarter Sessions held on 30th June, 1843. The Magistrates sitting on that occasion were:- the Revd. William Moore, D.D., Chairman; General Dyson, John Ballett Fletcher, Maurice Johnson, and Leonard Browne, Esqs., and the Revs. H. Fardell, Jas. Morton and Chas. Moore.

At the conclusion of the Court the Grand Jury were invited to inspect the building, and afterwards issued the following statement:-

'The Grand Jury having viewed and inspected the new Sessions-house, beg leave to express their gratification at the manner and excellence of the same, and their sense of the great necessity which existed for the erection of it. They find it commodious and convenient, and the architecture substantial and elegant'. (2)

(1). *White's History, Gazetteer and Directory of Lincolnshire, 1856.*   (2). *'Stamford Mercury', of 7th July, 1843.*

The Priors Oven

The Priors Oven is one of the few remaining portions of the former Benedictine Priory. A description, given in Camden's Brittannia, 1789, page 238, reads:-
"The prior's oven, an old strong vaulted building at the corner of the beast market by the gore, was the prison, and over it an arched chamber where refractory monks were kept.....and over that a lofty tower with a bell knelled at executions, and on solemn occasions......It is of brick and stone, very

Below: The Prior's Oven, 1820. From a Watercolour by Hilkiah Burgess.

strong, the arch concentring, and ribbed with Barnack rag, also the doorcase and foundation. But now only the lower vault remains, converted into a cooper's workshop, and a square room lately, built over it of brick".

In 1848 it was occupied by Anthony Joyes, blacksmith, and in 1885 by Mr. Tuddenham, fishmonger. Below is a view taken in the early 1900's.

Hall Place

Town Hall

The gift of John Hobson, of Spalding, it stood in the Hemp Market, now Hall Place, and was built about 1620. In the burial register of the Parish Church is the entry, "1611, November the 7th daye, John Hobson, Yeoman, whoe did give Towe hundred pounds towardes the Purchasinge of land and beuldinge A Towne hall within the Town of Spaldinge". (1) Underneath the hall were several shops, and according to the Will of the donor, were to be let for rents to be appropriated as to one-fifth to the Minister of Spalding, and the other four-fifths to the Town Husbands, for the poor of the parish. At the end of the eighteenth century a room for a card-assembly was added to the original building. Under this were rooms on the ground floor where the fire engines &c. were kept.

A description of the Town Hall in 1802 reads "It is a good brick structure, and its principal entrance is by a flight of about twenty steps from the N.W. end of the Market Place, and at the end of it, fronting the same, is a clock for the use of the town, surmounted by a large bell on which the clock strikes, and which is used to summon the inhabitants in case of fire, on parochial business, &c. It consists of a hall and record-room, the former is 47 feet long by 21½ wide....".(2) It was here that the Sessions of the Peace, Manorial Courts, Court of Requests and Courts of Sewers were held.

In 1853 the Spalding Improvement Act stated that,"...whereas the present Town Hall, and the buildings adjoining, situate at the north-west end of the market place in the town of Spalding, are in a dilapidated state, and are a great obstruction to the public thoroughfare,....it is expedient that the same should be removed...". (3) The Spalding Improvement Commissioners were authorized to provide a public building to be adapted and used as a corn exchange, market house, meeting place &c, and to pull down and remove the old Town Hall. In 1854 it was demolished and Samuel Dolman, of Spalding, builder, purchased the materials of the old Town Hall for £145 - 'The amount to be paid within three months with a rebate of £5'. He also contracted for the purchase of the mortar and rubbish on the old Town Hall site at 1/6d per load for delivery on the Cemetery Ground.

The Corn Exchange, the successor to the Town Hall, was opened in 1856.

(1). *"South Holland Magazine"*. Vol. 2. page 177.
(2). *"The Provincial Literary Repository"*. Vol. II June, 1802. pages 204 - 205 - footnote.
(3). *Spalding Improvement Act, 1853. sec. 52.*

The Fountain

The drinking fountain formerly in Hall Place, Spalding, was erected in 1874, by the Spalding Water Works Company, as a memorial to Miss Mary Ann Johnson (1794 - 1878), of Fairfax (Holyrood) House, Spalding, whose generosity enabled the mains to be extended to Little London and along Winsover Road and Holbeach Road.

On October 2nd, 1873, a meeting of the shareholders of the Company was held at the Corn Exchange. Mr. William Hobson, draper, occupied the chair, and was supported by Canon Moore, Edward Palmer Maples, timber merchant, Joseph Allen, grocer, and Alfred Hobson, draper, son of the Chairman. The Directors communicated to the shareholders an offer made by Miss Johnson to hand to the Company the sum of £1,500 to be expended by them in extending the water mains and especially upon Winsover Road (then also known as Bourn Road) up to Hawthorn Bank, and thence along the Hawthorn Bank up to the site of the proposed new Church of St. John Baptist, upon the Holbeach Road as far as the Pigeon Public House, and upon the London road "as far as the Pump near to Mr. Osgerby's House". This was conditional upon the Company erecting a drinking fountain upon each of the roads "at or near the extremity of each Main".

It was "Resolved that the Company desire to express to Miss Johnson their high sense of the liberality and munificence of her offer and that the same be gratefully accepted. That a sufficient portion of the £1500 be expended in erecting a drinking Fountain in the Market Place to her Memory (the consent of all necessary parties being obtained) and the balance in carrying out the proposed extensions and such further extensions as the Directors may think necessary. Ordered that a Copy of the above Resolution be transmitted to Miss Johnson".

The local press commented that "The gift will prove a great boon to the labouring classes in such localities, and will tend further to perpetuate here the honoured name of Johnson".

On 18th April, 1874, the Directors of the Spalding Water Works Company "Resolved that a Fountain be erected in Hall Place in accordance with the design prepared by Mr. Withers and that the Tender of Mr. Cooke at the sum of £269 14s 0d be accepted, the work to be executed in accordance with a Specification to be prepared by Mr. Withers and completed within three Months......".

It would appear that the work was completed within the time stipulated, for on 26th August, 1874, the Directors paid Mr. Cooke the balance due to him on the contract, together with an additional sum of £5. 3. 0d. "for extra work in Concrete for the foundation". Mr. Withers received £21 for preparing drawings and superintending the erection of the Fountain.

A few weeks after its erection the "Stamford Mercury", reported that as yet "no water flowed from it, and people were curious to know the cause of the delay in bringing it into practical use, as usefulness was undoubtedly a greater consideration with the benevolent lady, at whose cost it was erected, than ornament. Last week it was brought into operation, much to the amusement of the juvenile population, who in their usual exuberance of spirits on seeing something new must have a game, throw the water about, break two of the cups, and perform other little antics,very naughty but very natural with school boys. The fountain has cost £300. Three other fountains will shortly be erected - one on the London-road, one on the Holbeach-road, and one on the Hawthorn-bank. These will doubtless be of a less expensive character than the one in Hall-place". (no other fountains were in fact erected).

There were other problems for the Water Authorities for on 14th September, 1876, the Directors of the Spalding Water Works Company "Ordered that Notice be given to all persons using the water from the Fountain for domestic purposes that such use cannot be allowed and that in the event of their persisting to do so proceedings will be taken against them".

The Fountain remained the property of the Company until 1900 when the Water Works were purchased by the former Spalding Urban District Council. In 1954 it was removed to the gardens of Ayscoughfee Hall where it still remains.

Miss Johnson was the third daughter of the Revd. Walter Maurice Johnson (1757-1832), Vicar of Weston and Master of the Grammar School at Spalding, by his wife Frances, daughter of George Weller Poley, of Boxted Hall, Suffolk. The Church of St. John Baptist, Hawthorn Bank, with its adjacent school and vicarage house, together with an endowment of £300 a year, were provided by her - the Church being opened for worship in 1875.

Together with her sister - Elizabeth Ann Johnson - she left by Will provision for the building and partial endowment of the Johnson Hospital built in 1881. It is from these sisters that the hospital takes its name.

Writing in the South Holland Magazine for June, 1871, Canon Moore referred to Miss Elizabeth Ann and Miss Mary Ann Johnson as still living at Fairfax House "deservedly respected for their active benevolence". He went on to record that "On all occasions of public collections for the promotion of the welfare of their native town of Spalding, their names appear among the principal contributors", and ended by expressing the hope that "Long may they continue to live amongst us, highly esteemed for their works' sake: their memory will ever rank among the benefactors of this town".

Left: Photograph showing the original siting.
Right: As it is today in Ayscoughfee Gardens.

Above: Hall Place, early 1900's, showing the Fountain and the imposing establishment of Pennington & Son.

Pennington & Son (Fred Pennington),
GENERAL DRAPERS
...AND...
CARPET WAREHOUSEMEN.
Hall Place, Spalding.
TEL. No. 46.

The well known drapery firm was founded, in 1850, by Charles Maltby Pennington (1822 - 94), draper, silk mercer and milliner, who was assisted by the great business capacity of his wife. The undertaking developed to an extraordinary degree, and the business became one of the largest of its kind in the county. From a humble commencement Charles Maltby Pennington rose to a position of affluence, and became a considerable property owner in Spalding. He was a founder member of the Spalding Club in 1874. Many extensions were made over the years, including a large arcade. In 1929 the business was purchased by Mr. and Mrs. W. A. Wheeler. It continued to flourish, under the name of Penningtons, until May, 1941, when the premises were entirely destroyed during an air raid on the town. For some years after the bombing the firm carried on business with 12 separate departments scattered about the town. It later became part of the Keightley group of Boston and a new building was erected on the site. It continued to trade under the name of Penningtons until 1969 when it was closed down. A supermarket occupies the site to-day.

In addition to Penningtons, a number of other shops and premises in Hall Place and Market Place were destroyed or seriously damaged as a result of the air raid of May, 1941. In Spalding, the total number of premises, damaged, including many houses, was over 400. Five people were killed. Another air raid took place in August 1942, when more than 500 houses, business premises and public buildings were damaged. On this occasion there was no loss of life.

Above and below: Busy Tuesday market day scenes around the Fountain in Hall Place. In the background the premises of Scales & Sons, boot makers, 21 Hall Place; Frederick Jones, boot & shoe maker (22), and William Tomline, clothier at No. 23. c.1900.

Above: The interior of Pennington's tea lounge and refreshment room - about 1920.

Below: Hall Place, Pennington's, and the Market Place beyond - about 1920.

Right: Advertisement for Jones' Boot Depot. as seen in the photograph on page 65.
Below: Hall Place in the 1930's. The café and arcade of Pennington & Son can be seen on the right and on the left is the "Cross Keys", Commercial Hotel which closed in 1960. Compare the scene with that of the photograph opposite and what appears to be the total replacement of the horse by the motor car in less than twenty years.

ESTABLISHED 1800.

Jones' Century ..
Boot Depot,

22, HALL PLACE, SPALDING.

SOLE AGENT in Spalding and District for the Celebrated

Waterproof K Boots and Shoes
(LADIES', GENT.'S, AND CHILDREN'S).

Ladies' & Gent.'s Boots to measure.

Children's Boots, Shoes, and Slippers
in great Variety, and all fittings.

Ladies' Evening Shoes a speciality.
Large Assortment to select from, 3s. 11d. to 21s.

REPAIRS neatly and promptly executed.
Country Parcels returned same day.

Above: Kingston's Corner as it is today, and below, a view taken in 1907. This was described as probably the most dangerous place in Spalding, and the scene of numerous accidents. In 1907 - 1908 the corner was demolished, including the old offices of S. & G. Kingston, together with the adjacent premises and shops. A portion of the site at the extreme corner was thrown into the roadway having been purchased by the Spalding Urban District Council. On the remainder of the site, in 1908, the new offices of S. & G. Kingston were erected. The architect being Joseph Boothroyd Corby, of Stamford, who also designed the Kingston Cottage Homes, (South Parade), the Museum, and Christadelphian Hall.

Market Place

The Corn Exchange

The Spalding Improvement Act, of 1853, was entitled "An Act for Paving, Lighting, Watching, Draining, supplying with Water, Cleansing, Regulating, and otherwise Improving the Town and Parish of Spalding; for making a Cemetery; for erecting a Corn Exchange and Market House therein; and for other purposes". There were fifteen Commissioners - known as the Spalding Improvement Commissioners - elected by the principal ratepayers and landowners, five of them going out of office yearly, but being eligible for re-election. They had power to levy rates and borrow money for the above-named and other purposes.

Right: The Corn Exchange which was erected in 1855-6 as a result of the Act. Shown here about 1950.

Overleaf: An engraving by Hilkiah Burgess of the Market Place published on the 1st. January, 1822.

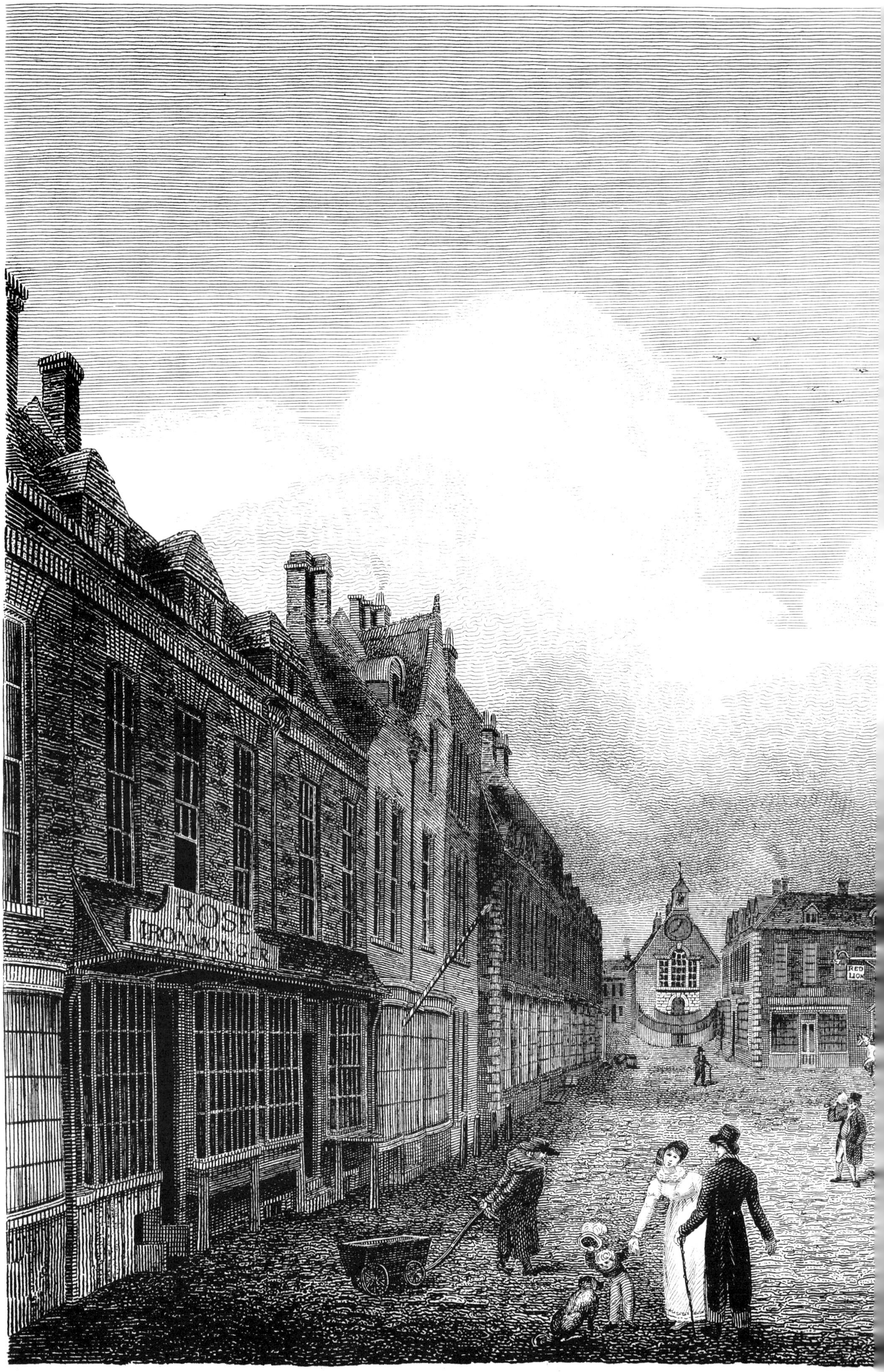
ROSE
IRONMONGER
RED
LION

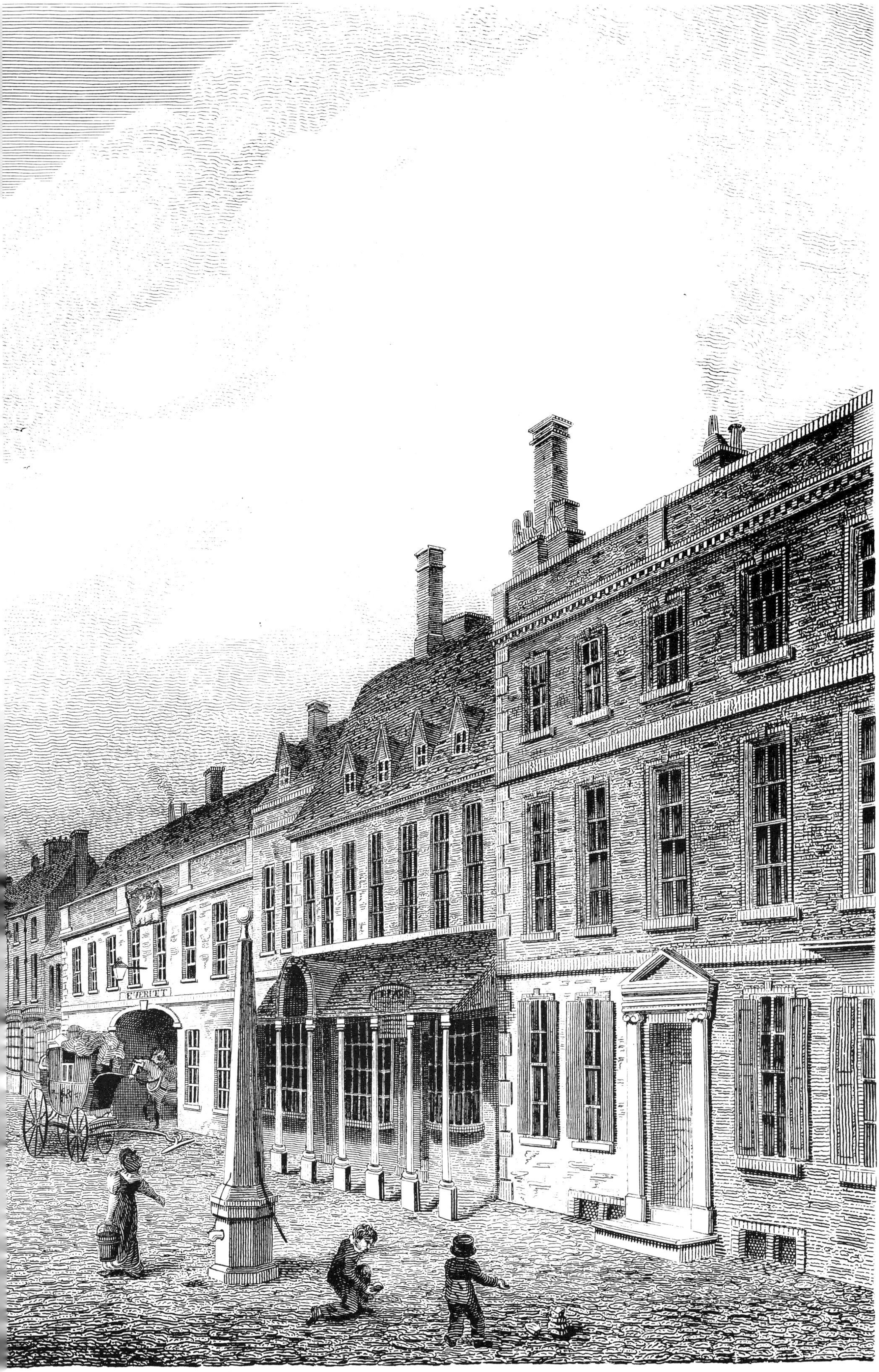

Above: A very early photograph of the Market Place prior to the building of the Corn Exchange.

The Commissioners who came into office on 1st September, 1853, purchased the Horse and Jockey site, between the Market Place and Double Street, from the Rev. W. Molson, for the purpose of erecting a Corn Exchange.

The old Town Hall, which stood in what is now known as Hall Place, was demolished in 1854, and the Corn Exchange was built by the Improvement Commissioners in 1855 - 56, at a cost of about £2,500. It was opened in March, 1856. The architects were Bellamy & Hardy, of Lincoln. The contractors William Sharman & Son, of Red Lion Street, Spalding. A description of the Corn Exchange is given in White's Directory of Lincolnshire for 1856, which reads:
"It is in the Elizabethan style, and has an illuminated clock. The Exchange Room is 73½ feet long and 42½ broad, and is neatly fitted up for the accommodation of corn merchants and farmers. The large room for assemblies, concerts, &c., is of ample dimensions and tastefully fitted up. A smaller apartment has been selected as a News Room".

On 9th May, 1856, Charles Rainey, was appointed Keeper of the Exchange, at a salary of £25 per annum.

Subsequently the rough land at the side of the Corn Exchange was converted into a Butter Market, which was opened on 14th July, 1857.

The Corn Exchange was demolished in 1972, and the South Holland Centre occupies the site today.

T. & C. Stubbs, 15

GENERAL, FANCY & FURNISHING DRAPERY WAREHOUSE.

DRESSES, MILLINERY, MANTLES, &c.

☛ FAMILY MOURNING. ☚
FUNERALS PERSONALLY CONDUCTED.
Washington Hearse, Shilbier, Mourning Coaches, &c.

3, MARKET PLACE, SPALDING.

Left: c.1890.

The Market Place, above, in the 1860s showing the shops, left to right, of: Joseph Pears, grocer and provision merchant and sole agent for W. & A. Gilbey's wines; Robert Donington, chemist and druggist; Edward Gilbert, bookseller, printer, stationer, and stamp office; Hobson and Sons, linen and woollen drapers, hatters and tailors; Stamford, Spalding and Boston Banking Co.

Hobson's Fire 1870

On the night of 27th March, 1870, the premises of Hobson & Sons drapery establishment in the Market Place was destroyed by a severe fire. The following report is from "The South Holland Magazine", for May 1870, pages 84 - 85:-

"The scene of the fire was terribly grand, even beyond description, and will long live in the memory of all who witnessed it. So rapid was the spreading of the flames that the new building where it is thought the fire emanated, was soon left floorless and roofless; and in a few seconds more, it extended its destroying powers to the old premises, and thus the whole house and shop with nearly all the stock of goods and furniture, were entirely consumed in the brief space of two or three hours. It was with considerable difficulty that the inmates were aroused to a sense of danger, some of whom, we understand, had to escape only partly dressed, to the Inns and neighbouring houses on the opposite side of the Market Place. At one time it was a matter of the greatest doubt whether the whole line of the principal shops and premises on that side of the street would not become a prey to the devouring element, but fortunately the night was calm and scarcely any wind blowing, so that the fire was kept confined principally to the premises of Hobson and Son. As it was, the roof of the Stamford Bank on one side, and the back of Mr. Appleby's premises on the other, had taken fire, and the Brigade therefore instantly directed their attention to these buildings, and by strenuous efforts kept the fire from doing greater destruction, but for which, in all probability both these buildings would have fallen an easy prey to the flames; of course, the Bank property was greatly injured, and Mr. Welden, the Manager, will be a considerable loser, both by fire and removal of his furniture. Mr. Appleby's house presented the appearance of a partial wreck, although it did not suffer much from actual fire, the greatest injury being occasioned by the falling of a chimney and sending the gable end of the house completely in. His stock and furniture as well as that of Mr. Donington next door, was much damaged by their removal to the Corn Exchange and other places. Generally speaking the inhabitants used their

Above: The ruins of the premises of Hobson & Sons, drapers, Market Place, after the fire of 27th March, 1870.

best efforts to prevent the fire spreading further, and too much praise cannot be accorded to the Revd. E. Moore, Vicar; Messrs. W. Cammack, Leaper, Pennington, Plumpton, Stubbs, Shadford, Driffill, Louth, &c. Strong remarks were made on all sides as to the inefficiency of the Spalding Fire Brigade in this instance, either from want of a leader or a proper supply of water. But whatever the cause, it was evident that there was a great difficulty in getting water applied; for had the Engines got to work as soon as the alarm was given, the front shop of Hobson and Son and its entire contents might have been saved. We are glad to learn that the books were saved, and insurances amounting to several thousands had been effected, but not to the amount of property destroyed by the fire. The estimated loss is from £10,000 to £11,000. The offices which will suffer are the Sun, the County, and the Midland. Whilst the flames were raging, an immense crowd had assembled in the Market-place, and every assistance was rendered to the sufferers, every one appearing anxious to lend a helping hand. On Sunday and Monday, great numbers of people visited the scene of destruction, to witness the removal of Salvage goods - and the workmen among the ruins".

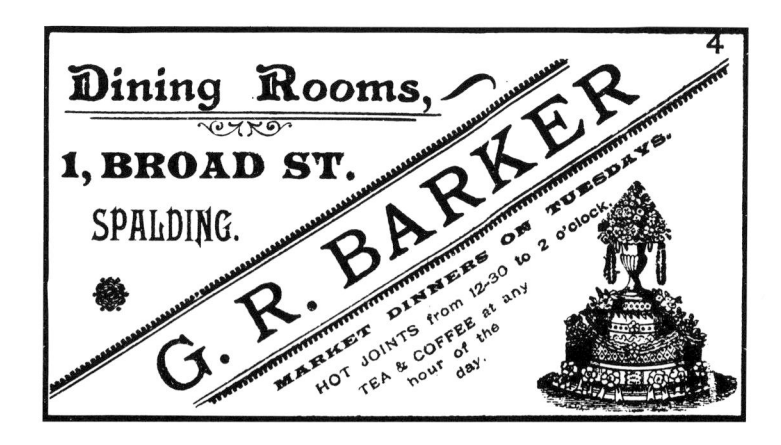

Left: c.1890.

Above: A view of the Market Place at the beginning of the Twentieth Century. In the foreground Spalding Urban District Council roadsweepers with hand dust cart. Omnibus outside the White Hart Hotel. The four storey building on the extreme left is that of Hobson & Co. drapers, erected in 1871, after their previous shop had been destroyed by fire. "The Stamford Mercury", of 7th April, 1871, reported "The new premises in the centre of the Market Place erected by Messrs. Hobson & Sons were opened for business on Tuesday. The lofty and spacious frontage of plate glass has an imposing effect. The superstructure is remarkably plain and heavy, and the great height to which the building has been carried dwarfs the architectural appearance of the bank and other adjoining premises".

HOCKNEY'S
Dining Rooms and . .
Confectionery Establishment,
Next Door to Corn Exchange, Spalding.

WEDDING, BIRTHDAY, & OTHER CAKES

Handsomely Ornamented. Any size not in stock made to order on the shortest notice.

Plum, Pound, Madeira, Rice, Cherry, Seed, Simnel, Tennis, Ginger, Cocoa-nut, Walnut, Sponge, Lunch, and a numerous variety of Cakes fresh daily.

All the Latest Novelties in French Confectionery and Italian Pastry

Fancy Biscuits & Tit-Bits for Afternoon Tea. A large Assortment.

Try Our Celebrated PORK PIES & SAUSAGES.

Fancy Chocolates and other Sweets in Great Variety.
Afternoon Teas and Social Gatherings Catered for

Left: c.1902.

May Hirings

Servants Annual Holidays as reported in "The Spalding Free Press", of 14th May, 1907:

The annual May Hiring Fair took place at Spalding on Friday, and was largely attended by farm servants and domestics of all descriptions. The wages given were, on the whole, about the same as last year's figures, and experienced men were quickly engaged at the higher wages. Male servants were hired at the following wage:- Ploughboys, £5 to £8; horsemen, £8 to £10; experienced men, £14 to £16; waggoners, £17 to £20; with 8s., 9s., and 10s., in addition, as standing wages, with certain other extras. For females, the rate of wages were as follows: General Servants, £10 to £14; Housemaids, £10 to £15; Plain Cooks, £16 to £18; and Cook-generals, £14 to £16. The weather was very favourable, and the usual May Fair attractions were greatly in evidence.

Right: Advertisement c.1902.

SPRING CLEANING.

During the Season, I will fit and lay all Floor Covering, Floor Cloths, Linoleums, Cork Carpets, &c., **Entirely Free of Charge**.

No Extra Prices. Goods will compare favourably with any bought in Spalding or elsewhere.

Stout Air-dried Linoleums

(thoroughly seasoned), 2yds. wide, 2/6, 2/11, 3/6, 3/11, and upwards. Or per sq. yd. 1/3, 1/5½, 1/9, 1/11½, and upwards.

Pretty Light Grounds for Bedrooms, Landings, Dressing Rooms, Lavatories, Bath Rooms, &c.

Inspection Invited. Call and see the various qualities and patterns.

FEATHER BEDS Re-dressed.

New Feathers Added if Required. New Ticks Made.
Purified Feathers Kept in Stock.

Cream and White Lace Curtains.

Handsome Designs. 1s. to 20s. per pair.

Madras, India, and Frilled Muslin Curtains.

Curtain Laces and Curtain Nets in Great Variety.

THOS. C. STUBBS, *Drapery & Furnishing Warehouse,* **Market Place, Spalding.**

Cattle Market

New Road, 1899

'While the sheep market has declined during the past twenty years, the beast market has on the other hand improved. In this, and in other connections, the holding of the market on Tuesday is a considerable advantage. Store stock are brought by dealers from Boston, Holbeach, Long Sutton, Wisbech, Sleaford, St. Ives, Louth, Alford, &c. The principal local dealers are Mr. James Tointon, who conducts a large business in "in-calvers", and store cattle, Mr. John Bunting, Mr. James Paddison, Mr. T. Phillips, Mr. J.T. Saxton and Mr. George Benner. Buyers of fat cattle come from Leicester, Nottingham, March, Cambridge, Peterborough, and Syston, one of the oldest, most regular and most familiar visitors being Mr. Joseph Driver, of the last-mentioned place. In 1887, as a fit method of celebrating the Jubilee of the Queen's Accession to the Throne, an attempt was made to induce the Improvement Commissioners to purchase the site of the then disused jail and adjacent grounds and transfer the beast market thereto. It was contended that an enclosure nearer the station properly arranged for the purpose, would be a great improvement upon the open thoroughfare - New Road and Westlode Street - where stock had to be held up in herds by drovers, and were an obstruction to the ordinary traffic, while making a squalid mess of the streets. The project, however, was abandoned, owing mainly to the opposition of the owners and licence holders of inns adjoining New Road, and the market continues to be held in the wide open street. The average number of store and fat cattle offered weekly for sale during the year has been about 200. The toll is 3d per head in the "fat", and 2d per head in the "store" division. For a bull, the toll is sixpence.' J.H. Diggle, 1900.

Above: A view of Spalding Cattle Fair, about 1908, held in the public streets. On the right wearing bowler hat is Mr. Fred Sly, then Chairman of the Spalding Urban District Council, who has had to leave the road, and take to the path with his cycle, the cattle monopolising the roadway. Mr. Sly, a farmer, of Holbeach Road, was Chairman of the Council 1908 - 9.

Below: Advertisements from just after the turn of the century, complete with telephone nos.
Opposite: Two more, from the late 1890's, prior to telephones being generally available.

ESTABLISHED 1870.

R. LONGSTAFF & Co.
F.A.I.

Auctioneers, Valuers, Estate Agents,

Fire Loss Assessors, Hotel and Tenant-Right Valuers a Speciality.

Weekly Stock Auctions—Spalding, Tuesdays.
Bourne, Thursdays.
Stamford, Mondays & Fridays.

All Sales carefully conducted.   Prompt Settlements.

Head Office—Sheep Market, SPALDING.

Offices at Market Place, Bourne, and
8, Ironmonger St., Stamford.

TELEPHONE NOS.—14X OFFICE; 14Y HOUSE.

TELEPHONE: NO. 60.

TOM A. WHITE,

*Auctioneer, Valuer
    and Estate Agent.*

SALES OF FAT & STORE STOCK Every Tuesday.
AGENT FOR ALL KINDS OF INSURANCES.

Sheep Market, SPALDING.

Below: New Road about 1928, on Market Day, viewed from Kingston's corner. George Hall's premises can be seen to the extreme right of the photograph.

GEORGE HALL & SON,

Auctioneers, Valuers, Land & Estate Agents, Accountants, etc.

Offices—NEW ROAD, SPALDING.

GENERAL PASSENGER & SHIPPING AGENTS.

AGENTS FOR

ALLAN LINE, QUEENSLAND ROYAL MAIN LINE, UNION CASTLE LINE (for the Cape), CUNARD LINE, DOMINION LINE, ABERDEEN LINE.

Passengers and Goods Shipped for all Parts of the World.

AGENTS for the MIDLAND RAILWAY COMPANY

And Receiving Office for Parcels and Goods,

At which INFORMATION AS TO RATES, &c., can be Obtained.

LIFE, FIRE, MARINE, ACCIDENTAL, EMPLOYERS' LIABILITY, MORTGAGE, and

GENERAL INSURANCE AGENTS.

Valuation for Probate for the New Estate Duties, and Enfranchisement of Copyhold Estates.

Agents for the Issue of Special Policies for Workmen's Compensation, Under Act 1880-1897, and Common Law, freeing Employers from all Liability, at Special Rates.

S. & G. Kingston

Auctioneers, Valuers,

AND

Land Agents,

Spalding & Long Sutton.

SALES OF FAT & STORE STOCK

AT SPALDING EVERY TUESDAY.

Spalding Monthly Horse Sales

First Wednesday in every Month, at Black Swan Hotel.

AGENTS FOR

Messrs. Joseph Fison & Co.'s Artificial Manures,

AND THE

North British & Mercantile Insurance Company.

Also at LONG SUTTON, for the

Atlas Fire & Life Assurance Co., and the

. . Midland Counties Hail Insurance Co.

Above: A photograph taken about 1900, of the Constitutional Club, in New Road, opened in 1892. These premises (which are now part of the offices of Messrs. Maples & Son, solicitors), were used until 1911. The history of the club dates from the time when Canon Moore allowed the use of a room near the Church; from there it moved to premises in the Crescent; then to rooms at the Drill Hall, in the Sheep Market, and finally to New Road. The next house, on the right hand side, No. 24, was the residence of the Rev. Samuel Yates, pastor of the Spalding Congregational Church (now the United Reformed Church), from 1877 to 1922. Note the iron posts used for holding cattle chains on market days.

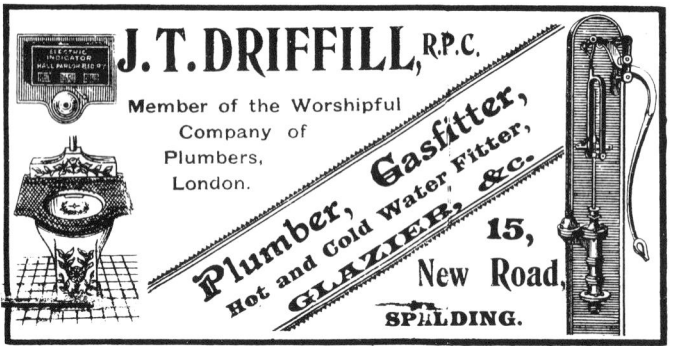

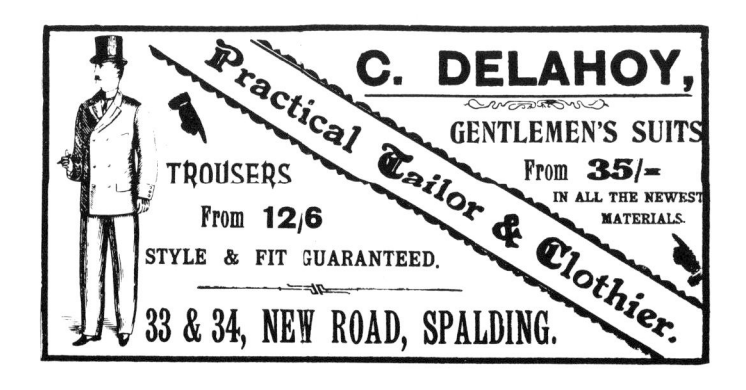

J. T. DRIFFILL, R.P.C.

Member of the Worshipful Company of Plumbers, London.

Plumber, Gasfitter, Hot and Cold Water Fitter, Glazier, &c.

15, New Road, SPALDING.

C. DELAHOY,

Practical Tailor & Clothier.

GENTLEMEN'S SUITS From 35/- IN ALL THE NEWEST MATERIALS.

TROUSERS From 12/6 STYLE & FIT GUARANTEED.

33 & 34, NEW ROAD, SPALDING.

Left: c.1890.

Horse Fair

Pinchbeck Road, 1899

'With the exception of an odd horse or two sold by auction, and an itinerant dealer's occasional drove of ponies and miscellaneous "crocks", horses do not appear for sale at the ordinary market. The September Fair is the principal day of the year for the show of horses, mares and foals. Nevertheless, the local authority has a bye-law on the matter which states: "Every person who brings any horse, mare, gelding, mule or ass into the market, shall cause such horse, mare, gelding, mule or ass to be placed in Pinchbeck Street, which is appropriated for the purposes of a horse-market. No person shall run or try the paces of any horses, in any other street, or place appropriated for use, or used from time to time, for the purposes of any market". The toll for a horse is 4d., for a "mule or ass", 2d. per head. Including the fairs, less than 500 horses "paid toll", at Spalding last year (1899).'

J. H. Diggle, 1900.

Below: Horse Fair held in Pinchbeck Road - early 1900's.

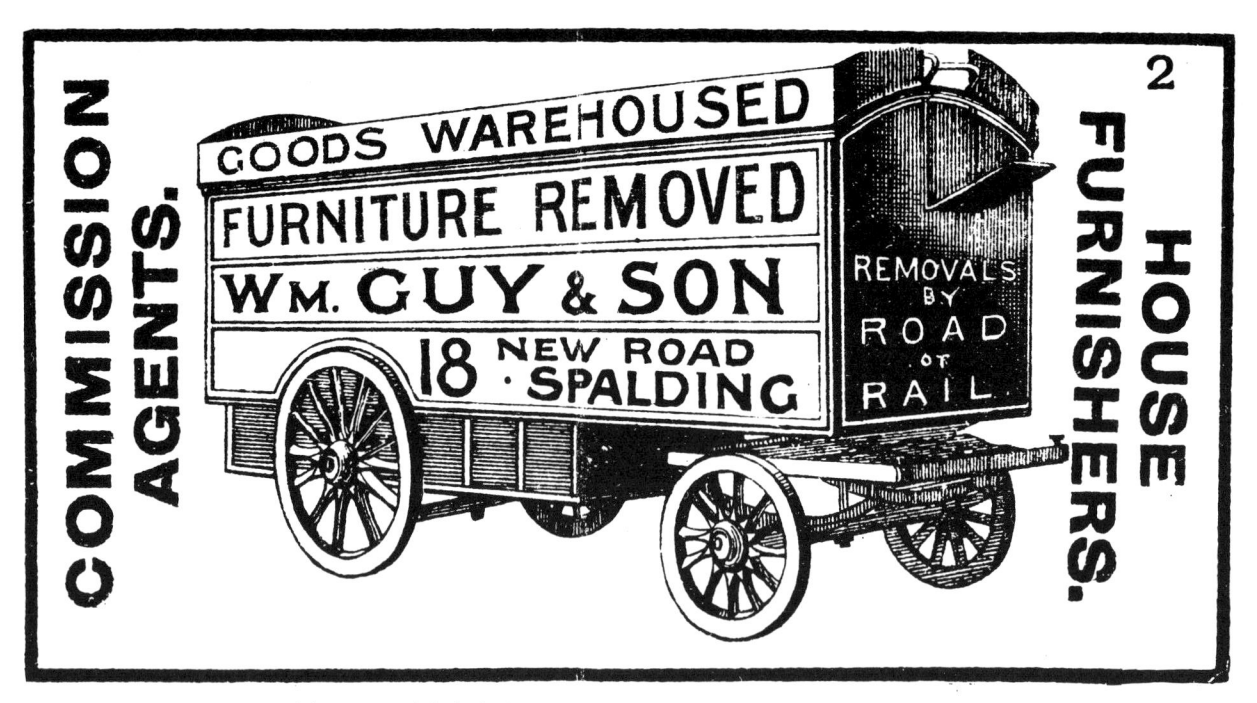

Above and left below: Advertisements from the 1890's.
Right below: The same firm as above, but from 1902.

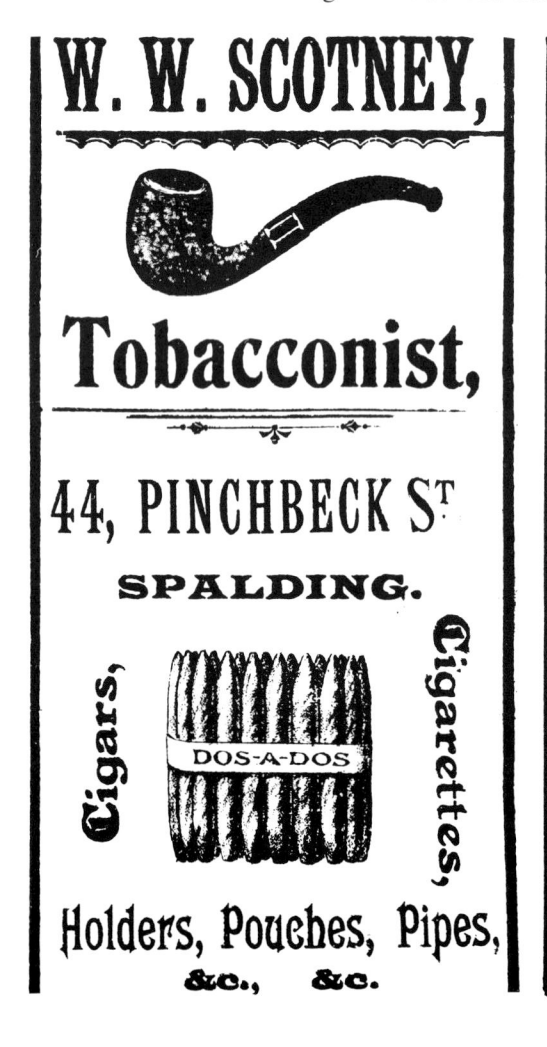

Trade and Commerce

Fairs and Markets

"Spalding hath a flourishing market weekly, on Tuesday, and five fairs yearly, viz. on the 27th of April for stock, hemp and flax, and town fair; the 29th of June, for horses and ditto; the 28th of August for horses only; the 25th of September, generally called the Summer fair and reckoned to be the largest, for horned cattle and other stock, hemp and flax and all other merchandize; and on the 26th of December, being St. Nicholas, to whom the monastry was dedicated, and thence, in all probability, the most ancient of them, for all cattle, merchandize, &c. The first two fairs were granted by letters-patent of King George 1. at the instance of the Duchess of Buccleugh, then possessor of the manor." (1)

In 1858 the Spalding Improvement Commissioners decided that the Horse Fair should be held in Pinchbeck Road. (2)

(1). *"The Provincial Literary Repository". Vol. 11. June, 1802. No.19. Page 201.*
(2). *Minutes of the Spalding Improvement Commissioners.*

Spalding Market, 1900

"The market now may be said to begin in earnest with the beast and sheep about 9 o'clock, and to continue until 12 o'clock. The butter, egg, poultry and fruit market occupies the attention of quite another class of buyers and sellers during the middle of the day. At 12 o'clock the first "Market Ordinaries" (1) are held, at the "White Hart", and "Red Lion" Hotels, and are attended by farmers and merchants. Previous to 1 o'clock, merchants arrive at the Corn Exchange to pay for produce purchased on the previous Tuesday, and to receive notices, by telegram, of the latest fluctuations in the corn market. At 1 o'clock, the Corn Exchange begins to fill, and a busy hour or so is spent, after which there is a general movement to the streets, the shops, and the inns, until 3 o'clock, when a large number go towards the station to catch the recognised return market trains. About the same time, the farmers who drive in to market prepare to depart; and by 4 o'clock, a large proportion of all classes are on their way home. Thus, the market from beginning to finish occupies little more than six hours, while probably the majority of the market folks are in the town not more than four hours. A striking contrast this with old-time habits, which, in the halcyon days of agriculture, kepts farmers at "market", two or three days and even longer.

Passengers by rail

A striking and growing feature of the market of 1900 is the number of market folks who take advantage of the special market trains and the cheap tickets for ordinary trains which all the railway companies now issue up to noon on Tuesday. Mr. T.N. Lewin, of the traffic department, Spalding station, has kindly furnished the following figures, which show the average number of passengers who arrived at Spalding station each Tuesday during the past twelve months:

From the:		
	Holbeach Line	600 passengers
	Sleaford Line	500 passengers
	Boston Line	450 passengers
	Peterborough Line	300 passengers
	March Line	300 passengers
	Bourne Line	250 passengers
	Total	2,400 passengers

(1). *A meal prepared at an eating-house at a fixed rate for all comers is called "an ordinary"; hence, the place providing such meals.*   *"Brewer's Dictionary of Phrase and Fable". 1970. page 785.*

Thus, between two and three thousand people come to Spalding market weekly on an average by train. The market trains are taken advantage of by a number of the largest farmers, who, instead of driving, as formerly all the way to Spalding, are driven to the nearest town or station in the morning, and are met after market.

Arrivals by road

This practice has necessarily reduced the number of vehicles which, some 30 years ago, after the pillion period had ended, and the improvement of the roads had begun, filled the yards of the principal inns as the horses crowded the stables. At the same time, the conveyance of butter, eggs and poultry to market, and the carriage home of heavy drapery, of agricultural tools and miscellaneous eatables, known as "shop-things", so obviously calls for a trap, that ostlers of most of the principal inns are still kept busy on market days. At the "White Hart", some 50, occasionally 60, traps are brought in, and other well-known hostelries - the "Red Lion", "White Horse", "White Lion", "Black Swan", "Greyhound", "Ram Skin", "Lincoln Arms", "Cross Keys", "Peacock", "Pied Calf", and "Little Bull", - have their share of customers.

The Carrier's Cart

Twenty-three carrier's carts and vans all told come to Spalding. The carrier's cart still lingers on the road, and is a time-honoured and time-killing institution, which, railways notwithstanding, it will be difficult to dispense with altogether. For its clients live at Bourne, Langtoft, the Deepings, Donington, Gosberton, Saracen's Head, Holbeach Bank, Fosdyke, Gedney Hill, Whaplode Drove, Pinchbeck West, Moulton Chapel, Crowland, and in other places remote from towns and railway stations. Crowland does not now attend Spalding market so well as formerly; nevertheless, it is served by a 'bus and several vans. "The loading up of these vans is a work of time, and great ingenuity is displayed by the carrier in accommodating the new kitchen utensils, the hat boxes, and the many shaped packages which the housewife is taking back to her expectant household. These lumbering vehicles, generally drawn by two unevenly matched horses, bring weekly a full load of country people, with their baskets on the top, and their live poultry in the travelling coup beneath".

The Market in progress

The system of selling cattle by auction has hitherto made little progress at Spalding compared with neighbouring towns, as Grantham, Lynn or Sleaford. Messrs. Laming & Son conduct a sale of fat and store pigs at the corner of the Sheep Market, near the "Pied Calf", and Messrs. S. & G. Kingston sell stock of all kinds - pigs opposite the Sessions House, and horses in Hall Place. A few sales by auction of wood and effects also take place in Hall Place and New Road. Other than these auctions the business is done privately, numerous dealers, factors, and commission agents acting as middlemen.........

The Corn Exchange

The marketing of farm produce in the Corn Exchange presents a different scene altogether. There, in a warm commodious hall - enlarged and embellished this year at a total cost of nearly £2,000 - the corn and cake merchant and the farmer, the miller and the seedsman, the agent with the ever-open order book are examining samples, marking sample bags, entering orders, making appointments, discussing prices, disputing deliveries, selling, buying, speculating, clustering round merchants' stands and learning, as judgement is pronounced on a sample, that the corn trade is no better. In whatever other department Spalding market may have declined, from the merchant and agents' point of view it compares favourably with - even surpasses - other Fenland towns of greater size and population. The merchants and middlemen who come to Spalding are legion. There is no mistaking them. They are brisk men who carry bags and an air of acquaintanceship with offices and town life making them distinct from the agriculturist, whose dealings with slow-moving cattle, stationary land, and whose waiting on the steady round of the seasons, make him less alert but more portly and reflective. There are now 75 stands used in Spalding Corn Exchange. Some merchants occupy a whole stand and pay £3 per annum, others share a stand and pay £2 each. About a score of dealers pay £1 each for the privilege of a "Walk"; 94 farmers and others have this year taken the 5s. ticket; while on an average 150 pay weekly the entrance fee of 2d. The highest number this year has been 240. Thus it would appear that the attendance at the Corn Exchange is about 400 weekly.

The Butter Market

The place appointed for the sale of butter, poultry, eggs and fruit, called conveniently the "Butter Market", has been described as "a congested passage and cellar extending from Crackpool Lane (Broad Street) to a narrow cobbled street at the back (Double Street).....". This year, in connection with the Corn Exchange enlargement, space has been added. The scene in the Butter Market is of a lively description. On the floor of the market there are hampers, also improvised stalls covered with white cloths, and upon them are great, cold, oval geese with the internal fat complete, while insinuating and obliging farmers' wives sit behind them; there are live poultry fluttering on the indented floor, and at festive seasons huge turkeys pinioned and crestfallen. Produce is much mixed. Here a buyer is negotiating for eggs at 8 a shilling, there "Normanton Wonders" are offered at 2s. per stone, close by, a dressed duck is changing hands, while, opposite, a farmer is exhibiting a cage of huge ganders and conversing with a cottager's wife, a patient vendor of cream cheeses under cooling cabbage leaves. The entire portion of the farmyard controlled by the farmer's wife is sampled here most Tuesdays.

The Market under Canvas

The whole available space in the Market Place, with part of Hall Place, is occupied by stalls, from which fish, meat, fruit, confectionery, vegetables, tools, cheap haberdashery, cutlery and trinkets of many kinds, are sold chiefly to the working classes. Local wheelwrights and the agents of agricultural foundries make in Hall Place a picturesque show of carts and wagons, and highly-coloured implements of the latest pattern. There are four portable offices stationed in the Market Place, and the noisy Vendor of tough crockery has space here as in other towns.

An Institution for Everybody

But Spalding Market is much more than a general mart for agricultural produce. The gathering together by common consent of the whole country-side is taken advantage of by many institutions - the County Council convenes its committee meetings, the Petty Sessions are held, the libraries are open. The solicitor, in his obscure sanctum, receives his clients one by one, his clerks receive the drainage, the acquittances, the tithe, and the insurance premiums, and aught besides. The town tradesman works under pressure during the day, the banks keep open an hour longer than usual. The active man seizes the occasion which brings numbers of customers within his reach, and gives his time sparingly. The circuit Superintendent meets the local "brother", and hears about the "cause", in the remote hamlet. Spalding, too, on Tuesday, is the rendezvous of many for whom "marketing", has become a habit, and who would greatly miss the gossip and the recreation associated with a little shopping and a pleasureable trip. And perhaps some who read this will be reminded that it was at Spalding Market - that universal trysting-place - where the first seeds of a romance were sown which blossomed into the companionship of a lifetime."

We must again be grateful to J. H. Diggle for the above description of the major role that the market played in the trade, commerce and indeed, everyday life of the Town.

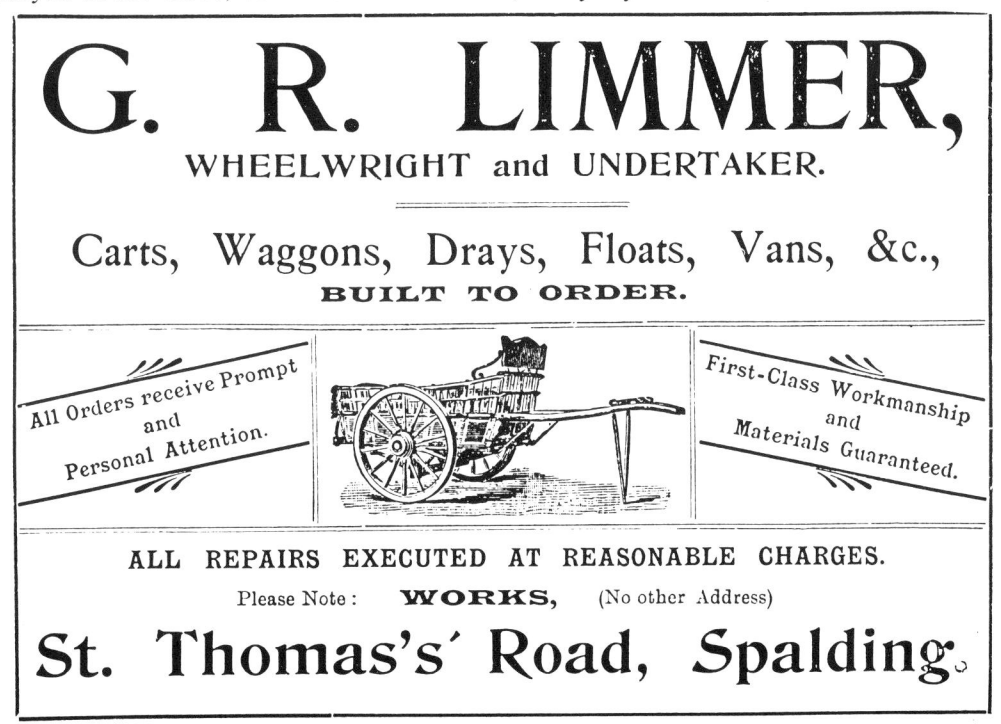

G. R. LIMMER,

WHEELWRIGHT and UNDERTAKER.

Carts, Waggons, Drays, Floats, Vans, &c.,

BUILT TO ORDER.

All Orders receive Prompt and Personal Attention.

First-Class Workmanship and Materials Guaranteed.

ALL REPAIRS EXECUTED AT REASONABLE CHARGES.

Please Note : **WORKS,** (No other Address)

St. Thomas's' Road, Spalding.

Henry Watkinson

H. Watkinson (1819-95), was a journalist born at Rookery Farm, Burwell, Cambridgeshire on the 17th July, 1819, the second son of John and Mary (Ball) Watkinson. The dramatist, Edward Fitzball (1792-1873), being his maternal uncle. He was educated at 'a very good Preparatory School', at St. Ives and later apprenticed to Wm. Watts, printer and bookseller, Wisbech, 1833-40. He joined the Independent Church at Wisbech in 1839, and for some years was active as a local preacher and Sunday School teacher, both there and at Nottingham. In 1840 he went to Nottingham as assistant to his uncle, C.N. Wright, printer, but by 1846 was himself in business in Spalding as a printer, bookseller and auctioneer. It was here that he was persuaded to publish a Spalding newspaper by his friend, John Gardiner (d.1883), who founded the Wisbech Advertiser in 1845.

The first number of the Spalding Free Press and Eastern Counties' Advertiser was published on the 5th October, 1847. In the earlier years of the paper he discharged the combined duties of proprietor, editor and reporter and he remained editor until 1874, when he entered into partnership with Walter Crust (d.1882), the latter becoming editor. Henry Watkinson was sole proprietor of the paper at the time of his death.

One of the original promoters of the Spalding Waterworks Company, he became a director in 1871, and chairman of the company on the death of Canon Moore, in 1889. He was a director of the Sleaford Waterworks Company; one of the managers of the Spalding Savings Bank; a member of the Hundred of Elloe Lodge of Freemasons, and a member of the Spalding Gentlemen's Society. At one period he owned and conducted the Sleaford Gazette.

He was married on the 6th November, 1845 to Jane, youngest daughter of Richard Hewitt, a surgeon in Spalding. He died on the 21st November, 1895, aged 76 years. (1)

Henry Watkinson, founder of the "Lincolnshire Free Press".

(1). *Henry Watkinson MSS. one vol.; in the custody of the Spalding Gentlemen's Society; SGS Newscuttings Books; "Spalding Free Press", 26th November, 1895; "History of Wisbech & Co." by F.J. Gardiner.*

The "Free Press"

Founded by Henry Watkinson (1819-95), the first number of the "Spalding Free Press and Eastern Counties' Advertiser", was published on 5th October, 1847. The first leading article came from the pen of the Rev. J.C. Jones, M.A., (1823-1917), pastor of the Spalding Baptist Church. From October to December, 1847, the "Free Press" appeared monthly. For the next two years it was published fortnightly. Towards the close of 1850 the proprietor announced that it would appear weekly, price 3d. The "Free Press" was first published on premises at the Corn Exchange end of the Market Place, later transferring to offices in Hall Place. In 1869, the "Free Press" consisted of four pages, two of which were printed in London, and the other two on an old-fashioned Columbian Press, which forty years later was still being retained as an interesting relic. The office was described as a modest little warehouse, which had been converted into a printing room; all hands, from the editor downwards, being compelled to take to the case and set type as publishing day approached. At that date - 1869 - the whole staff of every department of the business numbered only eight; the circulation was a 1,000 copies.

Henry Watkinson maintained full control for 27 years, until October, 1874, when he took into partnership Walter Crust, at that time chief reporter, and appointed him editor. In 1882 the two partners undertook a tour of the United States of America, and it was when they were returning home that Walter Crust died suddenly at New York, on October 11th, 1882, aged 33. He was succeeded by Joseph Wilson as editor. Joseph Wilson (1854-1909), had joined the staff in 1869, becoming a reporter in 1872. Many years later he recalled that "Practically I was the only reporter on the staff for some time. It was prior to the cycle age. What scores of miles I trudged along the country roads; many a time I have traversed the distance between Bourne and Holbeach on foot; what weary marches in quest of news I had into the surrounding villages; and then, after these long and tiring journeys the only desk available to me on which to transcribe my notes was the rack from which I vigorously set type in the intervals in which I was not in pursuit of news. Until the death of Mr. Watkinson, the only space possible even to the editorial department was a small partitioned enclosure in the corner of the composing room, while the click of type setting and the vibration of moving machinery were a constant and unwelcome accompaniment." (1). In addition to his professional activities Joseph Wilson was a "public man", being a member of the Spalding Board of Guardians, the Spalding School Board, and for a brief period the Spalding Urban District Council. A leading member of the Crescent United Methodist Church, he was a local preacher and temperance advocate.

Henry Watkinson lived on the premises up to 1895 in which year he died suddenly. Some years before he had retired from an active part in his business but still lived on the premises as did almost every other trader in the Market Place and Hall Place. At this time the editor was Joseph Wilson, reporters Alfred Crabtree and Samuel Jepson, advertisement manager Giles W. Ham, accountant and shop manager William White, and printing office overseer Alfred Ridlington. With the death of Henry Watkinson, the "Free Press" property came into the market and there was considerable competition for it but in the end it was secured by the heads of the different departments of the "Free Press" staff who joined together and in 1896 formed the Spalding Free Press Printing and Publishing Company.

In 1909 the staff numbered 33. The buildings accommodated a rotary newspaper machine, three linotype machines, and all the accessories associated with an extensive and constantly growing job printing department. What had formerly been the residence of the founder was occupied by the literary, reporting and art staff.

On 1st March, 1909, Joseph Wilson celebrated forty years connection with the paper, and a few days later, on Sunday afternoon, 7th March, 1909, while in the process of making preparations to carry out a preaching engagement in the evening, suddenly collapsed and died. He was 55. His sudden death caused a great sensation in the town and district where he had been so highly esteemed. A fellow journalist wrote that he was "one of the best of chums, the most discerning of editors, a pattern of family life". Alfred Crabtree then became editor, and on his retirement in 1923, was followed by Ernest A. Wilson, son of Joseph Wilson, who remained editor until the paper was acquired by the East Midland Allied Press in 1949.

Overleaf: Part of the front page of the first "Spalding Free Press". Note part of column 2 has been removed to accommodate the full editorial.

(1). *"Spalding Free Press", 9th March 1909.*

Spalding
And Eastern C

No. 1. TUESDAY,

ANNOUNCEMENT.

It is intended to publish a stamped sheet on the first Tuesday in every month, under the above title, price 2½d.; the present one is the first number of such issue. Below will be found a scale of prices for the insertion of Advertisements, which will on inspection, prove as low as is compatible with any chance of profit to the issuer. It is almost needless to expatiate largely on the benefits of advertising to the trading community; they are too well known to need any argument in their favour here. The only surprising thing is, that Spalding, with a population of about 8,000 has not long before been supplied with an advertising medium, when towns of about equal magnitude give existence to one and in some cases two influential and widely circulated weekly newspapers. Boston, with a population of 14,000, has not, it is true, till lately been able to support a weekly journal; but the success attending the spirited management by the present proprietor of the paper there, proves that it was not from any incapability in the place itself to become the seat of a widely circulating journal; but, that its capabilities were not skilfully brought out by the previous owners of the press there. Spalding, though not equal in size to Boston, possesses a neighbourhood, which, whether we look to the richness and extent of district, or the wealth and intelligence of its inhabitants, will suffer nothing in comparison with the latter. If Boston, then, can support a weekly paper Spalding surely can do as much for a monthly one; provided always it be conducted in that spirited and at the same time temperate manner, as to ensure it readers and sympathy from the public.

The proprietor of the "Spalding Free Press" looks to his advertising columns as the principal convenience he will be able to afford to the inhabitants of Spalding. In the other departments of the paper he will seek, by a careful choice of extracts and what is called "family reading" to relieve, for his fair readers, (for he hopes he shall obtain such), the heaviness which attends the mere business-like dulness of the advertising portion of the issue. The political department will be conducted on principles decidedly *liberal*. In the warmth of discussion personalities will be carefully avoided; and be it particularly understood, systems will be denounced, not men. All local abuses,

To ALL BOOKSELLERS And ALMANACK SELLERS.

22,000 COPIES OF NOBLE'S ALMANACK COMPENDIUM were published last year. The Edition for 1848 is now at press. Immediate orders should be given to prevent disappointment. Advertisements inserted on low terms (the circulation considered).

Noble's Parochial Account Books

are so well known, and are so very generally used, that little need be added to the enumeration of them. They are as follows:—

Noble's Improved Highway Account Book,

for keeping the YEARLY ACCOUNTS of Surveyors of Highways, is allowed to be the most complete and the cheapest Published. Price 4s. on fine paper, neatly Bound. The New Act on impounding of Cattle, and much other useful information has been just added.

"A Highway Surveyor's Account Book, by Noble, of Boston, has been brought under our notice, and we feel warranted in recommending it as the most simple and the best arranged book of the kind we have seen."—MARK LANE EXPRESS.

The Magistrates have repeatedly expressed their approbation of Noble's Highway Account Book.

however venerable, will be considered a fair mark for editorial comments and will be attacked with hostility but at the same time good humour. If in this short programme of the proposed action of the *bantling of the press* it is proposed to usher into the world, the writer has not conveyed to the public very studiously the course the *aforesaid bantling* is about to take, it is because he thinks very aspiring conceptions of the future greatness of infants are generally falsified; and that far better than any introduction to the world that any body or any journal can have, is, the experience of his or its good qualities which may be proved by the public after an acquaintance of some little time to enable them to do so.

Terms for the Insertion of Advertisements:

Stamford Mercury SCALE:— s. d.
One to three lines, ... 4 0
For every additional line, ... 0 3
Spalding Free Press SCALE:— s. d.
One to *four* lines, ... 3 0
For every additional line, ... 0 2

UNCLAIM

THE UNCLAIM the Bank of En Addresses, and Des persons entitled to amounts, being th Dividends and Stoc ing to many million accumulating durin teenth centuries, a now be recovered arranged under the Price 1s. each book ticular in stating require.

The whole bound W. STRANGE, 21, P all Booksellers.

Star Life

Chief Office, 44, M

Capi

James Hunter, Frederick Mild Thomas Sands, W. Skinner, Es

Chairman, Charles of *Deputy Chairman*,

William Betts, E John Churchill, Walter Griffith, John Lidgett, Es Wm. F. Pocock, William Merry, W. Daniel Owen, *Solicitor*, Rich *Bankers*, Messrs. M

THIS Society is devoted to th Members of the SOCIETIES, and that religious conn are effected upon a

ONE-HALF, at lea from ACCREDITED METHODIST SOCIET exclusive means of country, the most o

›ee Press,

ies' Advertiser.

ER 5th, 1847. Price

VIDENDS.

DEND BOOKS of
taining the Names,
of upwards 20,000
ms of money of all
of the Unclaimed
blic funds, amount-
y, which have been
ghteenth and nine-
hole of which can
t of kin. Carefully
te᎒ of the alphabet.
neath xtra. Be par-
cac letter you

in cloth, price 20s.
Row, London; and

---

ce Society.

reet, Bank, London.

000.

S.
ngton.
Nicholas-lane.
erpool.
tocton-on-Tees.
S.
d, Esq., Recorder
ry.
iah Buttress, Esq.,
m, H. Smith, Esq.
m, Tress, Esq.
o. F. Urling, Esq.
hn Vanner, Esq.
hn Wingrave, Esq.
hn Wood, Esq.

en Reece, Esq.
eters, Mildred & Co.

ut not exclusively,
ce of the lives of
AN METHODIST
rers and friends of
surances, however,
lives.
irectors are chosen
F THE WESLEYAN
sseses peculiar and
ng, throughout the
on relative
sunshine to be
educing the risks

TO ADVERTISERS.

THE WISBECH ADVERTISER,
AND
LOCAL CHRONICLE;

PUBLISHED on the FIRST SATURDAY IN THE MONTH, and *extensively* circulated in the Isle of Ely, the Counties of Cambridge, Huntingdon, Lincoln, Norfolk, Suffolk, and Northampton; and is forwarded by post to all parts of the world on the same conditions as all other newspapers.

Price *Twopence stamped* for general circulation, and will be forwarded by post on receipt of two shillings in postage stamps for a year's subscription.

Published by JOHN GARDINER, Bookseller, Stationer, and Patent Medicine Vendor, Wisbech, Cambridgeshire.

EXTRAORDINARY NOVELTY.
On *SATURDAY, OCTOBER 2nd,*
WAS COMMENCED
A BRILLIANTLY COLOURED SERIES,
OF THE NEWEST
LONDON AND PARIS FASHIONS,
The First Sheet containing
THE ENTIRE
FASHIONS FOR THE MONTH,
Elaborately Finished
IN THE FIRST STYLE OF ART,
And accompanied by plain instructions as to the mode, shape, and appearance of the various garments,
ADAPTED FOR WINTER WEAR;
THESE
Magnificently Coloured ENGRAVINGS,
PREPARED
REGARDLESS OF TROUBLE OR EXPENSE,
Are to be alternated with
A SPLENDID SUCCESSION
Of the most useful and ornamental
PATTERNS IN FANCY NEEDLEWORK,
COMBINING THE NEWEST DESIGNS
IN
BERLIN WOOLS, CROTCHET AND EMBROIDERY,
BOTH WILL BE
STAMPED TO GO FREE BY POST
TO ALL PARTS OF THE KINGDOM;
And are to be

GIVEN AWAY,

TO SUBSCRIBERS FOR
THE LADY'S NEWSPAPER,
Published every Saturday.

AS THE
BEAUTIFULLY COLOURED PATTERNS
Now in course of preparation, will effect an immense saving to those who devote time to the elaboration of
Elegant SUBJECTS IN NEEDLEWORK;
And as most of the Patterns are
OBTAINED BY
AN IMMEDIATE OUTLAY
OF
SEVERAL THOUSAND POUNDS
Expended for the

British Herbs for British Constitutio

CUL-   HE
PEPER'S   PIL

The best Remedy for indigestion and all d
of the Stomach and Bowels, Headache, D
Coughs, Colds, Eructations, Pains in the S
Bilious Complaints, Costiveness, Sickness,
Appetite, Incipient Consumption, &c., and a
Reviver of the System.

THE efficacy of this invaluable medicine
now been proved by numberless cases
and relief in the above complaints, the pr
are desirous of extending its advantages mor
sively to the public, than has hitherto be
Persons of the most delicate organization
this medicine with the fullest confidence, w
the same time, its powers are such as to rem
ease, however obdurate or deeply seated.
much the fashion, now-a-days, for partie
every nostrum to the furthest extent, that
prietors decline saying anything further in it
being convinced that a steady trial will conv
impartial persons of its efficacy.

Being compounded entirely of herbs and
ous gums, its action is gentle, and the violen
caused by most medicines directed against t
complaints (and which is ultimately so de
to the important organs of digestion, &c.), i
unfelt, and the disease gradually *melts* a
before the benign influence of this inestima
paration.

CAUTION To protect the public from base a
onrable imitations, of this genuine "Ex ract of
HERBS," her Majesty's Hon Commissioners of Sta
been pleased to order the words "CULPEPER'S HERB
to be engraved on he Government Stamp, in WHITE
a RED ground and none can be g nuine unless they
true test of authenticity

Sold in Boxes at 1s. 1½d each, stamp included, with
tions, and may be had wholesale of Mr Edwards, 67 S
Sutton and Co,, Bow Churchyard; Die richsen & C
street, London; and retail by all respectable B
Chemists, and Patent Medicine Venders

Agent for Spalding: Mr. H. Watkinson.
Press Office," top of the Market Place.

A CERTAIN CURE FOR CORN

GREGORY'S CORN KILL

IS a never-failing destroyer of Corns and b
its application is simple and gives insta
relief to the worst Corn that ever tortured hu
Corns do not require cutting or filing, whi

Spalding Free Press

On October 31st, 1923, the Directors of the "Spalding Free Press" Co. Ltd. gave a dinner at the Masonic Hall, Spalding, to commemorate the long and unique service with the Free Press of:-

Mr. J. W. White	(Secretary of the Company)	51¼ years
Mr. A. Ridlington	(Foreman Printing & Publishing Works)	46¾ years
Mr. S. Jepson	(Chairman of the Company)	43¾ years
Mr. A. Crabtree	(Editor of the "Free Press")	43¼ years

Total 185 years

An average of 46¼ years Service.

Messrs. S. Jepson and A. Crabtree retired that day.

Below: The four retiring Directors are shown in this photograph - Left to Right:-
A. Crabtree, Editor; J. W. White, Secretary; A. Ridlington, Foreman; S. Jepson, Chairman.

P. G. Burrell & Son

This was a furniture shop with premises in Red Lion Street which finished trading in the Spring of 1983.

Bulbs and Flowers

A Visit to Mr. J. T. White's Bulb Farm - 1899 by J. H. Diggle

"....it is about twenty years since Mr. White commenced the business which has now assumed such extensive proportions. He has upwards of 30 acres under bulb cultivation, and estimates that there are about 10,000,000 bulbs in his huge flower garden, which comprises of four or five separate fields. Ten millions can be better imagined than counted. Every bulb has at one time or other passed through the hands of sorter or planter, and with such a vast number in mind some idea of the patient labour involved may be conceived. Walking over the clean land, and amongst a million blades of green shooting from the symmetrical beds, one observes that the patches contain bulbs of different development. There are those of young offsets planted last autumn, those of a year older, and again a patch of three-year-olds. It requires from two to four years to produce what is known to the trade as a "good, fat, round bulb", of the first quality for sale.

The business has two branches - the bulb and the flower. There are, of course, subsidiary departments, such as tomato growing. Mr. Cunnington, of Moulton, and Mr. White have proved at the annual Chrysanthemum shows at Spalding that the local tomato is far and away superior to the miserable lobular fruit in the tomato line with which the foreigner supplies the grocer. But this branch of the business is subordinate. Mr. White grows bulbs to supply the trade, and the quality of his stock being high, they are in great demand. Like the growing of fancy potatoes, the original seed of special varieties costs money, and calls for the speculative spirit. It is recorded that a pedigree tulip cost no less than £200, and Mr. White has a patch of bulbs containing about 2 perches - 10 yards by 6 - which necessitated an outlay of £170. Mr. White is swift to see what are likely to be popular varieties. At the end of the summer comes the harvesting - the digging up, the drying, the selecting of the bulbs, and the execution of orders, the bulbs being despatched to their destinations in hampers so as to admit air circulating among them in bulk. Bulbs grown in Mr. White's "nursery" have been sent to Scotland, Ireland, France, Holland and America.

Cut Bloom

At this period of the year (April), thousands of cut blooms are sent to market - to London and all the great provincial towns in England and across the border, Glasgow and Edinburgh receiving consignments. At Easter-tide there is always an extra demand. The great spring festival call for flowers to beautify the homes of the people, to decorate the churches, and to brighten the wards of hospitals and institutions. Alack! There will be much disappointment all round this year. Easter is unusually early, and the frosts have been so continuous and keen that there are only, so to speak, a few handfuls of flowers, compared with the harvests of previous years. Last Good Friday Mr. White sent from Spalding station a consignment of cut bloom, with boxes, in all, 3 tons in weight, which means about 300,000 separate flowers. This year, for reasons stated, he has been able to send from five to ten thousand bloom only, and other growers proportionately. Of course, the flowers must go to market when they are ready. There are methods of forcing or retarding the blooming, but, once out, the flower is perishable. Mr. White was led to remark upon what he called the precarious nature of the business.

"I have had them," he said, "bring home as little as 1s. 3d. per thousand. If one happens to have a big lot in a good market it is all right; but when the market is down they have to go for next to nothing." Again, when the weather is hot they soon perish, and excessive rain has a damaging effect upon flowers in the open. The London and Provincial salesman is sometimes a source of trouble and loss.

Mr. White's premises at Little London are of a commodious kind, well adapted for every requirement of the industry. The glass houses are in all 250 yards in length and cover about a rood of land. The new rooms for bunching and boxing are airy and lofty, well lighted and adapted to enable a big bulk of bloom to be bunched and despatched quickly as the occasion demands. Mr. White gives close personal attention to the varied work, and he has the assistance of his two sons, and several men who have been associated with him from the origin of the enterprise, while in the height of the season, about 30 women and 20 men are employed. During the winter, work is found for about 15 men and boys. It is important to keep the bulbs clean. The plain work of weeding and hoeing 30 acres of land is in itself considerable. Bloom necessarily requires care in packing. About 72 dozens can be put in one box. It needs skill to wedge the delicate flowers in such a way that, when taken out and shaken, the bloom looks none the worse for the journey. It is obvious that if bulbs were allowed to develop without check, in the course of years, the crop would spread out as the proverbial horse shoe nail doubles and multiplies. Forcing, however, will soon reduce the stock. Mr. White forces about half-a-million annually under glass, and, at the present time of writing, ornati, tulips, and daffodils are being plucked and hurried off to market. Under the process of forcing, the bulb has been practically destroyed, and is usually thrown away. The sight of the tiers of boxes in Mr. White's storeroom, and the busy workers with the verdant field beyond, suggested the question: Is there not a danger of over production? To which Mr. White said: "There is certainly plenty of it now. We begin to find out that a hot week will flood the market, and demoralise the prices."

"But does not the demand for flowers in the large centres of population continue to increase in proportion?"

"Yes; when what formerly cost 6d. can be bought for a penny, it may be supposed the flowers have got down amongst the people."

"So that you and others are growing for the million?"

"Yes; there is a great sale at a low price."

It is 26 years since Mr. White came to Spalding. His first commercial success was the building up of the well-known business at the Sheep Market corner, now carried on under the style of Messrs. J. T. White & Son, which, under the management of Mrs. White and Mr. W. White, has become one of the most attractive repositories for fancy goods in the district....".

Thirty Years Later - J. T. White - a tribute by J. H. Diggle

"During the last of many conversations I had with the late Mr. J. T. White he spoke of his wonderful health, but gave a hint of the source from which trouble might come. It has now come with the swiftness not without compensation in relation to a man of his active habits and with such zest for life. Much will be said in the pulpit and Press of so notable a Spalding citizen - the perfect embodiment of the servant of whom it was spoken: "Then he that had received fine talents went and traded with the same and made them other fine talents"....To industry, temperance and thrift, the master keys to fortune, always bright in his hands, Mr. White added a rarer public virtue - consistency. In him prudence and stability, seemed personified. For half a lifetime he sat under the serious ministry of the Rev. J.C. Jones. But nothing austere mingled with the cheerfulness of his outlook on life inspired by a happy temperament and buoyant health. Advancing age seemed to pass him by. As has been well said, "Life never hardened him; his sympathies were always fresh and young."

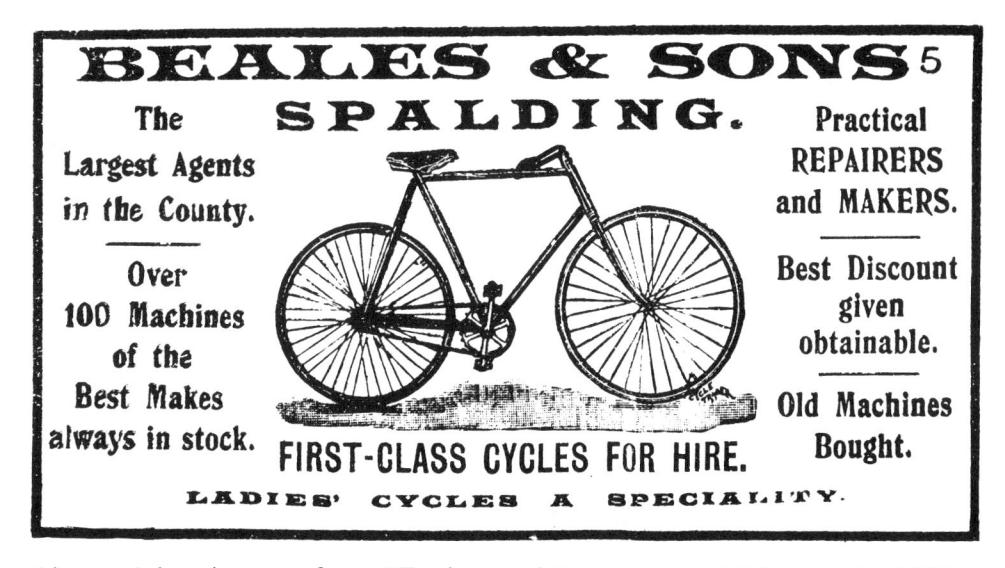

Above: Advertisement from "Environs of Spalding", published in the 1890's.

Joseph Mowbray

Left: Joseph Mowbray, the Baker, with his son Bertram outside the "New Bell Inn," (now Frost & Co. Solicitors), London Road, 1901. Joseph Mowbray had a Mill on Roman Bank, and, in 1892, a baker's shop at 16 Church Gate. In 1905 he was in business as a baker at 6 London Road.

WALDEN & SONS,

FAMILY GROCERS,

TEA DEALERS,

AND

Provision Merchants.

Best Prices given for New Laid Eggs.

3 & 4, LONDON ROAD,

SPALDING.

Walden & Sons

Opposite top: This photograph taken about 1900 shows the Grocers and Provision Merchants of 3 & 4 London Road.

Coconut matting and brush heads on display. William Nundy Walden commenced business on London Road in 1882 (he had another shop in Love Lane), and was joined by his son Fred Walden in 1887, and by his son William H. Walden in 1890. On their father's retirement in 1892, the brothers carried on the business which continued to expand, being the first in the neighbourhood to begin the systematic collection of eggs from the district for despatch to large centres. Note the advertisement above.

Right: Fred Walden (1867 - 1937), of Love Lane, Spalding, Grocer. Photographed standing in the dry bed of the River Welland, with Victoria Bridge behind, about 1930. Although a prominent business man he took little or no part in public affairs, but was a keen and active member of the Crescent Methodist Church in which he held a number of important offices. Of a genial disposition, he was greatly handicapped by deafness in his later years.

W. Fletcher

Above: The Outfitter's about 1910. The proprietor is standing in the doorway.
William Fletcher took a prominent part in the public life of the town, as a member of the Board of Guardians and Spalding Urban District Council. He served as Chairman of the Council in 1911 - 1912.
Below: Date - the 1920's. Two youthful employees in the doorway of 6 Market Place - left to right - the late John Smith and Horace Bailey. Note the advert. c.1890 opposite top.

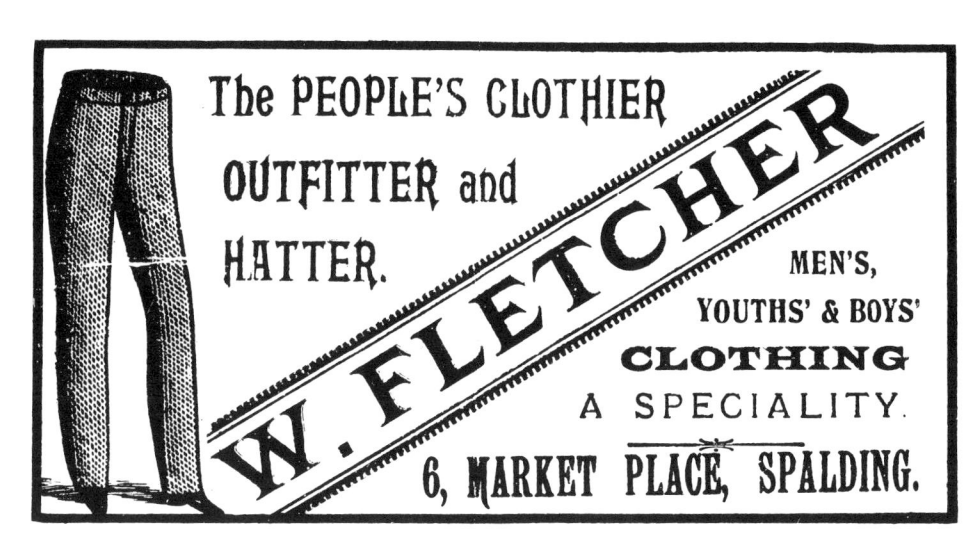

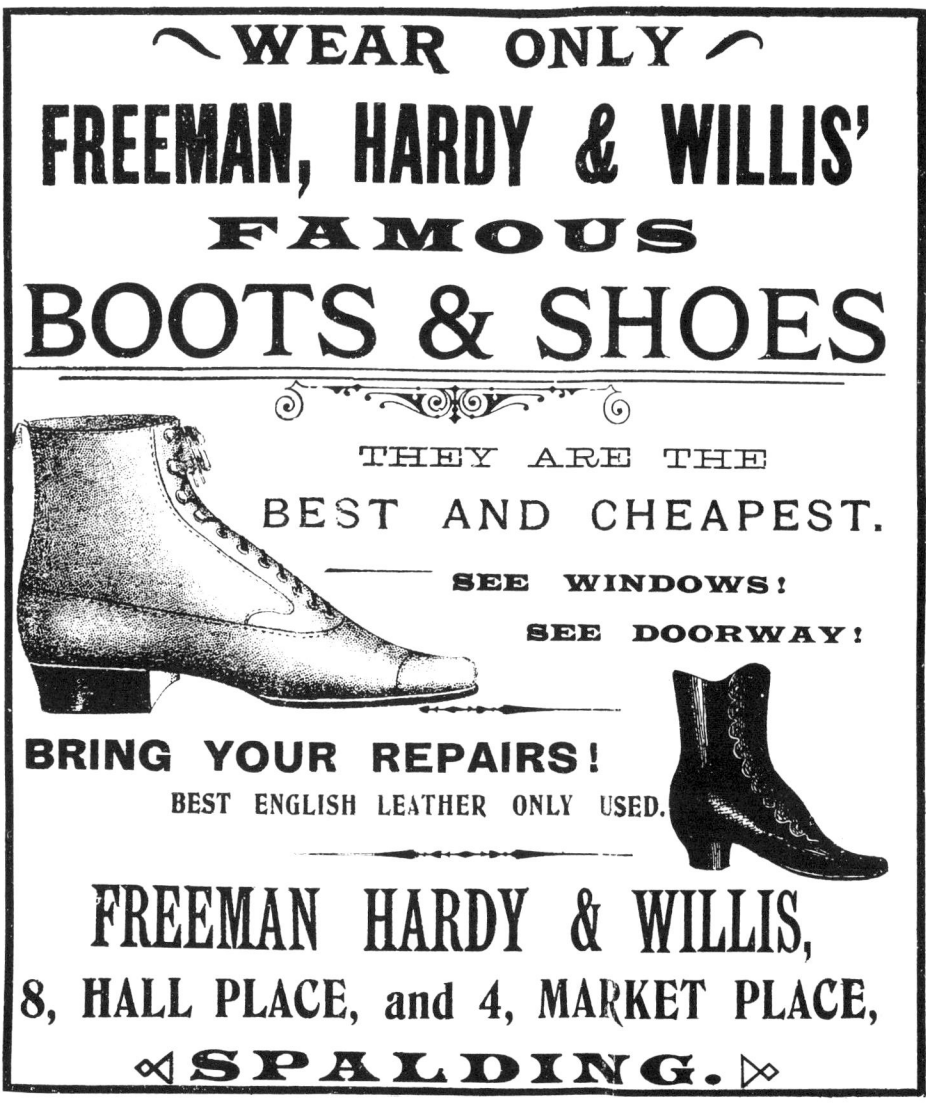

Advertisements from the 1890's.

Hallam & Blackbourn

No.23 Market Place, the premises of Hallam & Blackbourn, family grocers and provision merchants. According to 'Old Robin' Harmstone this building was erected in 1753. At the beginning of the 19th century it was occupied by Thomas Maples (1771 - 1832) one of the 'eminent merchants of the town', who was in business as a grocer, tea dealer, tallow chandler, and agent for Garfit, Claypons & Co. Bankers, of Boston. The banking side of the business was personally conducted by his wife, Mrs. Ann (Palmer) Maples (1774 - 1837), who may be considered the first lady bank manager in Spalding. Thomas Maples was also in business as a timber, wine and spirit merchant. In the furtherance of these three important commercial enterprises he had stage waggons running between Spalding and London, and also boats on the Welland, which made the voyage to Newcastle or London, to bring to the town coals and other supplies. In 1840 the grocery business was acquired by Joseph Allen, and was afterwards carried on by Robinson & Jennings, David Robinson and finally Hallam & Blackbourn.

```
Retail Establishment:                    Wholesale Offices and Warehouses:
18, Hall Place.  Tel. G.P.O. 37.         THE "SHIP," Double St.  Tel. G.P.O. 37x.

              HALLAM & BLACKBOURN,
              Wholesale & Family Grocers,
           Wine, Spirit & Provision Merchants,
                      SPALDING.

Sugars are sold upon the terms contained in the printed conditions of the London Sugar Dealers' Association.
```

Above: The wholesale offices and 'Ship' warehouse, Double Street, about 1910. Standing in the doorway - left to right - Thomas James (foreman - also the Authors Grandfather), Isaac Hallam, John Edward Blackbourn.

HALLAM and
BLACKBOURN,

Family Grocers,

SPALDING.

FOR FINEST

Home-cured Hams and Bacon,

Cured upon our own Premises.

Stilton, Gorgonzola, Leicester, & Cheddar Cheese

Of the BEST QUALITY always obtainable.

The building in the Market Place was demolished and replaced by the National Provincial Bank, which opened for business on this site on Friday, 2nd August, 1907. This development made possible the widening of Broad Street, a strip of land being purchased from the National Provincial Bank by the Spalding Urban District Council for £300. It was at this time - 1907 - that the Council changed the name of Crackpool Lane to Broad Street.

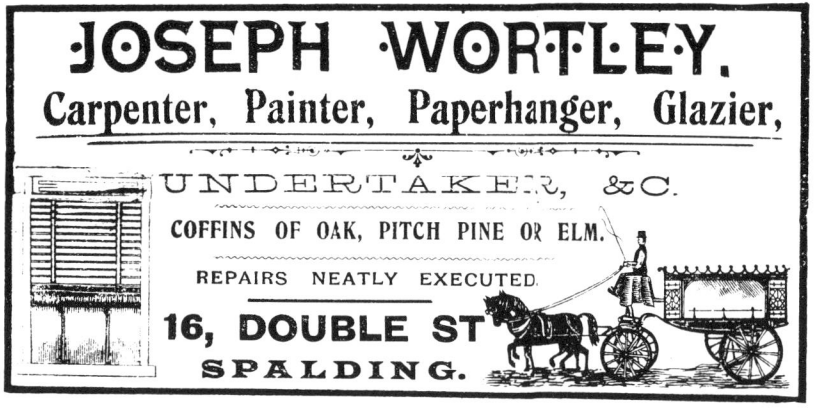

JOSEPH WORTLEY.
Carpenter, Painter, Paperhanger, Glazier,

UNDERTAKER, &C.

COFFINS OF OAK, PITCH PINE OR ELM.

REPAIRS NEATLY EXECUTED.

16, DOUBLE ST SPALDING.

M. DALTON & SON,
Furniture Dealers,

BEDSTEADS AND BEDDING.

WRINGERS, PERAMBULATORS & MAIL CARTS.

Carpets, Blankets, and all kinds of Furniture.

149 and 150, WINSOVER ROAD, SPALDING.

H. L. ENDERBY,
THE CHEAPEST SHOP IN THE COUNTY
— FOR —

PORTMANTEAUS,
Dress Trunks, Holdalls,

BAGS, HAT CASES

Legging Maker,
FOOTBALLS, SHIN GUARDS,
Cricketing Materials,
Athletic Requisites.

MARKET PLACE SPALDING.

Advertisements from "Environs of Spalding", published in the 1890's. (see back endpaper).

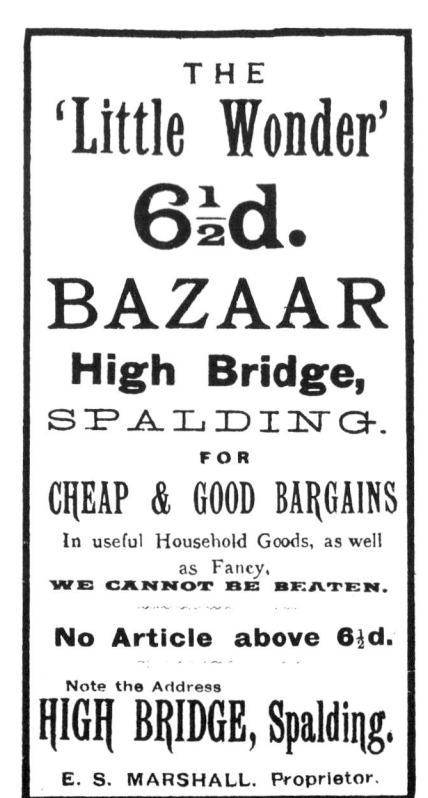

THE 'Little Wonder' 6½d. BAZAAR
High Bridge, SPALDING.

FOR

CHEAP & GOOD BARGAINS

In useful Household Goods, as well as Fancy,
WE CANNOT BE BEATEN.

No Article above 6½d.

Note the Address
HIGH BRIDGE, Spalding.

E. S. MARSHALL, Proprietor.

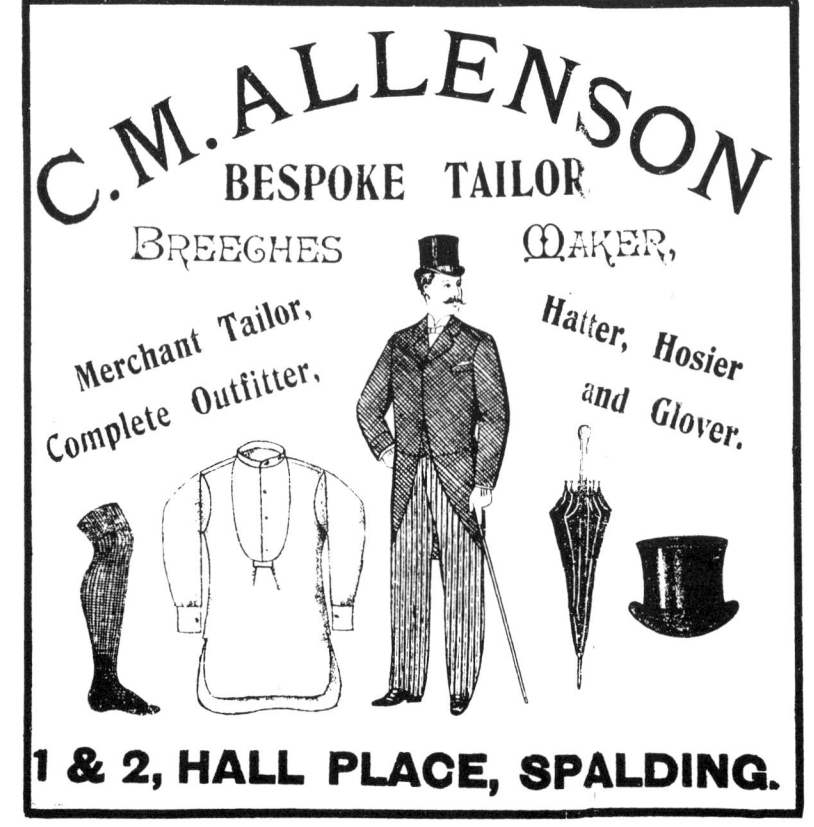

C. M. ALLENSON
BESPOKE TAILOR

BREECHES MAKER,

Merchant Tailor, Complete Outfitter,

Hatter, Hosier and Glover.

1 & 2, HALL PLACE, SPALDING.

106

Brick Making Yards in South Lincolnshire

"Years ago, there were several brick making yards in south Lincolnshire, in which the fen-land clay was shaped and burned in the old-fashioned way. The late Mr. C. Brett had a yard at Spalding, near the Pinchbeck road; Mr. S. Kingston made bricks at Spalding Common; near Pinchbeck Bars there was an establishment; while Mr. Hunt moulded the Deeping Fen clays to meet the local demand. It was possible, too, to find clay under the peaty soil of Crowland, while the ring of the Fen skating "pattern" was, in keen winter, heard at Holbeach on pits which have supplied that town with many of its weather-tight walls. This would be in the days when there were no railways to bring bricks from a distance. One by one these brickyards closed. And now, with the exception of Mr. Rawding's establishment at Gosberton, Mr. E.W. Gooch is about the only local brickmaker who still holds the fort. Councillor Gooch revived the Clay Lake business which, like the others, had fallen into decay; and now he there conducts a thriving little business, finding employment for half-a-score of hands. All the bricks are sold locally. Mr. Gooch is also a director, and one of the largest shareholders of the Bourne Brick and Tile Company, which has a siding connection with the Saxby line; and in which Messrs. Mays Brothers of Bourne, are interested.......At Bourne and Gosberton good facing bricks are made, but fine red facing bricks of the best quality are usually brought across the Midlands.......the plasticity of the clay has hitherto made it difficult, if not impossible, to make bricks on the semi-dry principle. There is an abundance of clay. Mr. Gooch has dug down 23 feet, and has not touched the bottom of the "Lake". The local clay makes a durable brick, too, but considering the peculiar advantages of other districts, and since being close to a railway is a sine qua non of success, Mr. Gooch does not anticipate any startling local development.......".

J. H. Diggle, 1899

Johnson's Bakehouse

The business was carried on from premises in Little London. Photograph about 1930.

Herbs are the only true Medicines of Nature.—SIR JOHN HILL.

The only Establishment in South Lincolnshire
For the Sale of ALL KINDS of English and American

BOTANIC REMEDIES,

BOTH IN A CRUDE AND PREPARED STATE, IS

NEXT DOOR BUT ONE TO THE POST OFFICE,
DOUBLE STREET, SPALDING,

SOLE PROPRIETOR,

DR. FRITH, M.A.M.R.

Diplomatized Member of the Society of Medical Reformers of England and America, (not registered in England).

All Articles purchased at this Establishment warranted Pure, whether purchased in the raw or prepared state, and at prices which will defy competition.

Wholesale and Retail.

DR. FRITH begs to thank the Inhabitants of South Lincolnshire for the unbounded confidence they have reposed in him, and the support they have accorded to him during the two years and-a-half he has resided at Spalding, and hopes to continue to merit the same by an assiduous attention to all orders for goods; and at the same time desires to state, that he has been successful in curing more than one thousand cases of Diseases during the above period.

Only one death has occurred under Dr. Frith's practice in that period.

Dr. FRITH'S Remedies for the HOOPING COUGH

Have been proved, so far, effectual in curing the most inveterate cases in about two weeks. QUITE HARMLESS. PURELY HERBAL.

Parents do not let your dear little ones suffer, when you can obtain relief at once, and cure them speedily.

None need Despair.

NO POISONS MADE USE OF
ADVICE FREE.

Thyme, Mint, Sage, and all Culinary Herbs
ALWAYS IN STOCK.

[*Please Observe the Address.*]

J. H. Measures,

Hole-in-Wall Inn, Spalding,

Has for Hire Horses, Dog Carts, Waggonettes, Smart 'Favourite' Brake (*to carry 18*), Broughams, &c.

SMART PAIR OF GREYS FOR WEDDINGS.

Horses may be Hired Separately. Funerals Attended.

TERMS MODERATE. Apply at the INN, or YARD (next to Temperance Hall), CRESCENT, SPALDING.

'VALENTO,' A Brilliant, Sparkling, NON-ALCOHOLIC WINE,
Prepared by a Patented Process from the Finest Valencia Grapes.

Kops Ale and Stout, A Popular Non-Alcoholic Beverage.

The Noted Billingboro' Mineral Waters.

J. H. MEASURES & SONS, Crescent, Spalding.

ESTABLISHED 1871.   PRIZE MEDAL 1875.

Packs of TESTIMONIALS for SAFETY and CHEAPNESS.

For all Removals, to and from all Parts.

THOMAS GUY, 21. CRESCENT. 21. SPALDING.

Prompt and Personal Attention.

THIS IS THE REMOVER OF THE DAY.

Please Address All Letters: NOT to his other Warehouses.

THOMAS GUY, CRESCENT, SPALDING.

Companion Books to the Present.

Spalding and Its Churches,

Being a description of the Parish Church, St. Peter's, St. Paul's, and St. John's, with 17 Excellent Views of the Churches, and 7 Portraits of Spalding Vicars. Price 6d.

Ayscoughfee and Its History.

Price 3d. A description of the Hall and Gardens, with Nine Illustrations; also a Poem by Richard Harris, Esq., K.C., entitled, "The Maid of Ayscoughfee."

Free Press Co., 5, Hall Place, Spalding.

Lincolnshire Agricultural Show 1887

This was the second time the Lincolnshire Agricultural Society held its show at Spalding, the first time being in 1872.

The street decorations were said to have been carried out with "good taste upon a liberal scale". From Venetian masts placed at short distances apart on either side of the street a continuous line of pennons stretched from pole to pole, each mast displaying a banner, and being further ornamented with shields and devices in different colours. In Hall Place and in the Market Place were laid out beds of palms, shrubs, and flowers set in a border of gravel. By a clever arrangement of ferns, which hid all pots and supports, these improvised shrubberies and gardens had all the appearance of reality. Many tradesmen and the inhabitants generally displayed flags, banners, mottos, and flowers in profusion. In every part of the town flags were erected on lofty poles or hung from windows, it being stated that about 8,000 flags were used.

Opposite: A view of the decorations in Church Street. The chemist's shop of Brelsford Asling is facing High-bridge. He was an active churchman, being churchwarden from 1858 to 1863 and again from 1869 to 1888.

Advertisements: opposite top, from 1867 and below from 1902.

Below: Views of the decorations in Market Place and Hall Place.

G.F. Birch, of High Street, 1851 - 1912

The ceaseless daily activity of a section of High Street recalls to mind the busy time when Steel's steam mills ground up fenland wheat for the artisan of the Midlands. This business has had its death-blow. The old has given place to the new. The big granaries, so long silent and bare, are now sack-laden and noisy with rattling chains and revolving wheels. The "jolly miller" has returned. The only difference is that food for men has given place to food for cattle. Gas engines, each of 40 horse power, are grinding barley maize, beans and clipping oats at the rate of 1,000 quarters per week. Outside, waggons are being packed with cake or loaded with feeding stuffs; and in the Welland, a sailing vessel is pitching her cargo of linseed into the black storehouse, which conveniently dips towards the vessel's deck.....Oat clipping is a special department, employing seven hands regularly at the mill. Oats are bought in the district and at markets by Mr. Birch's representatives; are delivered or brought to Spalding, clipped - i.e. the sharp ends are taken off - by machinery, and sent away again for oatmeal or horse corn, &c. Mr. Birch has just devised new machinery to save a large portion of labour, in connection with this work, which, it will be inferred, creates an enormous amount of carting and carriage. The clover, hay, and straw trussing and delivery department engages about 25 hands. The trussed and trimmed article goes to Birmingham, Sheffield, Halifax, Bradford and other towns. Mr. Birch has followed the example of most traders and has gone into farming. He occupies about 300 acres situated at Fulney, Lock's Mill and Cowhirne. And to these business responsibilities he has added that of owning land in the "high country", and various properties in Spalding including the house, premises, granaries, and office, in High Street, whence the ninety to one hundred men in his employ look for instructions.

The Secret of Cheerful Success

It is about 30 years ago since Mr. Birch came to Spalding - an orphan and absolutely dependent upon his own efforts. For a time he served Messrs. Robinson & Jennings as a journeyman. When at age he started in business for himself at the corner of St. Thomas's Road. The numerous enquiries for corn, offals, &c., led him to take up the feeding stuffs department. Grinding by wind followed. Wind was supplemented by steam, until some years ago the High Street premises were purchased. At these Mr. Birch spends most of his time, his two sons assisting in the business.

Mr. Birch has managed to make the burden of a big business a light one, for his cheery motto has always been, "Make business a pleasure", and the arrangement and conveniences of his house and garden in High Street illustrate another of his wise maxims, "Make home attractive". Mr. Birch has grown prosperous, and he has done it smiling. He is still well on the right side of 50. Few men with no backing at the first have made such rapid progress on the beaten track of plain trading. Few, indeed, can be conspicuously prosperous in a limited community. But there is no one who, having worked for and won that position, enjoys to a greater extent the good wishes of farmers in the district, and of neighbours and employees in the town of Spalding.

J. H. Diggle, 1899.

The best Aerated Waters in the world.

Made from the Purest Water Supply in the Kingdom,
ARE PRODUCED BY

LEE & GREEN,

OF

SPALDING, BOURNE AND SLEAFORD,

AND A TRIAL IS RESPECTFULLY SOLICITED.

Ask for them in all Hotels, Inns, and of your Family Chemist, and see that you get them.

ALSO THEIR NOTED

HOME-BREWED

GINGER BEER

—— IN ——

STONE BOTTLES.

TRY IT!

The study and production of a lifetime.

This favourite beverage has no superior in the trade.

TRY IT!

Messrs. LEE & GREEN are the sole possessors, by purchase, of the bottles and cases of the Economic Supply Co., Grimsby and London.

Above and below: Advertisements from the 1890's. It was about this time that Lee & Green purchased the Albion brewery, (page 21). On the other hand, due to the death of his son at 27, Joseph Henry Burg decided to sell the Cowbit Road brewery, (page 48). The purchasers were Soames & Co.
The premises were, until recently, occupied by Watney Mann, but, at the time of writing, are undergoing renovation work to be returned to residential use.

SOAMES & CO.
BREWERS
AND
Spirit Merchants,
SPALDING.

MILD BITTER & LIGHT DINNER ALES
A·K   A·K

BRANCHES:
BOSTON, SLEAFORD & SKEGNESS.

Tradesman's Excursion

Photographed about 1900. Left to right:
Dan Slaughter; lad unknown; R. C. H. Scales; H. W. Tippler; A. R. Colam; W. Crabtree; George Neaves; Beecham; J. Peet; R. Tippler; Inspector Rickett; George Barnett; Bert Harris; Fred Colam; George Jennings (grocer); Richard Glenn (coal merchant); G. W. Redford (stationmaster); George Goodwin (St. Thomas' Road); Arthur Harris; J. C. Harris (watchmaker); Cornelius Dalrymple Hall (auctioneer); C. M. Allenson (clothier).

No.2 platform later altered to No. 5. Note flat peaked uniform caps, and six wheeled saloons.

Below: Advertisement from 1866/7 (Spalding Monthly Magazine).

PRINTING.

A. PORTER, PRINTER.

THE TYPES ARE NEW.
THE WORK PROMPTLY EXECUTED.
THE CHARGES ARE MODERATE.
THE PRINTING DONE IN A SUPERIOR MANNER.

Church and Chapel

The Parish Church

In 1802 it is described as '...a light, airy structure, has a handsome spire steeple, and is kept very neat and clean within. The stone coggs or frostings of the steeple are so much decayed by the weather as to be easily broken off. There was formerly a noble gothic window over the west entrance of the church; but the good effect which this had on the uniformity of the building was done away many years ago when this window was wholly glazed with small oblong squares in lead. There not being pews sufficient for the accommodation of the inhabitants, an additional gallery was built by subscription, about the year 1797, on the north side of the middle aisle. To make the church still more complete, the parishioners have this year added to the harmony of the old peal of five bells, by increasing that number to six and recasting others, which formerly made rather too discordant a peal when it was intended to celebrate our public rejoicing days....' (1).

In 1823 the vicar was the Revd. Maurice Johnson, D.D. Born in 1756, the son of Colonel Maurice and Mary (Baker) Johnson, and grandson of Maurice Johnson 'the Antiquary', the founder of the Spalding Gentlemen's Society, he became vicar of Moulton in 1780 and of Spalding in 1782. He resigned as vicar of Spalding in 1825, but retained the living of Moulton until his death, which took

Below: South East view of Spalding Church, 1823. From a watercolour by Hilkiah Burgess (1775-1868). Spalding Gentlemen's Society's collection.

place in 1834. "The Lincolnshire Chronicle and General Advertiser", of 6th June, 1834, carried the following report of his funeral: "The remains of the Rev. Maurice Johnson, D.D., were deposited in the family vault, in the south aisle of Spalding Church, on Monday last. The funeral was very numerously attended. Besides a long line of carriages, and gentlemen robed in silk, there were between two thousand and three thousand spectators; and notwithstanding this great multitude, the greatest order and decorum were observed. Not one half of the people could get into the body of the church. The service was read, in a very solemn and impressive manner, by the Revd. Charles Moore, of Moulton. Maurice Johnson Esq., in his 19th year, grandson of the deceased, succeeds the reverend gentleman as proprietor of Ayscough Fee Hall, and the hereditary property of the family".

(1). *"The Provincial Literary Repository". Vol.II. July, 1802. No. 20. page 243.*

Above: c.1843. From "An Account of The Churches in the Division of Holland in the County of Lincoln", by Stephen Lewin. Boston: T. N. Morton. 1843.

Opposite: c.1870. From "The Fen and Marshland Churches"; A Series of Photographs, with short historical and architectural descriptive notes, and ground plans.

Two views of the church before and after the restoration by Sir Gilbert Scott in 1865 - 7. The first is of the North East view of the church in 1843. In the north wall of the chancel against the rood turret is a small window of three lights with Decorated tracery, and a large square headed window of five lights; while in the east gable of the chancel is a window of four lights with Perpendicular tracery. Canon Moore, in a paper on St. Mary and Nicolas Church (South Holland Magazine, April 1869) states that 'on the north side nearly the whole of the wall had been rebuilt, perhaps about a hundred years ago, and a square headed transomed five-light domestic window inserted. The roof of the chancel was a lead flat, carried on a double floor of timber; the upper flooring of meanly moulded fir beams; the under flooring of rough hewn oak (12 x 14 in.) both floors having the addition of many cross pieces,

114

forming together such a stock of material as would be a good supply for a timber yard. Much of this heavy timber was added to the roof in 1751, that date being found repeated four times on the main beams, and here was the reason. In one of the register books of the Parish is this entry: "Spalding. April ye 20, 1747. Memorand. That the churchwardens having given notice that the chancell wants to be Speedily repaired, the inhabitants present took the same into consideration and did find the same to be so, and that ye Rufe thereof ought to be raised, for that its Lying so Flat has decaid the timbers, and the churchwardens desire estimates be made for doing the same work and be Layd before the next vestry. St. Lyon, Minister, M. Johnson, John Bladesmith", and thirteen others whose family names are now extinct.... Perhaps for a piece of hideous construction, this chancel roof was the boldest attempt ever seen, and the fittings were equally discreditable.....'.

The second is a photograph about 1870. This shows the church after the restoration. Canon Moore gives the cost of the restoration as £10,000. He writes "The chancel roof has been restored to its original high pitch. The four-light east window has been removed, and three elegant lancet windows under one hood substituted. The north wall has been removed and an aisle added, which is separated from the chancel by two arches supported on clustered columns: this aisle is also covered with a high pitched roof, and the walls are pierced with traceried windows of very elegant design. The original design of the chancel, which has been strictly adhered to in the restoration, is of early English architecture; the new aisle is in the style of the Decorated period". (South Holland Magazine. April, 1869. pages 4 - 5).

Canon Moore

The Revd. Edward Moore, M.A., F.S.A., J.P., was born at Spalding, 24th May, 1811, being the third son of the Revd. William Moore, D.D. (1784 - 1866), by his wife Anne Elizabeth, the only daughter of the Revd. Maurice Johnson (1756-1834), of Ayscoughfee Hall, vicar of Spalding and Moulton.

He was educated at Spalding Grammar School, under his great-uncle, the Revd. Walter Maurice Johnson (1757 - 1832), and at Shrewsbury under Dr. Samuel Butler. He studied at St. John's College, Cambridge, and in 1835 was ordained deacon and priest by the Bishop of Lincoln. In the same year he became vicar of Weston St. Mary, chaplain of Wykeham, perpetual curate of Moulton Chapel, and Master of the Free Grammar School at Spalding. In 1837 he succeeded his brother, the Rev. William

Continued on page 118.

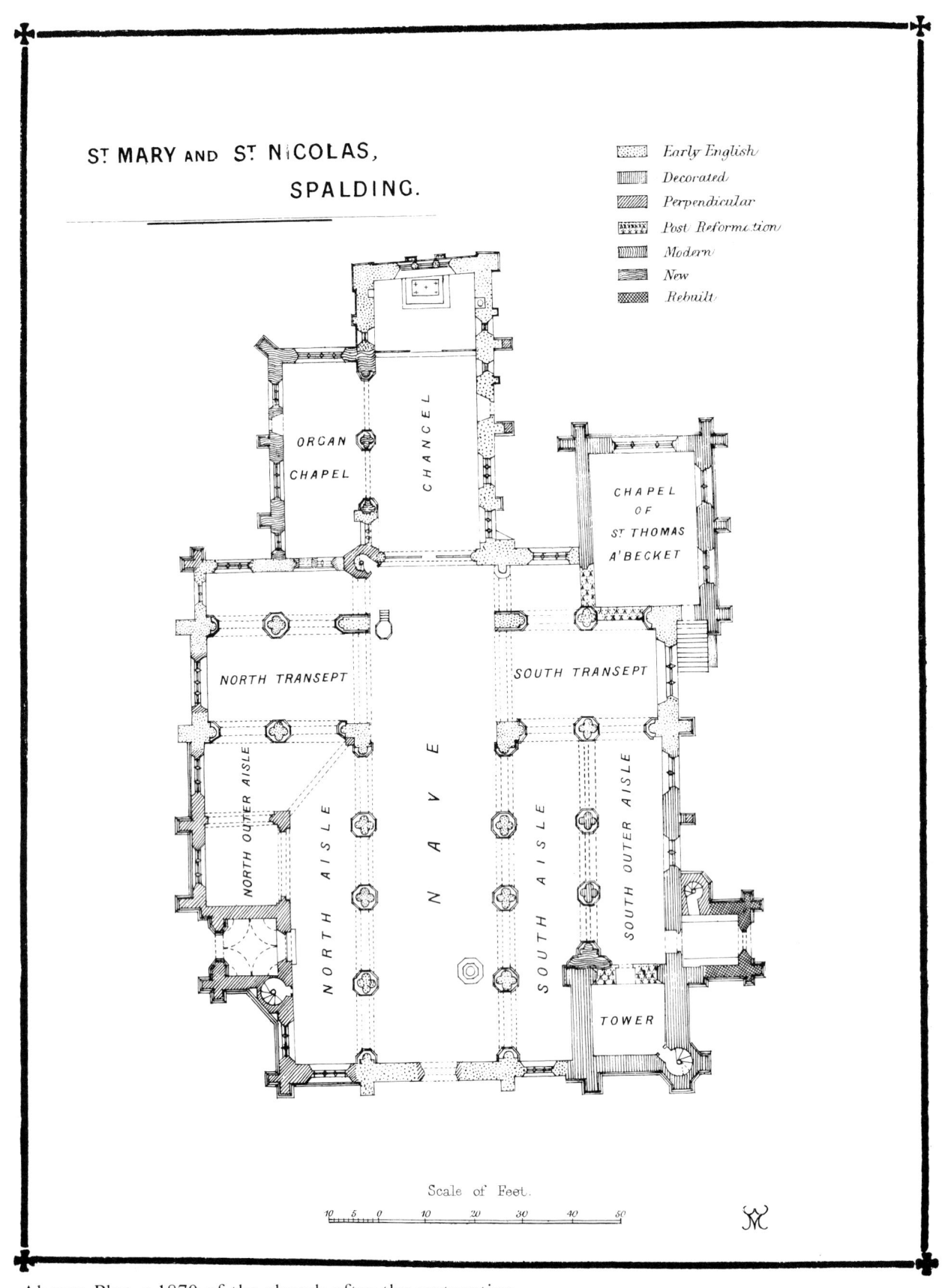

Above: Plan c.1870 of the church after the restoration.
Note the flight of stairs up to the schoolroom above the chapel of Thomas à Becket.

116

Left: The interior of the church showing the North and North outer aisles after the restoration.

Right: The interior of the church showing the South and South outer aisles after restoration but prior to the creation of St. Georges Chapel (after the Great War).

George Moore (1808 - 37), as perpetual curate of Whaplode Drove (where he resided for a few years), and resigned the curacy of Moulton Chapel. In 1866 he succeeded his father as vicar of Spalding, and resigned all his other clerical appointments, except that of Wykeham. He also retired as Headmaster of the Grammar School.

For over fifty years he was intimately associated with almost every sphere of public life in South Holland. He was connected with all the chief institutions and administrative bodies, and in each made himself felt and heard.

The restoration of Spalding Parish Church in 1865 - 67 was accomplished largely through his energy and zeal. For a time during the work he acted as clerk of works. The church of Weston St. Mary was restored, during his incumbency, with the liberal assistance of Lord Kesteven; the Church of St. John Baptist, Hawthorn Bank, was erected under his personal superintendence and opened in 1875; the Church of St. Peter's was opened in 1876; and in 1880, due to the generosity of Miss Charlotte Charinton, the Church of St. Paul at Fulney was built and endowed. In all these Canon Moore was the mainspring. Among other buildings in the town that owe their origin to his influence is the Johnson Hospital, built and partly endowed by the Misses Johnson, the structure being commenced in 1879 and completed in 1881.

He always took a prominent part in educational matters, being for thirty-one years Headmaster of Spalding Grammar School (1835 - 66), and subsequently chairman of the governors; he was closely connected with the Willesby School; he was the sole Manager of the National schools up to the time of his death; he instigated the building of the Goodfellow's school at Spalding Common; and although he strongly opposed the formation of a School Board at Spalding, when it was established, he obtained a seat on the first School Board, and retained it thereafter, serving for three years as chairman.

He was a regular attendant at the meeting of the Board of Guardians, of which he was an ex-officio member; for three years (1862 - 65) he served as a Spalding Improvement Commissioner, during which time he took an active part in buying the gas-works for the town; he was a Town Husband for many years; was chairman of the Spalding Waterworks Company; a Commissioner of Sewers for Holland Elloe, and interested in several of the local drainage trusts.

He was appointed a magistrate in 1857, and was known as one of the most active members of the South Holland Bench, succeeding his father as chairman in 1861, and retaining the position for fifteen years.

In politics Canon Moore was a Tory of the old school. While at college he was secretary of the Cambridge University Conservative Union, and in later years he took an active interest in the local Conservative Associations and in the Primrose League.

He was keenly interested in local history and antiquities, and in 1860, it was due to his initative and persistence, in face of many difficulties and some discouragement, that the west front of Crowland Abbey was saved from falling. He was a Fellow of the Society of Antiquaries, and an active member of the Lincoln and Nottingham Archaeological and Architectural Society. In 1834 he became a member of the Spalding Gentlemen's Society, was appointed treasurer in 1856, and elected President in 1872.

Over the years he gained a practical acquaintance with all matters of public importance to this locality, being a member of almost every administrative body, and developed an extraordinary capacity for business. In addition to regularly attending numerous church services, he rarely missed being present at the meetings of the public bodies to which he belonged, and so it followed that he led a remarkably busy life. Nearly every day he was engaged in public work, and the parsonage was a place of general resort by parishioners seeking advice upon legal or business questions, or for the purpose of settling disputes. It used to be a common expression for people who felt themselves agrieved to threaten to "go to Mr. Moore". He took great delight in every branch of public affairs with which he had to deal, and he was noted for the order and method he employed and his punctuality both in correspondence and in fulfilling engagements.

He was a man of stern, unswerving character, of indomitable pluck, and of great perseverance, doing that which he believed to be right, careless of whom he might offend, and utterly regardless of public opinion.

His dispensation of charity was great but it was strictly private. He was fond of "doing good by stealth", and he befriended, by numerous generous gifts, many poor families and many struggling cottagers, which the general public knew nothing of, as often the gift would pass through other hands, so that the receiver should not know from whom it came.

He was active until the very end of his life, and died after an illness lasting only four days, on 13th May, 1889, aged 77. He had married, in 1838, Elizabeth Sarah Stephenson (1813-89), only daughter of Richard Moses Stephenson, of Swineshead, who was his wife for fifty years and widow for nine weeks. She was described as a lady of amiable disposition, who led a remarkably quiet and peaceful life. They had no children, and were buried side by side in the porch of the church of Weston St. Mary.

The Parish Church viewed from the tower of Ayscoughfee Hall c.1900. In the foreground of the picture can be seen the roof of Holyrood House.

Wykeham Chapel

Wykeham chapel was built about the year 1311 by Clement Hatfield, Prior of Spalding, as the private chapel of his country house.

In the Spalding Priory Cartulary, under the year 1330, we read, that the Prior, "not only built the chapel of Wykeham, at no small cost, but also the whole manor or dwelling house there as it now is, and planted the trees there at the time of this present writing."

Dr. H.E. Hallam refers to "The magnificent chapel at Wykeham which stills remains to testify the wealth and grandeur of the Prior."

Clement Hatfield was Prior of Spalding from 1294 to 1318. He is described as a "great building and farming prior," and he left behind him a good reputation for the government of his house and the management of its property.

In 1305 he entertained King Edward I at Spalding, and in 1315 he likewise received King Edward II.

Richard Flemming, Bishop of Lincoln from 1420 to 1431, stayed at the grange at Wykeham in March, 1421. Spalding was the scene of the ordinations of the Saturday before Passion Sunday (March 8th) and Easter even (March 22).

On December 8, 1539, Spalding Priory with all its possessions, which included Wykeham grange, was surrendered to the Crown.

At this time we are informed that the Wykeham estate contained 200 ash trees of 40 years' growth - each tree valued at twelvepence. On September 1, 1543, the estate was purchased by John Harrington.

The following extract from the Patent Roll (34 Henry VIII), is of interest:

"The King to All to whom &c greeting. Know ye that we for the sum of £492.0s. 10d. paid by our beloved John Harryngton of Exton in our county of Rutland Esquire granted to him our whole Manor and grange of Wikeham with its appurtenances in the parishe of Spaldyng lately belonging, to the Monastery or Priory of Spalding...".

John Harrington was empowered to possess the estate as fully as the monastery had done "expecting nevertheless always to us and our heirs all the lead upon a certain chamber called the convent chamber and upon the chapel there, to have and to hold by the service, of a twentieth part of a Knight's fee paying to us and our heirs annually 53s. 7d....'.

In respect of this clause Ashley K. Maples (1868 - 1950), who carried out extensive researches into the history of Wykeham, commented:

"It appears therefore that Sir John Harrington incurred no liability for the maintenance of Wykeham Chapel and that there was no intention of retaining it in a state of repair for the reservation of the lead on the roof to the King obviously implies that the said lead was to be sold and that the rest of the building was not considered worth mentioning in the grant any more than the rest of the convent chamber".

Some years earlier John Harrington had served as head of the commission for the valuation and suppression of monastries in the county of Rutland.

At the time of the Lincolnshire Rebellion in 1536 he visited Peterborough and the Holland Division of Lincolnshire, including Spalding, and pacified the inhabitants who were about to join the rebels.

He was unsuccessful, however, when he commanded the prior of Spalding to be ready with as many men as he could to fight for the king, being told that the prior was a spiritual man.

The name of Harrington occurs, as Sheriff of Rutland, no less than 18 times between 1492 and 1602. Sir John Harrington held "Wikeham Grange", with 930 acres, in 1619.

In 1625 the chapel was repaired "by the pious care and generosity of Tyringham Norwood Esq. (a relation to and thereof farmer under, the Right Hon Sir John Harrington, Knight of the Bath and Baron Exton) who rebuilt the roof and raised the parapet walls about it ...".

Tyringham Norwood died September 16, 1629, and was buried at Wykeham. It would seem that he farmed the estate under the Harringtons.

His memorial inscription tells us that "He repayred this chappell in ye year of our Lord God 1625, and left maintenance for a preaching minister". His widow, Anne, was buried in Wykeham Chapel on August 21, 1633.

In a paper on Wykeham, Canon Moore wrote "Until 1782 this Chapel was regularly used for public service, being kept in repair by the parochial church-rate levied on the Wykeham estate, which was appropriated for that purpose. The parish accounts show that Mrs Ravenscroft's rate was thus credited in 1741".

In another paper on Wykeham Canon Moore stated that "According to the Registers of Baptisms and Burials of Spalding there appear to have been very many of both at Wykeham Chapel.

From 1626, the year after the recorded restoration of the Chapel by Tyringham Norwood Esq. when the baptism of Edward son of John Harrington Esq. on April 10 is registered down to July 1880 when the interment of Robt Everard Esq. of Fulney House is entered, there are nearly fifty entries of baptisms and burials besides some few marriages, recorded as celebrated in Wykeham Chapel.

These public services seem to have been conducted by the chaplain for the time and independently of the Vicar of the Parish. I could almost think sometimes, from the intervals of time without any records of Wykeham Chapel, that the Vicar of Spalding did not care to record these Chapel services; and this is rather confirmed by one of the entries being prefaced with 'I was informed' such a baptism took place at Wykeham."

In 1707 a silver chalice was presented to the chapel by Mrs Cordelia Cosh, of Wykeham. It bears the inscription "The Gift of Cordelia the wife of William Cosh for a Communion Cup for the use of Wickham Chapel 11th Novr 1707."

Her husband, William Cosh, lived at Cowhurn, and was a member of the Spalding Gentlemen's Society. (William Cosh and Cordelia Baxter were married in Spalding church July 5, 1692).

At this period (early 18th century) services were being held twice on Sundays.

James Thompson, of Ropsley, co. Lincoln, made the following bequest in his will (proved February 4, 1720):

"I bequeath to such person or persons as now is or hereafter shall be Minister and officiate the cure of souls within the church or chappell of Wykeham in the parish of Spalding the sum of thirty shillings to be issueing and payable out of my said Marsh called Wragg Marsh yearly for ever and above thirty shillings already charged upon the said Marsh and payable to the Minister of Wykeham for the time being".

When the property was sold in 1898 a declaration was made by one of the vendors that "no claim has been made upon or payment made by them in respect of the said sums for 20 years prior to the day of sale."

Maurice Johnson, "the Antiquary" (1688 - 1755), the founder of the Spalding Gentlemen's Society, became possessed of the advowson. By his Will, dated December 16, 1752, he did "...give grant devise and bequeath my Chapel at Wykeham in the Parish of Spalding aforesaid with the perpetual Donation and Nomination thereof and thereunto unto the Governors of the possessions revenues and goods of the free Grammar School of his late Majesty King Charles the second of blessed memory in the Town of Spalding in the County of Lincoln of the foundation of John Gamlyn gentleman and John Blankes and to their successors for ever ...".

In their gift it still remains.

Between 1706 and 1783 sixteen marriages took place at Wykeham. The first between Wm Thompson and Elizth Graves was at "Wickham Chapel", on June 4, 1706. The last was in 1783.

Canon Moore tells the story. "Before the introduction of railways, which has had the effect of exciting people to leave their homes and their own locality when they desire a days pleasure, Wykeham I have been told was a fashionable resort for parties residing in Spalding who wished to enjoy a holiday.

The last pleasure seekers who revelled under the protecting roof of Wykeham Chapel were a wedding party, celebrating the nuptials of Mr Green. They amused themselves by dancing on the flat roof of the Chapel: that same night the roof fell in."

In the parish Marriage register of Spalding is the entry "1783 Feby 12 Charles Green Esq. and Miss Sarah Shepherd married in the Chapel of Wickham in this parish by Geo.Maclellan, Minister."

The Revd. Geo. Maclellan was Master of Spalding Grammar School and doubtless chaplain of Wykeham Chapel.

In 1790 it was reported that "the walls are in good preservation; but the oak roof is in the most ruinous condition, some of the beams having fallen down and the remainder will most probably soon follow and let in the leaden roof which they now support; the glass windows are broken; the pews are in a dilapidated condition; the floor fast giving way; the octagon font broken in pieces; and the busts of Edward I and his queen Margaret, which supported the door arch, are destroyed.

On the inside of the east end are two niches in the wall, which appear to have had figures placed in them. On the top of the roof, to ascend which there is a flight of stone stairs, is affixed a small bell, with this inscription on it, 'SPALDINGS 1661'...".

At this time divine service was performed only about twice a year in the chapel. About a dozen families claimed a right of attending the chapel, and were said to be united in wishing it might be repaired, so that they might again enjoy the benefit of having the service of the church regularly performed there.

By 1802 the chapel was in such a state of decay and dilapidation that it had become imposible to perform divine service in it at all. The inside of the chapel was wholly exposed to the "pitiless pelting" of every storm.

The minister occasionally performed the church service to such as were desirous attending, in a room at the mansion-house near the chapel. The chaplain at this time was the Rev. Walter Maurice Johnson (1757 - 1832), a grandson of Maurice Johnson, "the Antiquary", he was Master of Spalding Grammar School from 1792 to 1826, and also Vicar of Weston from 1805.

He resided at "Masters Lodge", Church Street, Spalding, and was the father of the Miss Johnsons who left, by Will, funds for the erection of the Johnson Hospital.

Canon Moore, who was Chaplain of Wykeham from 1835 to 1889, writes that "The debris of the roof lay on the floor of the Chapel until the year 1835 when the lead was sold and the proceeds applied towards the reflooring and reroofing of St. Mary's Chapel which was used until 1881 as the Grammar School in Spalding.

"The timbers of the roof were cleared out together with a great deal of old woodwork about the year 1838 and buried in the moat which was then in process of being filled up by the recent purchaser of the estate ... From this time, and for several years after portions of the old Roman Bank upon the estate were carried away into the pits adjacent to Cowhirn."

The Wykeham estate was owned by the Ravenscroft family from 1684 until about 1787, when it came into the possession of Charles Butler (1750 - 1832), of Wykeham, and of Thurlow House in Great Ormond Street, London, barrister-at-law and Bencher of Lincoln Inn, K.C.

He was said to be the first Roman Catholic admitted to the Bar after the Relief Act, 1791. After the death of Charles Butler the estate was sold and purchased by Robert Everard (1795 - 1880), of Spalding.

In 1870 it was proposed that the marriage of Miss Sarah Elizabeth Everard and Edward Montague Earle Welby, Esquire, should take place in the chapel.

However, some objection as to the legality of marriages at Wykeham was raised, and they were married at Spalding Parish Church on February 3 of that year.

The South Holland Magazine for March, 1870, in reporting the marriage, notes that "The Bride, who will inherit great wealth, is a very amiable young lady, and has, by her kindness and courtesy, won the esteem of all who knew her. The family of Welby has been connected with South Lincolnshire for centuries, and is as old as our Churches, with which they have ever been prominently connected as patrons and benefactors."

In 1880, Robert Everard, Deputy Lieutenant of South Lincolnshire and JP of Fulney House and Wykeham, was buried in the chapel. His widow, Mrs Sarah Everard, who died in 1903, aged 93, was also buried there. Known, affectionately, as "Lady Everard", she was said to be the last person in Spalding to drive in her carriage and pair.

In 1927, the then owner, arranged for the repair of the defects in the walls, and the careful restoration of the mullions and tracery in the windows under the supervision of Mr Walter Tapper, ARA, RIBA.

The following is a list of chaplains of Wykeham, together with the dates of appointment:

1792	Walter Maurice Johnson
1832	William George Moore
1835	Edward Moore
1889	Thomazin Albert Stoodley
1894	Edward Martin Tweed
1940	Basil Gordon Nicholas
1946	Lancelot Smith
1977	John Charles Moon

Since 1977 the Rev J.C. Moon, Vicar of St John Baptist, Spalding, has been chaplain of Wykeham.

The Parish Church of Saint John Baptist

The church was erected at the sole cost of Miss Mary Ann Johnson (1794 - 1878), of Fairfax (Holyrood) House, Spalding, who also purchased the land, paid for the erection of the day school and vicarage, and contributed to the endowment of the benefice. Miss Johnson spent nearly £20,000 on St. John's, and also, left by Will, a sum of £1,000 for the distribution of coal to the poor of the parish.

Miss Johnson would have liked the church to be built on London Road, but this was not possible, and after several other sites had been unsuccessfully sought after, Hawthorn Bank was settled upon.

The architect was Robert Jewell Withers, of the Adelphi, London, and the builders Huddlestone and Son, of Lincoln. The building of the church, school and vicarage was entrusted to a committee, but Canon Moore had practical control, and conducted all the negotiations with the architect.

The foundation stone was laid by Miss Johnson on 12th February, 1874, and the church was consecrated on 24th June, 1875, by Christopher Wordsworth, Bishop of Lincoln.

The school was opened on 31st May, 1875, with Miss Clara Brummitt, as headmistress, a post she retained until 1913.

Canon Moore's nephew - the Rev. Augustus William George Moore, M.A. (1841 - 1897), - was appointed the first Vicar in 1875. A High Churchman, and noted as an effective and sympathetic preacher, he was described as a man of unusual versatility and remarkable vigour. As parish priest he worked unsparingly, and had no Sunday away on holiday before 1892, and possibly not after that. He took an active part in the public life of the town as Town Husband, trustee of the Johnson Hospital, feoffee of the Spalding Living, member of the Spalding School Board, member of the Spalding Gentlemen's Society and as a Freemason. He died in 1897 aged 55. His successor was the Rev. Grant William Macdonald, M.A. (1846 - 1923), the great grandson of Flora Macdonald, of Milton-in-Skye, the heroine who saved the life of the Young Pretender after his defeat at the Battle of Culloden in 1746. He served as Curate at Holbeach 1872 - 79, and Vicar of Holbeach St. Mark's 1879 -97, before being appointed to St. John's. He published a number of authoritative works on local history including "Historical Notices of the Parish of Holbeach &c." and "The Holbeach Register &c." He retired in 1913, and was succeeded by the Rev. Arthur Henry Morris, previously Rector of Crowland.

A Census of Religious Worship taken on Sunday, 27th November, 1881, revealed that 213 were present at St. John's in the morning, and 152 attended the evening service.

Left: The Rev. A.W.G. and Mrs. Edith Moore (seated) and family with governess. About 1880.

Below: The Parish Church of Saint John Baptist, Hawthorn Bank, Spalding.

St. Peter's Church, Priory Road

St. Peter's Church, in Priory Road, used as a Chapel of Ease to the Parish Church, was built in 1875-6, according to designs by Sir Gilbert Scott (1811-78). Ten years earlier, at the time of the restoration of the Parish Church, the building of a new church had been proposed, and a site in Priory Road (then known as Abbey Gardens) purchased for £500, and the foundations prepared. The cost of the restoration works at the Parish Church however, absorbed all the available funds, and the undertaking had to be postponed.

The church was finally completed in 1876, at a cost of £10,000, mainly contributed by Canon Moore, Miss Mary Ann Johnson, Miss Charlotte Charinton, T. M. S. Johnson, Esq., and a few others. It was built of red brick with stone facings, and consisted of a nave, with north and south aisles, chancel, with two vestries, and an organ chamber on the north side. A spiret, at the west end, contained a bell exhibited by the founders at the Great Exhibition of 1851. The font was the one used in the Parish Church before restoration. Accommodation was provided for 500 worshippers.

The building was consecrated by Christopher Wordsworth, Bishop of Lincoln, on 6th July, 1876. The attendant ceremonies were overshadowed and curtailed due to the tragic death of the Parish Church Sexton, William Stretton, aged 39, who died from injuries received as the result of an accident which occurred when he was at work on the site a few days previously. The register of SS. Mary & Nicolas records his burial on 1st July, 1876.

The religious census of 27th November, 1881, revealed that 128 were present at morning service, and 313 attended in the evening.

In 1901 the church was entirely re-seated, the chairs being replaced by pews.

The church contained two memorial tablets. One recorded that the pulpit and screen were a thanksgiving offering for the deliverance from sickness of Elizabeth, the wife of William James Eland Hobson, of Spalding, draper, Easter, 1885, and the second the death of Sidney Victor Borrer, a choirboy, aged 11 years, in 1906.

In 1917, during the First World War, regular services were suspended. For many years thereafter a part of the building was used as a school, also for sporting, social and other purposes.

In 1967, the building was purchased by the former Spalding Rural District Council, at a cost of £5,750, for the purpose of providing additional space for car parking at the offices of the Council. The church was demolished in 1968.

St. Paul's Church, Fulney

St. Paul's Church, Fulney, was almost the latest work of Sir Gilbert Scott (1811 - 78), but he died before the plans, based on suggestions from Canon Moore, could be carried out, and the work was completed by his son. The contractors were S. and W. Pattinson, of Ruskington. The foundation stone was laid by Miss Charinton on 18th October, 1877, and the church was opened by Christopher Wordsworth, Bishop of Lincoln, on 27th October, 1880. The whole cost of the site and buildings, together with an endowment of £300 per year was defrayed by Miss Charlotte Charinton (1801-88), of Spalding. Her expenditure on St. Paul's was in excess of £30,000. Canon Moore acted as Miss Charinton's representative during the building of the church, which remains a memorial to his zeal and energy, for he was intimately associated with the scheme from its inception to its completion.

Miss Charinton, who resided on the Terrace at Spalding, came from a long established Gedney Hill family. Though possessed of considerable wealth she lived very quietly, and contributed largely to good works in the various parishes where she had property. She contributed generously to the restoration of the Parish Church at Spalding and the erection of St. Peter's Abbey Church. At Gedney Hill she mainly restored the Parish Church, and presented a carved pulpit in memory of her father. Her private charities were scrupulously hidden and known to few except herself and the recipients. The family of Charinton was well known at Gedney Hill for several generations but with the death of Miss Charinton the name became extinct.

The first Vicar was the Revd. Richard Guy Ash, M.A., (1848-1935), who was a native of Long

Below: St. Paul's Church, Fulney from Fulney Lane.

Sutton. He was educated at Leeds Grammar School and at Wadham College, Oxford. A learned scholar, he became Professor of English History at Aberystwyth in 1879. He was curate at St. Mark's, Lincoln 1877 - 78, and appointed Vicar of St. Paul's in 1878, where he remained in charge until his death in 1935. A keen angler and cyclist, he was well known throughout the county as a sportsman. He served as Chaplain to the Spalding Poor Law Institution, was a Town Husband, a feoffee of the Spalding Living, a trustee of the Spalding Savings Bank and a member of the Hundred of Elloe Lodge of Freemasons.

On Sunday, 27th November, 1881, a Census of Religious Worship revealed that 122 persons were present at the morning service at St. Paul's and 117 attended in the evening.

St. Paul's Church, Spalding - Sir G. Gilbert Scott, R.A. Architect.

The Catholic Church, Henrietta Street

The church of The Immaculate Conception and St. Norbert, in Henrietta Street, the school and presbytery were provided by the generosity of Thomas Arthur Young (1805 - 91), of Kingerby Hall, Market Rasen, Lord of the Manor of Kingerby. A devout Catholic and a well-known philanthrophist he also provided the funds for the building of Catholic churches at Gainsborough, Crowle, Market Rasen and Grimsby.

In February, 1873, it was reported that the priest of Boston hoped to establish a Catholic Mission at Spalding. At that time Mass was said once a month in a rented room, the altar furniture, linen and vestments being brought over each time from Boston. Thomas Arthur Young purchased the house on the corner of St. Thomas's Road and Henrietta Street, and offered it to the Norbertines as a base for a

Catholic Mission. The opening of the new Catholic Oratory of The Immaculate Conception and St. Norbert took place on Wednesday, 8th December, 1875 with High Mass and Sermons at 11 a.m. and evening service and sermon at 6 p.m. It was said that the inaugural Mass was celebrated on a makeshift altar made from boxes and a table. Father Thomas van Biesen, the first Parish Priest arrived in Spalding on 22nd December, 1875.

A private residence was first adapted, but within six months the building of the present Oratory, in Henrietta Street, was commenced, the contract price for the first part of the work being £800. The opening services were held on 13th November, 1876, when Dr. E.G. Bagshawe, Bishop of Nottingham, celebrated Mass. Further property was acquired, and by the end of the 1870's, between £4,000 and £5,000 had been expended on an ambitious programme of building with a view to establishing an Oratory, Day School, and a Convent.

In a letter to Everard Green, dated 24th December, 1878, Father van Biesen wrote "You will be glad hearing that Catholicism is making some progress in your native town, we have now a small convent with boarding and day school although the number of pupils is very small; and we are just now enlarging our chapel the foundations for a chancel have been laid and as soon as winter is over we will continue ...".

In another letter to the same correspondent, dated 21st April, 1879, the Rev. Thomas van Biesen reported "Our little chapel is well filled on Sundays at the evening service, not so much in the morning as there are in Spalding only 51 Catholics; we have a goodly number in the villages but they do not come regularly. Among the converts we have in Spalding, the principal are Mr. and Mrs. Parkinson and their Son, 2 children of the farmer Williamson, Miss Measures etc....".

The day school had a very hard struggle at first owing to the Education Department's refusal to recognise it for grant on the ground that it was unnecessary.

The religious census of November, 27th, 1881, revealed that accommodation was provided for 200 worshippers. On that Sunday 64 were present at the morning service, and 69 attended in the evening.

The church was consecrated by Dr. Heylen, Bishop of Namur, in 1904. So many people wished to be present at the consecration that it was decided to admit by ticket only.

**Thomas Arthur Young (1805 - 91),
The Portrait.**
In a letter, dated 18th September, 1879, Thomas Arthur Young wrote "My portrait is at Spalding given in full length figure with Hat and Umbrella. You will please exhibit that photo and tell the Company the Story of the Umbrella........ The narrative might prove advantageous to go and do in like manner.

The entire works at Spalding, Crowle and elsewhere were all accomplished by the simple frugal adoption of the Umbrella, having relinquished - Groom, Horse and Carriage for 35 years. The Umbrella had been my daily companion, a staff in fatigue, a shade against heat, and a shelter from rain".

At the time of the General Election, of January, 1906, it was estimated that there were 200 Roman Catholic electors in the Spalding Division, and the Conservatives claimed that the education question would result in practically all these voting for their candidate, E. M. Pollock.

Father Clement Tyck succeeded Father van Biesen in 1903. A well known and highly respected figure he served as Parish Priest until 1921. In September, 1908, a Lady Chapel in the form of a grotto, a copy of the famous grotto of Lourdes, was added to the church. It was the work of a Belgian artist, Jacques Coomans, of Antwerp. In 1915 seven stone carvings, the work of a Belgian scupltor, J. Tuerlinckx, of Malines, were added to the exterior.

Father Aloysius Firth became Parish Priest in 1921, and remained until 1940. Succeeding Parish Priests have been Father Norbert Ellis, 1940 - 57; Father Joseph Dodds, 1957 - 60; Father Gerebern John Pelgroms, 1960 - 82; and, since 1982, Father Oliver Martin.

St. John's Free Church of England, Pinchbeck Street

The Free Church of England movement arose in Spalding in 1873, when William Thomas Capps, of High Street, timber merchant, and William Eusebius Dandy, grocer (of the firm of Stableforth & Dandy), together with several other influential residents seceded from the Church of England as a protest against what they considered to be the introduction of ritualistic practices into the Parish Church services. Meetings were held in the Corn Exchange, and afterwards in the old Assembly Rooms in Broad Street. In 1874 a corrugated iron place of worship was erected in Pinchbeck Street at a cost of £2,000. The building was neatly and comfortably fitted inside, having a chancel, organ and communion table. Outside there was a tall spire containing a large bell. Seating accommodation was provided for 520 persons. In the following year a Sunday School was added. This was situated at the back of the church, and the foundation excepted, was made entirely of wood. There were then about 80 Sunday School scholars.

For several years the church flourished. On Sunday, 27th November, 1881, there were 136 present at the morning service, and 126 who attended in the evening. In the early 1880's dissensions arose. Attendance fell. There were financial problems. Except during the first few years of the movement there was always a considerable financial deficiency for one or two of the more affluent members of the church to make up - W. E. Dandy contributing from £30 to £50 a year as his share of the extra expenses. In April, 1890, following a meeting of the congregation it was decided to close the church, and offer the building for sale, the last service being held on 5th October, 1890.

There were four ministers during the 17 years the movement was in existence in Spalding. They were the Rev. P. X. Eldridge (who later became a Bishop in the Reformed Episcopal Church), the

The photograph shows the spire of St. John's Free Church - the church itself being largely hidden by trees.

Rev. C. W. Lamport (appointed Pastor, in 1881, at a salary of £120 per annum), the Rev. G. S. Lee (who later joined the Church of England, and became Rector of Benniworth, near Lincoln), and the Rev. A. R. Gaze.

The building was then used by the Salvation Army, but was soon found to be too big for their requirements, and they moved to the schoolroom, which they occupied as their barracks. The church was eventually purchased by a Spalding furniture dealer, who sold the seats to the Vicar of Spalding for one of his churches, and turned the building into a furniture warehouse. It was later used by the Spalding Motor Company as a car showroom, and finally occupied by H. Leverton & Co. Ltd. as a showroom, drawing office, store shed and electrician's workshop. The site is today occupied by the offices of Messrs. Roythorne & Co., of Spalding, Solicitors.

Baptist Church, Chapel Lane

The Spalding Bapist Church is the oldest of the Nonconformist Churches in the town with a history going back to 1646. In that year, a visiting preacher, Henry Denne, was arrested for "preaching and baptising by immersion". He was taken into custody on a Sunday morning so that he might not preach, for, as the record says "the people resorted to him very much, and there was no small occasion of their taking offence".

After the passing of the Toleration Act, in 1689, it became possible to erect a meeting house, and in that year "one cottage and garden situate in Spalding between the lands of Mr. Walpoole on the West lands of Thomas Hudson on the East abutting on the common sewer called the Westload towards the South and upon a lane called Deadman's Lane (now Swan Street) towards the North then in the tenure of Widow Stennett . . .", was purchased from Elizabeth Burton, of Pinchbeck, widow for £24, in order to provide "a meeting place and burial place for the present church of baptized believers in Spalding commonly though falsely called Annabaptists and for that use to succeeding generations for ever . . .".

On this site a meeting house was built at a cost of £83. 0s. 1d. It was destroyed in the Great Fire of Spalding which occurred on 2nd April, 1715. By the following February a new place of worship had been erected. This served the cause until 1811, when it was taken down and a new chapel built. This building was demolished in 1828, and a new chapel and schoolroom erected at a cost of more than £800. The opening services took place on 6th February, 1829.

In 1807, a baptistry was made in the chapel ground, posts being placed round it to carry a rope to hold back the people. The inside was pitched and a cover put on the top. On the first Sunday in June, 1829, five people were baptised, there being 1,000 spectators at the ceremony, followed by a great evening meeting.

The Marriage Act, of 1836, enabled Nonconformists to be married in their own chapels. Previously, with the exception of the Quakers and the Jews, all marriages had to take place in the Church of England. In its issue for 10th November, 1837, "The Lincolnshire Chronicle", reported the marriage:-
"On Wednesday week, at the General Baptist chapel, Spalding, of Mr. Robson, baker, to Hannah, eldest daughter of the late Mr. Sudbury. This is the first marriage under the new Act which has taken place at Spalding".

In 1842 the church was enlarged at a cost of £500. The alterations included a new baptistry being made inside the chapel. In 1855 it was found that more room was needed in the chapel. The schoolroom was accordingly taken into the chapel at an outlay of £150. After this step was taken, great inconvenience was experienced in conducting the Sunday School. This created a desire for a new schoolroom, and in 1865 a new schoolroom was built, taking in the burial ground, traces of which can still be seen by the tombstones still remaining on the wall of the chapel.

In 1848, the Rev. J. C Jones, M.A. commenced his pastorate - the longest in the history of the church - one which was to last for 65 years.

The census of Religious Worship taken on 30th March, 1851, recorded 450 present at the morning service, and 500 in the evening.

On 16th October, 1857, the following members were chosen as new trustees:-
Edward Foster senr, gardener; John Foster, yeoman; Samuel Atkin, builder; Tyrer Johnson, gentleman; Thomas Sharman, cordwainer; William White, senr, coachmaker; Frederick Charles Southwell, clerk; John Richard Measures, draper; George Limmer, wheelwright; Edward Lawson,

1885-1886 *From Nellie Coley*

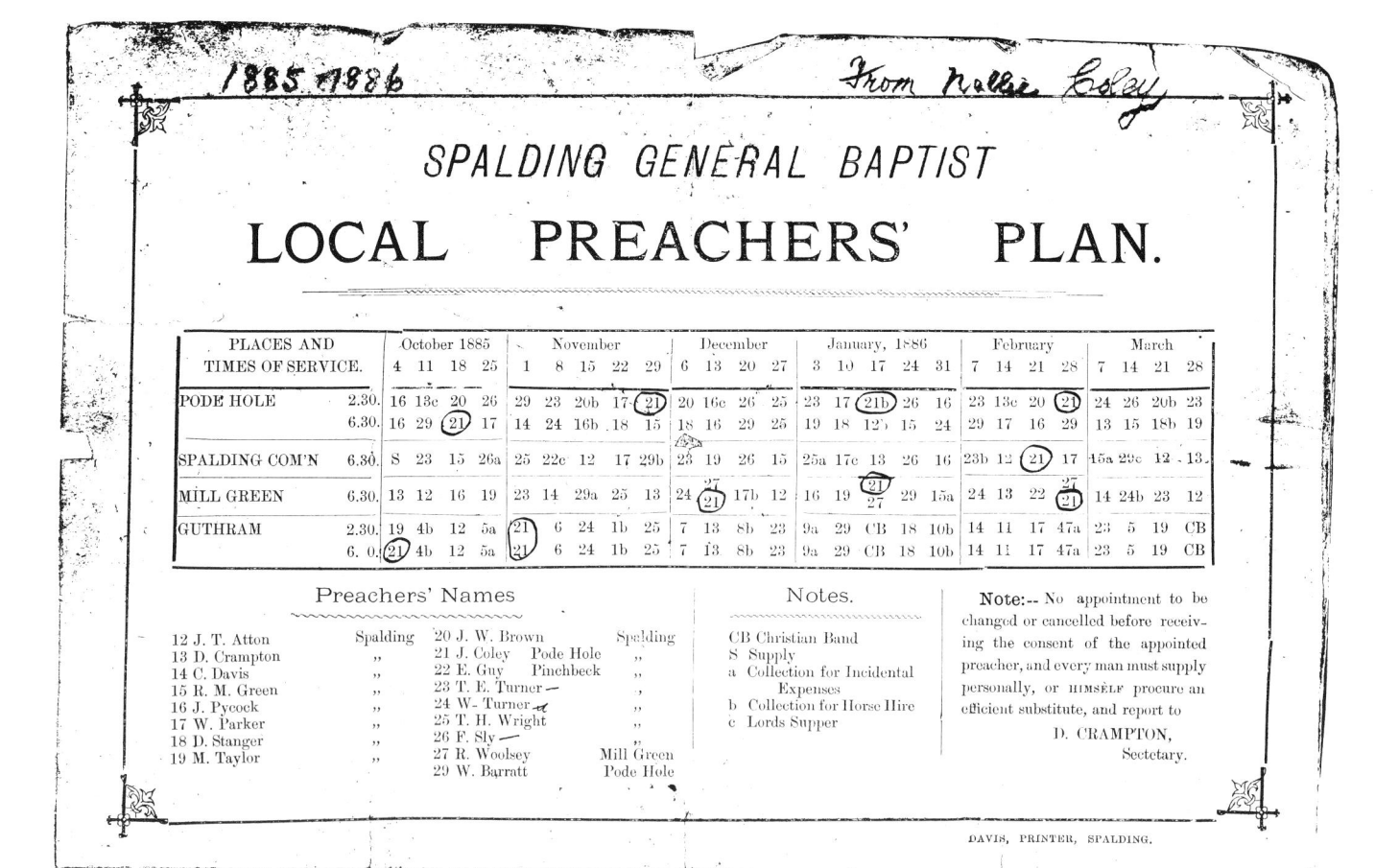

SPALDING GENERAL BAPTIST
LOCAL PREACHERS' PLAN.

PLACES AND TIMES OF SERVICE.	October 1885 4 11 18 25	November 1 8 15 22 29	December 6 13 20 27	January, 1886 3 10 17 24 31	February 7 14 21 28	March 7 14 21 28
PODE HOLE 2.30.	16 13c 20 26	29 23 20b 17 (21)	20 16c 26 25	23 17 (21b) 26 16	23 13c 20 (21)	24 26 20b 23
6.30.	16 29 (21) 17	14 24 16b 18 15	18 16 29 25	19 18 12b 15 24	29 17 16 29	13 15 18b 19
SPALDING COM'N 6.30.	S 23 15 26a	25 22c 12 17 29b	23 19 26 15	25a 17c 13 26 16	23b 12 (21) 17	15a 29c 12 13
MILL GREEN 6.30.	13 12 16 19	23 14 29a 25 13	24 (21)/27 17b 12	16 19 27/(21) 29 15a	24 13 22 (21)/27	14 24b 23 12
GUTHRAM 2.30.	19 4b 12 5a (21)	6 24 1b 25	7 13 8b 23	9a 29 CB 18 10b	14 11 17 47a	23 5 19 CB
6. 0.	(21) 4b 12 5a (21)	6 24 1b 25	7 13 8b 23	9a 29 CB 18 10b	14 11 17 47a	23 5 19 CB

Preachers' Names

12 J. T. Atton — Spalding
13 D. Crampton — ,,
14 C. Davis — ,,
15 R. M. Green — ,,
16 J. Pycock — ,,
17 W. Parker — ,,
18 D. Stanger — ,,
19 M. Taylor — ,,
20 J. W. Brown — Spalding
21 J. Coley — Pode Hole ,,
22 E. Guy — Pinchbeck ,,
23 T. E. Turner — ,,
24 W. Turner — ,,
25 T. H. Wright — ,,
26 F. Sly — ,,
27 R. Woolsey — Mill Green
29 W. Barratt — Pode Hole

Notes.

CB Christian Band
S Supply
a Collection for Incidental Expenses
b Collection for Horse Hire
c Lords Supper

Note:— No appointment to be changed or cancelled before receiving the consent of the appointed preacher, and every man must supply personally, or HIMSELF procure an efficient substitute, and report to

D. CRAMPTON,
Secretary.

DAVIS, PRINTER, SPALDING.

---

painter; William Fawn, builder; Joseph Pannell, grocer; Dean Swift, junr, yeoman; Charles Curry, tailor; John Thorpe Matthews, coachpainter; Robert Smart, gardener; John Chatwin Jones, minister; John Thomas Newling, grocer; Wm. Hy. Bennett, carpenter; Henry Everard, of Spalding, late of Gosberton, Baptist Minister there.

The census of religious worship which was taken on Sunday, 27th November, 1881, revealed that 240 attended the morning service, and 262 were present in the evening. Seating accommodation was available for 600.

On 2nd September, 1883, the death occurred of Thomas 'Daddy' Sharman, at the age of 87. He was brought up as a shoemaker, and for many years lived on the site of the railway station. Later he carried on a boot and shoe business in the Market Place. In many respects he was a remarkable man. He was self-educated, was a great reader, had an excellent memory, and made himself thoroughly acquainted with the works of many of the best authors, especially the poets, of whom Milton and Cowper were probably his greatest favourites. A member of the church for over fifty years, and a deacon for over a quarter of a century, he was mainly instrumental in the settlement of the Rev. J. C. Jones in Spalding. A very acceptable local preacher, and an earnest and popular Sunday School teacher, he was always ready to assist other denominations, and to co-operate in all movements connected with the moral and spiritual well-being of the town.

In 1898 the church appropriately celebrated the Jubilee of the Rev. J. C. Jones as pastor. The venerable minister continued to serve the church for another 15 years, finally retiring in 1913. When he died, in 1917, at the great age of 93, his strong character was epitomised in the text taken from 1 Corinthians xv. 58, "stedfast, unmoveable".

The Rev. Harry Spendelow was Pastor from September, 1914 to February, 1935. He came to Spalding from Grimsby, where his ministry at the Victoria Street Tabernacle had proved very successful. He was a firm upholder of Free Church principles, and, like his predecessor, was a Passive Resister of the Education Act. He was a member of the Spalding Board of Guardians, a Governor of the Spalding Grammar School and the Johnson Hospital, and a member of the Holland Education Committee. He resided in Spalding after his retirement, and up to the time of his health failing, continued to render sevice for the Free Churches in the town and district. He died in 1944. Succeeding ministers have been: the Rev. A. Rattray Allan, 1935 - 43; the Rev. J. Scott Thorburn, 1943 - 52; the Rev. Kenneth Allen, 1953 - 59; the Rev. Peter King, 1959 - 64; and the Rev. John Hance since 1964.

Left: Preachers plan for 1885 - 86.

Above: Local Mission Poster.

Right: The Chapel as seen today.

The Revd. J. C. Jones, M.A., (1823 - 1917)

The Rev. John Chatwin Jones, M.A., was born at Castle Donington, near Derby, on 7th July, 1823, the son of the Rev. John Jones, Baptist Minister. At the age of 17 he was baptised and received into the Baptist Church at March. He entered the General Baptist College, and on the completion of his studies successfully competed for Dr. Williams' Scholarship in the University of Glasgow. In the summer of 1846, when on vacation, he undertook a preaching engagement at Long Sutton. Among the congregation was Thomas Sharman, of Spalding, a shoemaker, one of the deacons of the Spalding Baptist Church. There was then a vacancy in the pastorate of the Spalding Church. Greatly impressed by the young student's preaching Thomas Sharman strongly commended him to the notice of the deacons at Spalding. On 21st January, 1847, he was invited to preach for six months, and on 1st October following was asked to take the pastorate at Spalding at a stipend of £100 per annum with two Sundays for vacation. After completing his studies at Glasgow, where he graduated M.A. he returned to Spalding, and was ordained to the ministry on 30th June, 1848. Thus commenced the longest pastorate in the history of the Spalding Baptist Church - one which was to last for 65 years.

He was a magnificent preacher in the hey-day of his power, and it is recorded that a friend of his who held an important position on the Great Northern Railway would often on a Sunday morning come from Hitchin to Spalding, on an engine specially appropriated for the purpose, in order to hear him preach. He was famed for his keen intellect, impressive personality, rhetorical brilliance, and expositary preaching. In one year 122 persons were baptised, and on another occasion over 30 young men, members of the Bible class, were baptised. In 1908 it was calculated that he had preached at least 8,000 sermons in the town where for six decades he had been a resident. He retired, after preaching his last sermon as pastor, on 6th July 1913, the day before he celebrated his 90th birthday. The next day he presided as usual, as Chairman, at the fortnightly meeting of the Board of Guardians.

He wrote the leading article for the first number of "The Spalding Free Press", which appeared 5th October, 1847. For many years he was an ardent Liberal politician, but he became estranged from that party by Mr. Gladstone's Home rule policy, and gradually forsook party politics, although he supported H. R. Mansfield, the successful Liberal candidate for the Spalding Division in the General Election of 1906. He was an outspoken opponent of the Boer War, and his house was attacked by a mob during the celebrations held in Spalding to mark the relief of Mafeking. He was a Passive Resister to the Education Act of 1902.

He took a prominent part in local affairs, being, with one brief interval, a member of the Spalding Board of Guardians from 1862, becoming vice-chairman in 1886, and was elected chairman, in succession to the Rev. J. T. Dove, in 1906. This post he held until his death. He also served as a member of the Spalding School Board and as a Governor of the Spalding Grammar School.

For a long period he conducted a boys' day and boarding school in The Terrace, and later in High Street.

It was said that he had no recreations beyond friendly disputation - which he loved and in which he always came out best - and fishing for pike.

He married, at Spalding, in 1850, Sarah Ann, daughter of David and Ann Newling, of Spalding. They had a family of three sons and six daughters.

For about forty years he resided at Charnwood, Pinchbeck Road, where he died, on 14th January, 1917, in his 94th year. He left estate of the gross value of £14,412. 4s. 6d., with net personalty of £2,340. 1s.

Charnwood, Pinchbeck Road

For about 40 years, from the mid 1870's, the residence of the Rev. J. C. Jones, M.A., (1823 - 1917), who was for 65 years - from 1848 to 1913 - Pastor of the Spalding Baptist Church. A man of great strength of character, and deeply held convictions, he vigorously opposed the war waged by the British against the Boers in South Africa from 1899 to 1902, and incurred some unpopularity thereby.

On Friday and Saturday, 19th and 20th May, 1900, celebrations took place in Spalding to mark the relief of Mafeking after a seven month siege by the Boers. Shortly before midnight on the Saturday evening a hostile crowd gathered in front of Charnwood, yelling and hooting, fireworks and other missiles were thrown through the dining room window, breaking three squares of glass and doing other damage, the heavy iron gate was hurled from its hinges, and a miniature bonfire held in the garden. It is said that the venerable minister - he was 77 years of age - sat quietly smoking through it all, and had to be restrained by his family from going out to confront the mob.

After the death of the Rev. J. C Jones, Charnwood was for many years the home of Tom A. White (1885 - 1941), auctioneer, valuer and farmer, who was the youngest son of John Thomas White (1847 - 1930), one of the pioneers of the Lincolnshire bulb industry.

Society of Friends, (Quakers)

Below: View of the Friends' Meeting House and Burial Ground taken in 1961.

There have been Quakers in Spalding since the 1650's. The records of Spalding Monthly Meeting of the Society of Friends commence in 1667. The early Friends were severely persecuted in South Holland. One of the leaders of Lincolnshire Quakerism, John Whitehead, of Fiskerton, dated an epistle entitled "A Tender Visitation of Heavenly Love", from 'Spalding prison this 19th day of the Ninth Month, 1664'. The site of the present Meeting House and burial ground was purchased in 1698. Two cottages standing on it were converted into a Meeting House, which was licenced for public worship in 1706. It stood on part of the present burial ground near to the Double Street entrance, and was demolished when the existing Meeting House was erected at the Westlode Street end in 1805.

Memorial stones recall former Quaker families - Bateman, Burgess, Chantry, Hawkes, Hopkins, Massey, Nainby and Neave.

The stones in the foreground record the names of George Hall (1831 - 1918), and his son, Cornelius Dalrymple Hall (1857 - 1926), both auctioneers. George Hall, described as one of the most remarkable men Spalding ever knew, was one of the leading public men of his day. Cornelius Hall, was for many years honorary secretary of the Spalding Shipwreck Society. He also took part in the wider activities of the Society of Friends, particularly in the cause of peace, in the interests of which he on several occasions attended Peace Conferences at The Hague and elsewhere on the Continent.

Above: View of the interior taken in 1961 before the Meeting House was restored. At the back is the Ministers' gallery, and below the Elders' bench. In front is the ancient oak table, and on each side the 'coffin stools'. (Are these the two buffet stools made by John Roberts in 1770, for which John Massey, on behalf of the Meeting, paid him ten shillings and six pence?). During the period 1964 to 1970 the Meeting House was restored through the generosity of Henry and Christine Burtt, of Dowsby. Additional facilities were provided, including the addition of a two-bedroomed flat for a Warden.

A Good Quaker

John Hawley was a Quaker who resided "within the compass" of Spalding Monthly Meeting of the Society of Friends during the 18th century. In 1762 he left Spalding to live in Leicestershire. On leaving Spalding he asked that Spalding Friends send a Certificate of Removal to the Friends in Leicestershire testifying that he was a member in good standing. The Certificate reads as follows:

To Friends of Old Dalby Monthly Meeting in the County of Leicester.

Dear Friends,
Our Friend John Hawley a Member of our Monthly Meeting, being removed into the compass of yours: and requesting of us a Certificate for that purpose: We in compliance therewith, and agreeable to

the Rules of our Society, send these to Certify you, that He has been of a sober inoffensive Life & Conversation, just in His commerce and dealings amongst Men, rather chusing to suffer loss to himself, than streanuously to insist upon what was his lawful right; thus by His peaceable disposition He gain'd the respect of his Friends, as well as those with whom He had dealings; as such we recommend Him to your Religious care, earnestly desiring He may be preserv'd during the residue of His time here, in such a state of Humble dependance and resignation to the divine Will, as will truly fit Him for a Mantion in eternal Bliss, whenever it may please divine Providence to call Him from Works to Rewards, with the salutation of dear Love we conclude your real Friends.

Signed in and on the behalf of our Monthly Meeting held at Spalding (by appointment) the 15th of the 10th Month, 1762 by John Massey, Henry Hammond, Joseph Massey, Jacob Hutchinson, Thos. Claxton, Isaac Theaker, John Hutchinson, John Copeland, William Hutchinson, Benjamin Kent, John Massey Junr.

"Ebenezer" Particular Baptist Chapel, Love Lane

Below: A view of the chapel and burial ground taken about 1902.

Built in 1770 it was "..the Chapel or Meeting House situate in Spalding in the County of Lincoln belonging to and for the use of the Society of Protestant Dissenters professing the Doctrine of Free Grace and commonly called Particular Baptists in Spalding...". It was erected principally through the assistance and exertions of Mr. Leonard Pape, "grazier, gardiner and seedsman", who was buried in the ground adjoining the chapel. Several of the early members and founders were opulent Fen farmers. In 1787, due to the increase of the congregation it became necessary to enlarge the building, pews being erected throughout. In 1802 it was described as "a neat and even handsome house of prayer". The first pastor - a Mr. Clark - who was minister for "about 15 or 16 years" was buried in the

"Chapel yard". His successor, James Craps, served from 1786 to 1812, and was remembered as a "zealous and beloved pastor". He was buried in the chapel, close to the pulpit steps.

Internal dissensions occurred during the first half of the 19th century. On two occasions some members left the church, and established separate congregations. These, however, only had a brief existence. In 1871 the chapel underwent restoration. Mr. John Vincent, fruit merchant, of Winsover Road, became pastor in 1872, and served until his death in 1880. He was succeeded by the Rev. Thomas Newbold. He left in 1884. On Sunday, 27th November, 1881, there was an attendance of 55 at the morning service, and 113 in the evening. There was then seating accommodation for 150. Mr. Joseph Wortley, builder and joiner, of London Road, seems to have been the last regular pastor. At the beginning of the 20th century there was no settled minister, the services being conducted by the members of the Society. After 1916 the chapel was no longer used by the Particular Baptists. For a time it was a warehouse. In due course it was again used as a place of worship, the last religious body to worship there being the Assemblies of God.

The chapel was sold in 1948, and became the headquarters of the scout and guide movement in Spalding, and known as 'Moose Hall'. It was finally demolished in 1984.

Wesleyan Methodist Church, Broad Street

Methodism was comparatively late arriving in Spalding, but by the early 1790's meetings were being held 'by appointment', and thereafter the number of adherents increased rapidly. The first chapel was built in The Hole-in-the-Wall in 1795. This served the cause for thirty years. It was afterwards used as a Soup Kitchen, and eventually became the property of Doningtons, the Chemists, who were still using it as a warehouse at the beginning of the twentieth century. The second chapel was erected in Broad Street, in 1826, on part of the site once occupied by the House of Correction, which had recently been demolished and replaced by a new prison in the Sheep Market. The chief supporters of the project were Augustin Pridmore, gentleman (who contributed £935), George Donington, farmer, John Longstaff, farmer, and William Brown, merchant. The chapel was set back from the road, practically out of sight, and hemmed in by cottages, pig-sties, and stables. Sixty years later Canon Moore could still remember the following epigram which circulated on the night of the opening of the chapel:-

Reader! if thou hast time to spare,
Turn o'er St. Matthew's leaves,
You find how once a 'house of prayer'
Became a 'den of thieves'.
But now the case is altered quite;
Oh! reformation rare!
This recent 'den of thieves' to-night
Becomes a 'house of prayer'.

In the early days services were crowded. People walked miles to attend the quarterly love-feasts, entrance to which was by ticket only. These were generally held in the afternoon, and at times people could not gain admission. Membership of the circuit was 373 in 1825, rising to 620 members in 1830, and to 821 in 1835. For a short while an organ, lent by William Brown, was used, but the congregation would not allow it to remain, as 'not being suitable for a Methodist place of worship'; and the singing was usually led by one man, assisted on special occasions by the fiddles, flutes and piccolos of the members. On Sunday, 30th March 1851, a Census of Religious Worship was taken. This revealed that in the morning the general congregation numbered 262, and the Sunday Scholars 200. In the afternoon the general congregation was 28, and in the evening 330. The census return was signed by Henry Longbottom (ironmonger), Chapel and Society Steward.

In 1851-2 dissensions arose as a result of the 'Methodist Reform' movement. Ultimately a very large number of members left the church, and, known as Wesleyan Reformers, met for worship in the Assembly Room (which stood on the site now occupied by the Spalding Club). Later they joined with others to form the United Methodist Free Church. The Broad Street Church was, for a time, much enfeebled, for the Reformers took with them not only members, but the whole of the Sunday School, and all the portable property. A faithful core of members, however, remained, and 'soon set to work to fill in the breach that had been made'. In two years a school of fifty children had been gathered out of the streets. By the 1860's the cause had revived.

On Sunday, 27th November, 1881, a census of religious worship revealed that there was an attendance of 176 at the morning service and 233 in the evening. There was seating accommodation for 450.

Right: The church and schoolroom complete with railings which were subsequently removed during the Second World War

Below: Artists impression of the new building from "The Free Press", of 8th March, 1887.

In 1886 it was decided to build a new church. This - the present church - was erected on a site adjacent to the old chapel. The stone-laying took place on 8th July, 1886, with the Rev. M. C. Osborn, of London, as the principal speaker. The chief stones were laid by Ald. W. Jackson, J.P., of Grimsby; Hugh Wyatt Esq., J.P., Mayor of Lincoln; R. Dowson Esq., of Asfordby; Robert Donington; James Sewell and Edward Tawn. "The Stamford Mercury", of 16th July, 1886, reported:-

"The total amount raised by the day's services was over £500, a sum which, it is said, has never been equalled by any Nonconformist body in the town as a result of a similar day's services. A large crowd witnessed the laying of the stones in the afternoon, many being accommodated with seats on a spacious grandstand erected at the expense of Mr. Joseph Dobson."

The church was opened for public worship on March 3rd, 1887, by the President of the Conference (Rev. R. Newton Young, D.D.), the Rev. F. Greeves, D.D., ex.President, preaching in the evening. The proceeds for the day amounted to over £230. The architect was F. Boreham, F.R.I.B.A., of London, and the contractor was J. Holmes, of Wainfleet.

It had been intended to use the old chapel as a schoolroom, but when the new church had been seen by the side of the old one, it was at once decided to pull down the old chapel and build new schoolrooms in keeping with the new church. This was soon carried out and the schoolroom was opened on 3rd November, 1887. The cost of the whole scheme was £4,700.

Among the leading members during the second half of the 19th century were the brothers James and Robert Donington. They were born at Whaplode Drove, the sons of George and Rebecca (Ogden) Donington. Their father was one of the pioneers of Methodism in South Lincolnshire.

James Donington (1830-95), settled at Spalding in 1856, where he carried on an extensive business as an ironmonger. He served the church in many capacities, but his outstanding service was as a local preacher, and he was acknowledged to be the most acceptable local preacher in the district. It was no uncommon thing for him to walk fourteen miles to Swineshead, preach three times and then walk home again at night, without help of any kind, ready for his business next morning at seven o'clock. He was an active Liberal politician, and being a ready and effective speaker his services were greatly in request on the platform.

Robert Donington (1832-95), was 'cradled in Methodism'. In 1863 he commenced in business as a chemist in the Market Place. He took an active part in public life. He became a member of the Spalding School Board on its formation in 1877, and on the retirement of Major Shadford succeeded him as chairman. For several years he served as a Guardian of the Poor. He was a strong advocate of temperance. A devoted member of the Spalding Wesleyan Methodist Church 'he served the Church of his choice with a diligence and faithfulness that knew no weariness'. In 1886-7 he was one of the leading

Above: The principal entrance. Over the doors are carved figures symbolically representative of Faith, Hope and Charity.

spirits in connection with the erection of the church and school in Broad Street, serving as treasurer to the scheme, and acting as honorary clerk of works.

Another prominent worker was George Longbottom (1845-1919), of Spalding, draper, being a partner in the well-known firm of Hobson & Co. He joined the Wesleyan Methodists at Spalding in 1860, and commenced to preach in 1862. He was one of the ablest and most appreciated of local preachers. "His were the briefest of sermons from the most unusual of texts. Hence the popularity he enjoyed as a lay preacher, for sermons were long and heavy, for the most part, when he did most of his pulpit work". He filled almost every office in the church it was possible for him to hold, and he was a trustee of almost every place of worship in the circuit. He was affectionately remembered for the quaint and unusual observations he so often made in the meetings of the church and its fellowship, hospitable and generous, he was described as "...one of those gentle, kindly souls beloved by all".

George Longbottom's great-grandfather was said to have been a very intimate friend and fellow worker with John Wesley, and one of the first of his itinerant preachers.

Thomas Jessop Skinner (1849-1909), of Bridge Street, grocer, represented essentially the spiritual side of the society. A native of Boston he came to Spalding in 1872. Converted when about 16 years of age, he commenced his work of Sunday School teaching and visitation of the sick immediately, and in 1902 it was stated that his name was "a household word in every home in Spalding where sickness or sorrow has come, among rich and poor alike". He served as a Sunday school teacher, class leader, temperance advocate and worker, and leader of the Sunday Night and Week Evening Prayer meetings. At the time of his death he was described as "...one of the oldest and most esteemed members".

On October 19th, 1893, it was resolved, at a Leaders' Meeting, that "Collections be made at the Chapel Doors on Sunday next on behalf of the Miners' Wives and Children who are suffering in consequence of the Coal strike".

The placing of a new organ in the church was delayed until the church had become well-seasoned, and ready for its reception. It was opened on April 16th, 1896, by Dr. H. Keeton, organist of Peterborough Cathedral, and was erected by Forster & Andrews, of Hull. The cost was £450. This was said to have given a finish to "what all visitors and residents in the town readily admit the prettiest and best equipped church and schoolrooms in the district".

In 1918 the Society Stewards were Messrs. S. Culpin and H.A. White, and the poor Stewards Messrs. T. Biggadike and P. Bratley; the representatives to the local Sunday School Council were G.W. Gibbs, T. Biggadike and D. Waldock, and the representatives to the Free Church Council were G.W. Gibbs, R.S. Donington, S. Culpin, P. Bratley and R.B. Stoakley.

Recent ministers have been the Revds. W. Langford Brooks 1945-49; William G. Fielder 1949-55; Joseph Wilson 1955-62; G. Henry Dunford 1962-67; Alfred G. Du Feu 1967-72; Anthony H. Gledhill 1972-78; John W. Smith 1978-86; Brian W. Rogers, 1986-.

Primitive Methodist Church, St. Thomas' Road

The exact date when Primitive Methodism became established in Spalding is unknown. It was in 1821 that a building, previously used as a carpenter's shop, was adapted for use as a place of worship by the Primitive Methodists. This meeting-house was in Malting House Square (off the Sheep Market, next to the Prior's Oven). In 1852 a site was obtained in the Crescent, and a chapel built, which was opened on 20th February, 1853, when "crowds of people could not gain admittance and were compelled to return home". This building was later to become the Temperance Hall, and used as a place of worship by the Railway Mission. Within less than twenty years the chapel in the Crescent was considered unsuitable, and a site being secured in St. Thomas' Road a new chapel erected. The Primitive Methodist Magazine for November, 1871, reported that "....In the erection, strength, beauty and comfort are thoroughly combined, and it is pronounced the neatest building and the best piece of work in Spalding.....".

The Chapel was opened on 8th October, 1871, when the Rev. John Phillips, of London, preached "eloquent sermons morning and evening", and the Rev. W.C. Preston, the pastor of the Spalding Congregational Church, in the afternoon to a crowded congregation. The chapel provided accommodation for 400 people, and the entire cost of Chapel, Schoolroom, Copper House etc. was upwards of £800.

Above: Spalding United Nonconformist Sunday School Festival, about 1900. The Primitive Methodist Sunday School joining the procession at the junction of Spring Gardens and St. Thomas' Road.

The Revd. John T. Stead

Primitive Methodist minister. Born at Oldham, 1847. Entered the Primitive Methodist ministry, 1870. Minister of Spalding and Holbeach, 1881 to 1886. 'He was a diligent pastor, and his visits to the villages were gladly anticipated. Devotion to duty, carefulness of detail, and intense piety were the chief characteristics of a long and useful career'. Died in London, 1934.

The United Methodist Church, The Crescent

The United Methodist Free Church arose as a result of the 'reform agitation' within the Wesleyan Methodist Church in the late 1840's and early 1850's. At Spalding a very large section of the Wesleyan Methodists left the parent body and joined the new denomination, then known as Wesleyan Reformers. The first public services were held in the Assembly Room, Broad Street (on the site now occupied by the Spalding Club), on Sunday, 4th April, 1852. Services were conducted there for five years. William Booth (1829-1912), later to be the founder of the Salvation Army, but then a Methodist, was the first salaried minister from 1852 to 1854.

In 1856 land in the Crescent was purchased, and a chapel built capable of seating 700 persons, with Sunday School accommodation at the base. The contractors were Charles Brett and John Moore, both members of the church, and the chapel was opened on 14th July, 1857. The total cost was £1,305. In the same year the majority of the Wesleyan Reformers amalgamated with the Wesleyan Association of 1835, forming the United Methodist Free Church. During the next twenty years the cause made great progress. Congregations were so large, even at ordinary services, that chairs were placed in the aisles, and eventually stout pieces of board were obtained to fix across the aisles from pew to pew as required. The Sunday School was the largest in the town, with 600 scholars.

After little more than twenty years it was evident that the chapel was no longer adequate for the needs of the congregation. It was demolished in 1878, and a new one, known, to members and friends, simply, as 'The Crescent', was erected. The builder was John Moore, jun., a member of the church and secretary of the Sunday School, and the architects were Bellamy & Hardy, of Lincoln. The cost of the work was nearly £4,000. It was described as the largest and finest Nonconformist place of worship in the neighbourhood. The opening services were conducted by the Rev. John Adcock, of Manchester, on 22nd May, 1879.

On Sunday, 27th November, 1881, there was an attendance of 339 at the morning service and 456 in the evening. A new organ was introduced in 1884, and in 1900 a new church parlour and accessories were erected on the north side of the chapel, at a cost of over £200, the money being provided from the

The building of 'The Crescent' chapel 1878-79. Note the social implications of the scene and in particular how each individual displays his status by what he is carrying.

20th century Fund. In 1902 the church had 180 members, and the circuit 407. The Sunday School had over 500 scholars and 60 teachers.

The undisputed leader at the Crescent from the day of the opening of the first chapel until his death was Major Shadford (1816-1902). Free Methodism at Spalding largely owed its position to him, and the chapel was sometimes termed by outsiders, not inappropriately, as 'Shadford's Chapel'. He came to Spalding in 1839, established a successful business as a chemist in the Market Place, and took an active part in the public life of the town. Other leading figures included Charles Brett, builder, Philip Clark (1820-1909), farmer and grazier, Richard Culpin (1844-1908), bulb grower, Isaac Elsom (1822-1910), rope maker, his wife Eliza Elsom (1824-1911), Henry James (1864-1951), corn factor, William Jepson (1838-1933), builder, George Shadford (1838-86), chemist, John White (1832-1907), baker, and Joseph Wilson (1854-1909), journalist, editor of "The Spalding Free Press", from 1882 until his death.

During May 1929 Jubilee services were held. Thursday May 23rd, 1929, being described as a "Day of Re-Union and Rejoicing". Many former members, who had moved to other parts of the country, returned to take part in the celebrations. 1932 saw 'Methodist Union' when the Wesleyan Methodist Church, the Primitive Methodist Church and the United Methodist Church re-united to form the present Methodist Church.

Sadly the great days of 'The Crescent' were now over. A new age had dawned. A faithful and devoted body of members remained, but it was a dwindling and predominantly ageing congregation. Serious structural defects in the building were developing. In the 1950's Methodism in Spalding was re-organised, and it was decided, after much heart searching, and to the acute distress of many who had worshipped there all their lives, that 'The Crescent' should close. The final services were held on 22nd May, 1955. At that time there was a membership of 88. The building was sold and soon after demolished. The post office occupies the site today.

Above: 20th May, 1910. Memorial service for King Edward VII. Over a thousand people attended the united memorial service of the Free Churches of the town, held in the Crescent Church. The photograph shows the congregation leaving shortly after 3 o'clock.
Below: An advertisement from "The Free Churches of Spalding", 1902.

Companion Books to the Present.

Spalding and Its Churches,

Being a description of the Parish Church, St. Peter's, St. Paul's, and St. John's, with 17 Excellent Views of the Churches, and 7 Portraits of Spalding Vicars. Price 6d.

Ayscoughfee and Its History.

Price 3d. A description of the Hall and Gardens, with Nine Illustrations; also a Poem by Richard Harris, Esq., K.C., entitled, "The Maid of Ayscoughfee."

Free Press Co., 5, Hall Place, **Spalding.**

SPALDING NONCONFORMIST CHOIR UNION.

ON
MONDAY, FEB. 1ST, 1915

AT 8 P.M., A

PATRIOTIC CONCERT

Under the Patronage of Lieut. The Hon. F. McLAREN, M.P., R.N.V.R., W. S. ROYCE, Esq., J.P., T. O. MAWBY, Esq., J.P., and Members of the Spalding U.D.C., and the Local Ministers,

IN AID OF THE

BELGIAN RELIEF FUND & SPALDING NURSING ASSOCIATION

WILL BE HELD IN THE

CRESCENT CHURCH, SPALDING

National Choruses & Songs of the Allies including the British, Belgian, French, & Russian National Anthems,

MARTIAL MELODIES, PATRIOTIC SONGS, &c.

PRINCIPALS:

SOPRANOS:
Miss EDITH FIELDING and Miss EVELYN WILLSON.

CONTRALTOS:
Miss ELSIE JAMES and Miss GRACE CONQUEST.

TENORS:
MR. CHARLES WHITE and MR. J. EARLEY.

BASS:
MR. R. B. STOAKLEY and MR. CHAS. WHEATMAN.

Miss MAY RICHARDS (Violin).

Piano, **Miss Gladys Greenall,** A.T.C.L. Organ, **Mr. Haydn Chester,** A.R.C.O.

Conductor: PROFESSOR BERNARD FOWLES, L.R.A.M.

President - - Rev. H. COOK.

Programmes 6d. Each. May be obtained from any Member of the Choir Union.

Printed by the "FREE PRESS" Co., Ltd., Hall Place, Spalding.

The First World War - Patriotic Concert. 1915.

Below: A Portrait group, taken in front of the United Methodist Church, in the Crescent, of the Spalding Nonconformist Choir Union, after giving a very successful patriotic concert, under the conductorship of Bernard Fowles, L.R.A.M., with Haydn Chester, A.R.C O., at the organ, and Miss Gladys Greenall, A.T.C.L., at the pianoforte.

The names reading from left to right, are:-

Bottom Row:	Miss G. Conquest; Miss Elsie James (Mrs. Leveritt, the Author's Mother); Miss R. Chapman; Miss Evelyn M. Willson (Mrs. Fardell); Miss E. Conquest; Miss E. Edwards; Miss I. Fovargue; Miss G. George; Miss May Allenson, daughter of Mr. J.H. Allenson, tailor; Miss Annie Walden, daughter of Mr. Fred Walden, grocer.
Second Row:	Miss A.E. Osgerby; Miss C. Atkin; Miss A. Hollingworth; Miss E. Fielding; Miss A. Wadsley; Miss J. Cox; Miss G.A. Hill, (Mrs. Fred Walden); Miss G. Brown; Mrs. Young and Mrs. Robinson.
Third Row:	Mr. J. Earley (secretary); Mr. H. Price; Miss Hilda Stiles, Spring Gardens; Miss Lindsey; Miss Emma Hewson, Westlode Street; Mrs. R. B. Stoakley; Mrs. Would and Mr. Charles Major White (treasurer), baker, the Crescent.
Top Row:	Mr. Herbert Arthur White, baker, the Crescent; Mr. Walter James, Albion Street; Mr. R.B. Stoakley; Rev. Herbert Cook, superintendent minister of the United Methodist Church; Mr. John Willson; Mr. William R. Murrell, printer and stationer; Mr. R. Tippler; Mr. Ernest A. Wilson, journalist, later editor of the 'Lincolnshire Free Press'.

Left: The "Quad-Crown" poster which advertised the concert.

General Booth's Spalding Days

In 1852, William Booth, a young man of 23 arrived in Spalding to be minister of the Free or Reformed Methodists in the Spalding Circuit.

He was of course later to become world famous as General William Booth (1829-1912), the great evangelist and founder of the Salvation Army.

Unfortunately the records of the Free Methodist Church in Spalding for the period of William Booth's ministry are no longer extant, but the following extract from The Lincolnshire Free Press of 12th December, 1899, is of interest.

Although unsigned it was almost certainly contributed by the editor Joseph Wilson (1854-1909), himself a devoted member of the United Methodist Free Church, and a local preacher.

We are told that "General Booth was practically one of the founders of the Spalding Free Methodist Circuit. It was in 1852, when a young man, 23 years old, that he first came to Spalding. The circuit was then in a critical condition.

William Booth infused such boundless energy into his two years' work that his enthusiasm proved contagious; and when he left the Spalding district in 1854, he had established a new organisation on a permanent and prosperous basis. It has never looked back since.

William Booth as he looked a few years after leaving Spalding.
(Picture by courtesy of the Salvation Army).

There are only five members of the Crescent Chapel now remaining who were on the roll when General Booth was in the circuit, and one of them is Mr. M. Shadford, with whom the General has 47 years been on terms of closest intimacy, and whose guest he is during his present visit to Spalding.

Indeed, we are divulging no secret when we remark that, but for the tender memories that surround this district in connection with Mr. and the late Mrs. Booth, the General would not have been visiting Spalding yesterday and Boston today (Tuesday).

It is worthy of note that General Booth's first service in Spalding was conducted in the old Assembly Rooms, which occupied the site now devoted to the Gentlemen's Club; and it was during his residence in the Circuit that steps were taken for the erection of a chapel in the Crescent."

The Spalding Free Methodist Circuit was the outcome of the Reform movement of the late 1840s and early 1850s. In William Booth's time the circuit covered an area which extended from Boston to Holbeach Drove, via Spalding. (In later years it was divided into the Spalding, Holbeach and Boston circuits).

The only railway that existed was that from Spalding to Boston. The early ministers were "travelling preachers" indeed, and the circuit had to be traversed on foot, except when a kindly farmer took pity on the "poor parsons".

General Booth has described how he left his home on a Saturday, walked to his Sunday appointment, spent the whole week perambulating the villages — visiting the folks during the day and preaching at the little Bethel in the evening — and returning home at the end of it.

In 1909, when over 80 years of age, he referred to his experiences in the Spalding circuit and said: "It was fine exercise, I was a weak and puny fellow when I went to the Fens, and they told me my days were numbered. What do you think of me now? Those long journeys on foot, and the splendid hospitality of the Lincolnshire people simply made me."

A letter written by William Booth while living in Spalding is preserved in the library of the Spalding Gentlemen's Society. (It was presented to the SGS by the late Mrs. O. B. Elsom in 1968).

Dated "Red Lion Street, Spalding, February 2nd 1852" it is addressed to "my dearly beloved brethren and sisters in Christ in connexion with the Wesleyan Methodist Society Holbeach Drove, but more especially to those who have so recently given their hearts to God and gained a hope of Heaven, this cometh greeting.

With many prayers for your happiness on earth and your preservation to share in the nightless, cloudless boundless and eternal felicities of a residence with Jesus Christ throughout all eternity. Amen and Amen."

In a six page letter he implores his brethren to "Be *earnest* be *hopeful,* be *confident,* be *united,* and above all love one another with an affection that is very *tender* and *enduring* and God shall, God *will,* bless you in a wonderful and glorious manner".

He asks for the prayers of his congregation that he "may be assisted with power to preach my Master's word and seek the wand'ring souls of men", and ends his epistle "In conclusion I would say to those who have now for the first time found their way to Christ or whom having backslidden have come again to the fountain, pray much in private, meet regularly in Class, to seek the salvation of other souls and until we meet on earth or in Heaven, I remain in much affection Yours faithfully in the ministry of the Gospel, William Booth".

A newscutting from "The Lincolnshire Free Press", dated 23rd August, 1910 in the library of the SGS contains the report of an interview with Mrs. Charles Brett, of Spalding, who had just celebrated her 99th birthday, having lived in the town for 96 years.

It reads "...Mrs. Brett has been associated with the Free Methodist (now United Methodist) cause in Spalding ever since its formation, and has vivid recollections of the first minister who was none other than General Booth, the great founder of the Salvation Army, himself.

Then, as now, the passion for soul-saving burned strong within him, and when, as he frequently did, he called at the house after his meetings, it was easy to tell by his manner whether those meetings had been successful or not.

If they had, he would leap up the steps like a school-boy, humming snatches of some favourite hymn tune.

A few years ago, the General sent a signed portrait of himself to Mrs. Brett to show that he had not forgotten an old friend...".

In 1902 the "Free Press", published a 75-page booklet on 'The Free Churches of Spalding'. In the section devoted to the story of the United Methodist Free Church we are told that "Free Methodism has existed in the town just over half-a-century; and it is a remarkable fact that the two chief ministerial and lay pioneers of the movement — General Booth and Mr. Major Shadford, of Spalding — still survive and are attached friends.

There are several members of the Crescent Church at the present time who were on the original register; but those who now worship at the Crescent who can claim half-a-century's association with the cause in Spalding include Mr. M. Shadford, Mr. P. Clark, sen, Mr. J. White, Mr. W. Jepson, Mr. I. Elsom, Mrs. C. Brett, sen, and Mrs. I. Elsom.

The Spalding Free Methodists had no building of their own during the first years of their existence. They met in the old Assembly Rooms (which occupied the site where the Gentleman's Club now stands), and for several years the work of building up a church and congregation and founding a Sunday School devolved exclusively on laymen.

The first minister who laboured in the circuit was the Rev. William Booth (now the famous General Booth), and to his unselfish devotion, inexhaustible energy, and great organising capacity, in those early years Free Methodism in the Spalding Circuit owed not a little of its subsequent success.

It is interesting to note that Mrs. I. Elsom, of Pinchbeck-street, was welcomed into church membership by and received her first ticket from General Booth, in the old Assembly Rooms, nearly 50 years ago, and that ticket she still retains.

From 1852 to 1854, General Booth worked in the circuit, and it was during his ministry that the idea of erecting a chapel in Spalding was suggested. It was not until 1856, however, when the late Rev. G. R. Rawson was minister, that a site was secured in the Crescent for £110, and on the 31st December of that year the foundation stones were laid.

"On July 14th, 1857, a new chapel, capable of seating about 700 people, and with Sunday School accommodation at the base, was publicly opened. The architects were Messrs. Bellamy and Hardy, of Lincoln; the builders were the late Mr. Charles Brett and the late Mr. J. Moore; and the total cost was £1,305 15s 11½d."

By the late 1870s a new and larger chapel and school premises were needed, and the old chapel was demolished and a new one erected on the same site (now occupied by the Post Office). Opened on 22nd May 1879, it had seating accommodation for 1100 persons, and was described as "without doubt the largest and finest Nonconformist place of worship in this neighbourhood".

It will be remembered, affectionately, by many residents of the town and district.

Major Shadford was born at Tetford, near Horncastle, in 1816. His relatives were devoted Methodists. He was apprenticed to a chemist at Horncastle; spent three years in London; and in 1839, started in business at Spalding.

In the same year he was elected Superintendent of the Wesleyan Methodist Sunday School, Broad Street, and for 63 years held successively the position of Superintendent of that and the free Methodist Sunday Schools.

He held many public offices, including that of Chairman of the Spalding Improvement Commissioners, Chairman of the Spalding School Board, Vice-Chairman of the Board of Guardians and Alderman of the Holland County Council.

His chief claim to honour, however, was his long, intimate, and unsparing devotion to Free Methodism. He died on 25th June 1902, aged 86.

Joseph Wilson's connection with Free Methodism was lifelong. Born in 1854, the youngest of a family of ten, he commenced work at the age of eight. He joined the Free Press in 1869, becoming editor in 1882, at the age of 28. A local preacher, a Sunday School teacher, he was an active worker in every department of the Free Methodist Church. He was also noted for his devotion to Temperance movement.

He was connected with many institutions in the town and district, and was a member of the School Board and the Board of Guardians. Joseph Wilson was brother-in-law to Sir William Randal Cremer, MP (1828 - 1908), the founder of the Workmen's Peace Association, and the advocate of international arbitration.

In 1903 W. R. Cremer was awarded the Nobel Peace Prize, worth then £8,000, which he devoted to the cause of peace. Knighted in 1907, Sir William Cremer achieved world wide renown in connection with the propagation of Peace principles.

William Randal Cremer and Charlotte Wilson were married at Spalding in 1860.

TO BREWERS, INNKEEPERS
AND OTHERS.

ON THE PREMISES

SPREAD EAGLE INN,
PINCHBECK-STREET, SPALDING,

TO BE SOLD BY

AUCTION,

BY

CHAS. DOLBY,

ON TUESDAY, THE 6 DAY OF SEPTEMBER NEXT,
AT SEVEN O'CLOCK IN THE EVENING,

Subject to such conditions of sale as will be then produced, (unless previously disposed of by private contract, of which due notice will be given,)

ALL THE ABOVE OLD LICENSED AND WELL FREQUENTED INN OR

PUBLIC HOUSE

Most desirably situated in one of the principal entrances to the Town, and in the immediate vicinity Of the Beast Market.

Possession will be given at Michaelmas next. For further particulars apply to Mr. W. T. CAPPS, Hall-Street, Spalding, or to the AUCTIONEER.

Spalding, 17th August, 1853.

Edward Gentle, Printer, Albion General Printing-Office, Sheep-Market, Spalding.

United Reformed Church and Sunday School

Previous page: Advertisement of the sale of the 'Spread Eagle Inn', purchased by the Independent (Congregational) Church, for £350. Subsequently demolished and the Sunday School erected on the site.

The history of the church goes back to the early part of the 19th century. Services were first held in a room in Red Lion Street, which had been an auction mart. So much success attended the effort that it was decided to build a chapel. The 'Independent Chapel', in Pinchbeck Road, was opened on 8th March, 1821. The total cost of the building was £1,200. Underneath the chapel, 26 vaults were provided for the internment of the dead, each vault being capable of receiving four adults. Galleries were added in 1857 at a cost of £300.

In 1856, the schoolroom was built upon the site formerly occupied by the 'Spread Eagle' public house. The public house had been an inconvenient neighbour, as 'the music of the sanctuary blended somewhat strangely and disturbingly with the more lively strains of the fiddle next door'. Designs for the schoolroom were prepared by William East, and the contractor was William Brown, both of Spalding. The total cost, including purchasing the site, erecting the hall and providing the furnishings was £800.

In 1847 Edward Palmer Maples, timber merchant, William Barber, draper, William Hobson, draper, and William Proctor, clerk, were elected deacons. The occupations of some of the early members included those of farmer, grocer, weaver, clock case maker, miller, boatman and boat builder, carrier, servant, carpenter, and Scotch draper. In 1880 it was decided to appropriate a pew in the chapel for the poor from the Union Workhouse.

The Census of Religious Worship taken on Sunday, 30th March, 1851, revealed that 216 attended in the morning, and 185 in the evening. There were 76 Sunday Scholars. Thirty years later, an unofficial census of religious attendance, on Sunday, 27th November, 1881, listed 189 at the morning service, and 144 in the evening.

In 1902 it was reported that since 1877 'various structural improvements have been effected; additional class-rooms have been built; a minister's house purchased; and the chapel re-pewed and thoroughly renovated. The buildings are entirely free from debt'. At that date the deacons were Alfred

Hobson, H.M. Proctor, E.B. Proctor, W.A. Southwell, F. Catt, C.B. Crust, and J.W. White. There were 160 Sunday school scholars, and 23 teachers. In 1904 the membership of the church was 202. In 1910 the front was re-faced by building a wall one brick thick close up to the front wall of the chapel.

In 1877, the Revd. Samuel Yates, from Runcorn, became pastor, and commenced what was to become the longest pastorate in the history of the church, lasting 45 years, until his retirement in 1922. A great scholar and eloquent preacher, he played a prominent part in the establishment, in 1901, of the Council of the Spalding Evangelical Free Churches, and became its first President. He died in 1928. He was succeeded by the Revd. Herbert Burn, from Brigg, who was to serve the church as pastor for thirty years. Few churches have had the experience of a span of 75 years with only two ministers, both of whom rendered outstanding service not only to the church but also to the public life of the town and district.

Mr. J.W. George, in his 'Brief History of Spalding United Reformed Church' writes:
'Herbert Burn was a man of great spiritual stature, he preached the word of God faithfully, and undertook his pastoral duties with dignity, zeal and sincerity. He was a friend and confident to all, and by his cheerful disposition bound the members of the church together into a happy family of spiritual fellowship. His influence extended far beyond the bounds of the church, into the town of Spalding

Below: A view of the interior before the renovations.

where he served on almost every committee of importance, throughout the county of Lincolnshire where he served as Secretary of the Lincolnshire Congregational Union, and nationally where he served on the Council of the Congregational Church of England and Wales, and as a Director of the London Missionary Society. He was ably supported by his wife, Mrs. E. Burn, and by his sister-in-law, Miss L.A. Wise.'.

Owing to ill health the Revd. H. Burn retired on 30th April, 1953. Succeeding ministers have been - the Revd. R.W.G. Talmey, 1954-63; the Revd. V.L. Tudor, 1963-75; the Revd. Stanley Whiffen, 1976-82, and the Revd. Margaret Howard from 1983.

In October, 1972, the United Reformed Church was formed by the Union of the Congregational Church of England and Wales and the Presbyterian Church of England.

Christadelphian Hall, New Road

A view of the Christadelphian Hall, in New Road. Opened in 1908. The site was formerly occupied by two cottages. It is faced with red Gosberton bricks. The architects were J.B. Corby & Son, of Stamford, and the builders Watson & Co. of Spalding.

Christadelphians have been in Spalding since the early 1870s. In 1874 a Spalding member wrote that 'after more than three years' solitary sojourning' she had been joined by another member from Leicester. In 1879, a room 'capable of holding from 100 to 150' had been obtained. There were then six members. These included a 24 year old Spalding clothier, Amos Jane, who with his wife, Elizabeth Ann, were for many years among the leading members, and gave lifelong devotion to the cause. On Sunday, 27th November, 1881, there was an attendance of 9 at the morning service and 14 in the evening. Until the hall was opened, members of the ecclesia met for worship in hired premises, including the Temperance Hall in the Crescent, and latterly at the Mechanics' Institute in Red Lion Street. The hall was opened on 19th July, 1908, the first public lecture, in the new building, being given that evening by the editor of 'The Christadelphian', Mr. C.C. Walker.

High Days and Holidays

Spalding United Nonconformist Sunday School Festival

The first Nonconformist United Festival was held at Spalding on the occasion of Queen Victoria's Coronation, in 1838, when about 800 children took part. This annual gathering became one of the chief events of the year in the town. The children and teachers gathered in the Market Place, and proceeded to Mr. E.P. Maples' field, where a marquee was erected. Edward Palmer Maples (1803-91), of High Street, timber merchant, took a prominent part in the public life of the town, and was a member of the Spalding Congregational Church.

The photograph below, taken in 1875, shows the band, scholars, and teachers in the Market Place. The Festival usually attracted a large number of people from the neighbouring villages. The occupiers of the business premises on the left hand side of the Market Place were C. Tyler, tobacconist; F. Rhodes, chemist; J.T. Pears, grocer; R. Donington, chemist; R. Appleby, stationer; A. & W.J.E. Hobson, drapers (Spalding's Skyscraper); Stamford, Spalding and Boston Bank; Osborn, draper; A. Hall, hatter, &c. T. Hiley, currier; T.Smith, butcher; H. Watkinson, "Free Press".

On the right hand side - Augustus Maples (formerly Henry Maples), wine merchant (now Lloyds Bank).

A unique feature was the dinner of roast beef and plum pudding in the marquee. In 1854, 303 puddings, 22 stones of beef, 40 quartern loaves, and 8 gallons of milk were consumed by 1200 children and 200 teachers.

In 1881, when 1500 children assembled in the Market Place, the younger ones were in waggons decorated with evergreens and flags, and the older ones on foot bearing banners. They were preceded by the Nottingham Sax Tuba Band. At night there was a display of fireworks.

In 1902 the Nonconformist Sunday Schools embraced about 2000 scholars and teachers.

Right: Advertisement from 1902.

Below: Spalding United Sunday School Festival early 1900's.
Teachers and scholars of the United Sunday Schools assembling in the Market Place. From its establishment in 1838 the Sunday School Festival was one of the outstanding events of the year in Spalding.

Bibles and Hymnals. . . .
Books for Presentation & Rewards.
Birthday, Text, & Devotional Works.

'Free Press' Co., Spalding.

Fancy Goods in Great Variety,
At much below usual Prices.

Photo Frames, Albums, Stationery Cabinets and Desks, Inkstands, Paper Knives, Letter Racks, Postcard Stands, Telegram Cases, Cigarette, Card, and Letter Cases, Wallets, Purses, Ladies' and Gent.'s Hand Bags, Glove and Handkerchief Boxes, with Local Views.

'Free Press' Co., Spalding.

EIGHT SPALDING . .
✴ Pictorial Postcards
FOR SIXPENCE.

Spalding Parish Church; ditto (another View); Ayscoughfee, Holyrood, & Church; St. Peter's Church; St. John's Church; St. Paul's Church; Lock's Mill (Flood Time); Picturesque View on the Welland.

OBTAINABLE ONLY FROM

Free Press Compy., Ltd.,
5, HALL PLACE, SPALDING.

74th United Sunday School Festival. 29th June, 1911

Above: A view of part of the procession emerging from St. Thomas's Road and proceeding along Winsover Road. Those taking part comprised members of the Wesleyan Methodist, Baptist, United Methodist, Primitive Methodist and Pode Hole Baptist Sunday Schools.   They numbered:-

School.	Scholars	Teachers	Total
Wesleyan	230	48	278
Baptist	200	50	250
United Methodist	475	51	526
Primitive Methodist	100	20	120
Pode Hole Baptist	80	14	94
	1085	183	1268

For refreshments   300 puddings,   400lbs of beef,   85lbs of butter,   13.5lbs of tea,   8.5 stones of sugar,   120 quartern loaves,   80 quartern plum cakes,   48 quartern seed cakes, and 14 gallons of milk were supplied.

Above: A view of the inside of the tent at 6 a.m. on Festival Day. Ministers and laymen belonging to the different schools carving the roast beef for the dinner.
Opposite page: As this poster shows, in later years the Festival often included an excursion to the seaside.
Below: At work in one of the Methodist Schoolrooms making the plum puddings, a work which lasted for a week.

SPALDING UNITED NONCONFORMIST

Sunday School Festival.

LONG DAY AT SEASIDE.

Corridor Excursion to

HUNSTANTON

THURSDAY, June 22nd, 1922.

SPALDING Depart 7.45 a.m.   HUNSTANTON Arrive 9.50 a.m.
Returning from Hunstanton on same day only at 7.15 p.m., arriving at Spalding 9.25 p.m.

RETURN   6s.   FARE.

Children under 3 years of age, free; above 3 and under 12, half-price.   No luggage allowed. The tickets are not transferable, and will only be available on the dates, by the trains, and at the stations named; if used on any other date, by any other train, or at any other station than those named, the tickets will be forfeited, and the full ordinary fare charged. The Company give notice that tickets for this Excursion are issued at a reduced rate, and only on condition that the Company shall not be liable for any loss, damage, injury, or delay to Passengers arising from any cause.

The Public are invited to join this Excursion.

TICKETS may only be obtained from Mr. J. E. Ayre, Cunningham's Drove, Mr. H. Hardy, St. John's Road, Mr. H. A. White, The Crescent, Mr. C. Thompson, 73, Pinchbeck Road, Mr. A. H. Freir, Pode Hole, or

Hon. Secs. { Rev. G. H. KINGSWOOD, 21, Cross Street.
W. F. ATTON, 10, Station Street.

Buy your TICKETS early to avoid disappointment, as we have only a limited accommodation.

W. R. MURRELL, PRINTER, SPALDING.

National Occasions - The Coronation of King Edward VII

The Coronation Festivities at Spalding and the Children's Treat as reported in "The Spalding Free Press", of 12th August, 1902.

"... the little folk gathered at their respective schools and were presented with Coronation medals. They then went in procession to the Market Place, where they were massed, the infants being conveyed in some fourteen waggons. Is it necessary to say that, bright with decorations of various kinds and in high anticipation of what was to follow, the children were in the liveliest of spirits? A large crowd of people gathered and exhibited great interest in the proceedings. Prizes had been offered by Mr. F. George for the best decorated waggons, but, with the exception of one of the Goodfellows' vehicles (lent by Mr. J.R. Perkins) no real effort at decoration had been attempted. This waggon was, therefore, an easy first, and that of Mr. J.T. White was placed second. The National Anthem was sung by the children in the Market Place, and three lusty cheers were given for the King and Queen. The large army of men and women of the future were then marched to the respective schools for refreshments. The children's tea was a large undertaking, but all was carried through without a hitch. Mr. E.H. Andrew was hon. sec. of the committee which arranged at what centres the respective schools should have tea, and that gentleman was also responsible for organising the plan on which the children should gather in the Market Place. Mesdames J. Wilson and W. Guy, Sister Eva, and Miss E. Maples were entrusted with the responsible duty of settling quantities, and ordering food and superintending its distribution to the proper centres, and most efficiently they discharged these duties. The food provided for the youngsters included 240 loaves of bread, 80 4lb cakes, 1000 buns, 1000 rock cakes, 1000 scones, 240 jam sandwiches, 70lb butter, 12 stone sugar, 26lb tea, 20.5 gals of milk. The children numbered over 2000 and were in the charge of their respective day school teachers......The food was ample and excellent; the workers were numerous and indefatigable; and the order and arrangements were all that could be wished."

Below: The children in their waggons in the Market Place.

National Occasions.
Memorial Service for King Edward VII, 1910.

Procession to Spalding Parish Church on the Day of the Kings Funeral, 20th May, 1910.

The procession is shown taking Kingston's corner, headed by the Silver Band, followed by the Territorials, the Police, the Fire Brigade and the Freemasons. The procession passed along Hall Place, through the Market Place, over High Bridge to the Parish Church for the memorial service. Some seven hundred persons were in the procession.

Coronation of King George V - Celebrations at Spalding. 22 June 1911.

The Celebrations at Spalding on 22nd. June, 1911 as reported in "The Spalding Free Press", of 27th June, 1911. and headed:

The Market Place Ceremony
Territorials fire a "Feu de Joie"(overpage).

"After the service (at the Parish Church) the procession was reformed in Church Street, and again headed by the Silver Band, marched to the Market Place. Here the Territorials, among whom we noticed that veteran Bugler Hunt, were drawn up in double line at the Hall Place end facing the Corn Exchange, the various other bodies forming the procession being grouped in a square in front. The rest of the Market Place was packed with an enthusiastic crowd, while every window looking on to the Market Place was crowded by sightseers. The Territorials, who, in the absence of Major Barrell in London, were in command of Sergt. G.T. Allen, fired a feu de joie with three rounds of blank ammunition, the Silver Band playing six bars of the National Anthem between each round. The firing concluded, the Territorials came to the Royal salute, and the National Anthem was played by the band.

Then Mr. W. Fletcher, J.P., the Chairman of the Urban Council, from a waggonette placed in front of the Red Lion Hotel, called upon the citizens of Spalding to give three hearty cheers for his Majesty King George V. This over, the various bodies marched off, and the crowd dispersed.

Above: The scene as described in the article on the previous page.

Below: An advertisement from the "Spalding Monthly Magazine", of 1867.

ARTIFICIAL TEETH.

MR. SWIFT, DENTIST,

CORNER OF PINCHBECK STREET, NEW ROAD,
SPALDING.

The Artificial Teeth constructed by MR. SWIFT, so closely resemble natural ones as to escape detection; are durable, light, and do not decay, or change colour; they restore the power of speech and mastication, can be adapted to the most sensitive gums, and when required, without extraction or any other painful operation.

No exorbitant extra charges, a stated fee being contracted for, which in all cases will be found most reasonable.

A SATISFACTORY FIT GUARANTEED.

CONSULTATIONS FREE.

In the Public Eye

The Lincolnshire Regiment at Spalding, 1897

The second battalion of the Lincolnshire Regiment leaving Spalding en route for Billingborough, on Friday, 3rd September, 1897. The battalion consisting of 524 men and 21 officers, under the command of Lieut.Colonel H.R. Roberts, had arrived in the town, from Bourne, during the previous afternoon, and camped in Cley Hall Park, which had been placed at the disposal of the regiment by Henry Clark, J.P. (1821-1910). During the time the troops were at Spalding the camping ground was visited by crowds of spectators from the town and the surrounding villages, foot troops not having been seen in the locality for a number of years. During the evening an open air camp fire concert was held, and the following morning, about nine o'clock, the battalion left Spalding.

Below and overleaf: The following six photographs show the progress of virtually the entire regiment through the Market Place. Note how the spectators have a tendency to follow the band through into Hall Place.

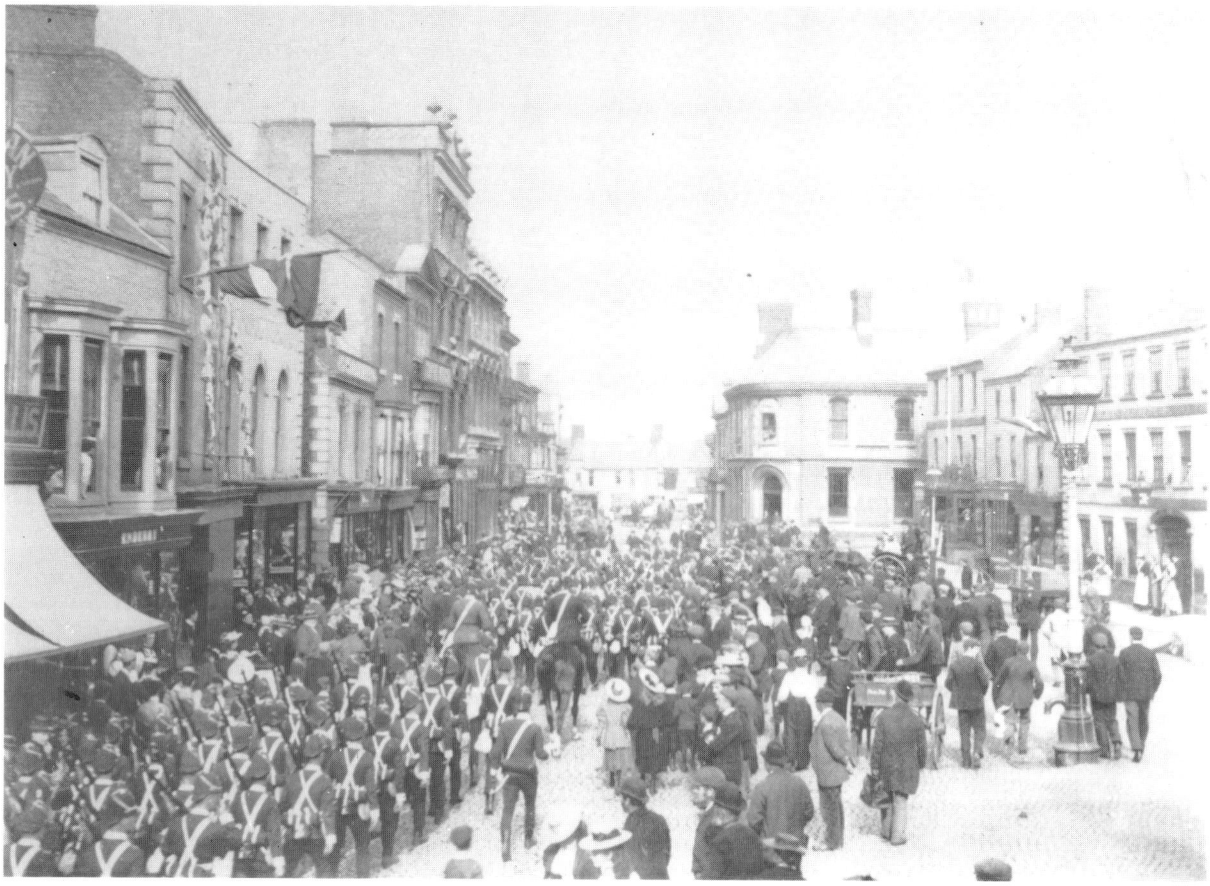

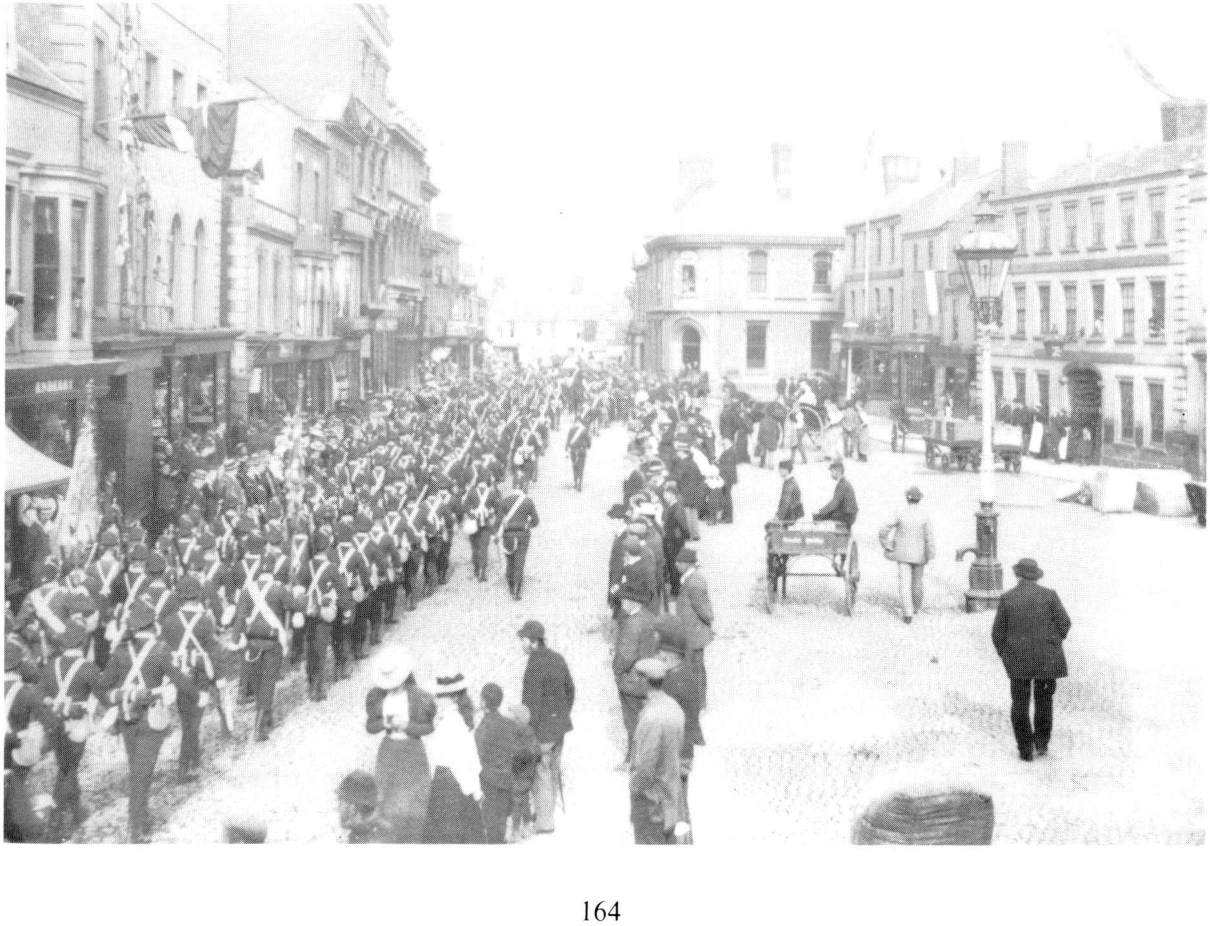

FREEMAN
HARDY
&
WILLIS
4
HARDY & WILLIS

N HARDY & WILLIS
FREEMAN
HARDY
&
WILLIS
4
FREEMAN HARDY & WILLIS
GOODWIN

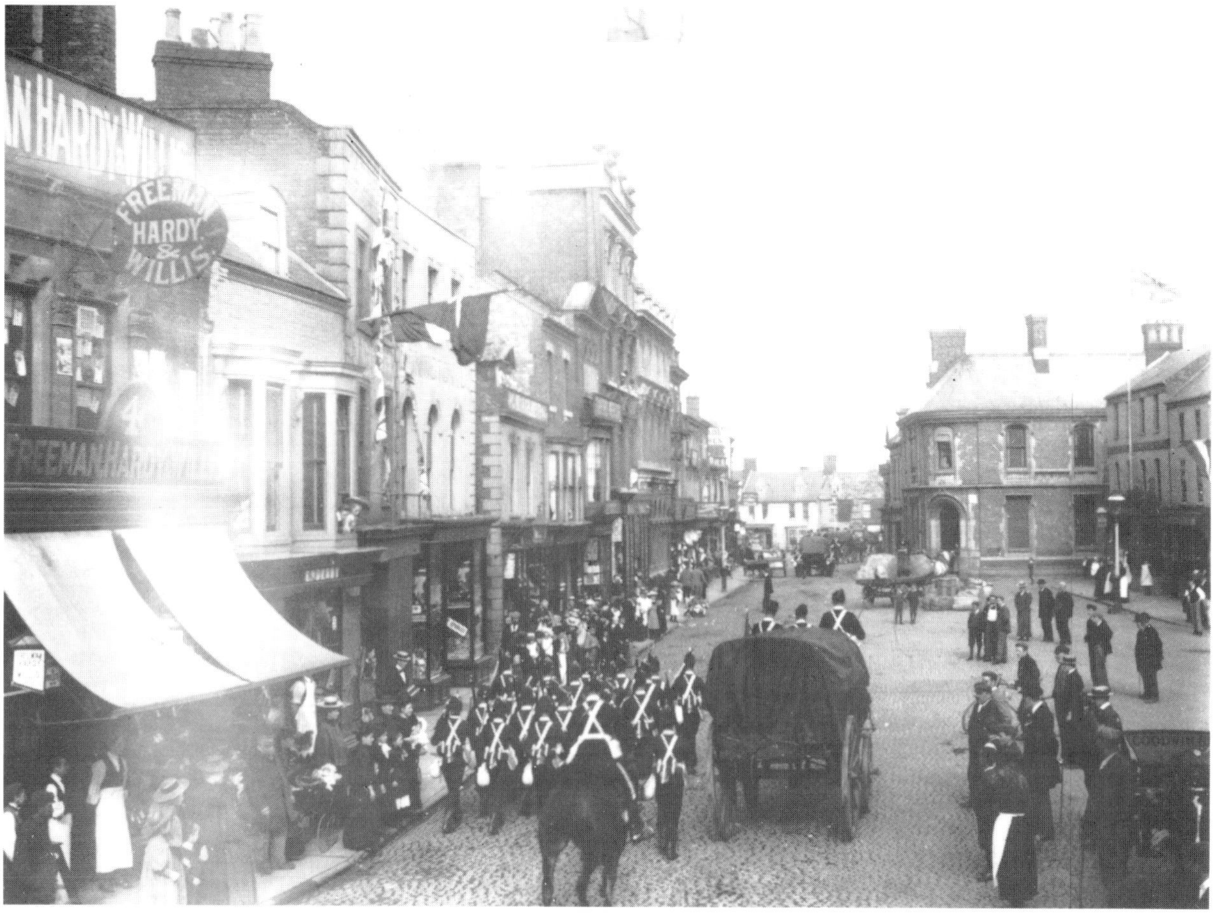
FREEMAN
HARDY
&
WILLIS

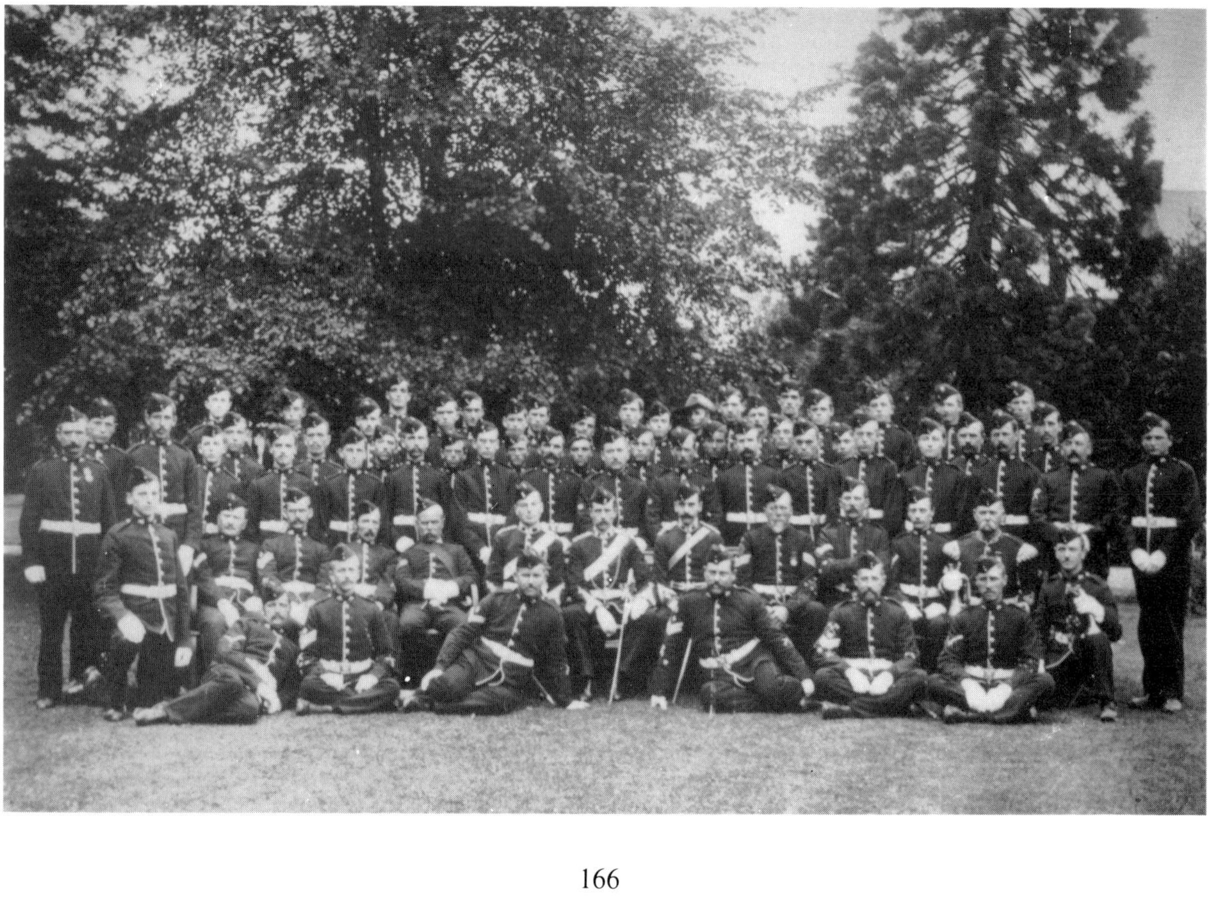

The Volunteers

Opposite below: The Spalding Volunteers, "F" Company of the 2nd V.B. Lincolnshire Regiment on the occasion of a church parade at Spalding in 1898 when a presentation was made to Captain E.V. Atkins, Officer Commanding the Company, on his leaving the district. Captain Atkins will be seen sitting in the centre of the second row from the front. Next to him, on the left, is Lieut.Colonel G.J. Barrell. The photograph, was taken in the grounds of Holland House, and at the time the Spalding Volunteers were about 80 strong. They wore scarlet tunics, blue trousers with red stripes, and white belts. The Volunteers were very proud of their band.

In the photograph the three Seymour brothers are seen seated in the front row, together with many other Spaldonians including Sergt. Barwis, Bugler Hunt, Messrs. Duckworth, F. Pooles, A. Fawn, S. Greaves, Harrison, A. Butler, G.R. Barker, T. Cutforth, T. Gibbons, G. Green, Ward, S. Smith, A. Preston, C. Watson, Cooper, W. Cotton, & Co.

The Drill Hall, Haverfield Road

Erected in 1913 for the "F" (Spalding) Company of the 4th Battalion Lincolnshire Regiment (T.F.) It was then described as 'a commodious building, and well equipped for its purpose. It is faced with red heather bricks and has dressings of Ancaster stone and cornices of wood' (1). The foundation stones were laid on 20th February, 1913, by the Hon. F.W.S. McLaren, M.P. for the Spalding Division, and Lt. Col. J.W. Jessop, Officer commanding the 4th Lincolns. The opening ceremony took place on 9th October 1913, and was performed by Major General E.C Bethune, C.B., C.V.O., Director General of the Territorial Forces of Great Britain.

The architects were Scorer & Gamble, of Lincoln, and the contractors Stapleton & Co. of Spalding.
It is now used as the South District Office of the Lincolnshire County Library.

(1). *"Spalding Free Press" 14th October, 1913.*

George Hall

From "The Spalding Guardian", of Friday, April 12, 1918

Passing of Mr. Geo. Hall (1831 - 1918).
The Story of a Remarkable Career.
Romantic Marriage with an Admiral's Grand-daughter who was the relative of peers.

In the fulness of eighty and six years, Mr. George Hall, of Spalding, one of the most remarkable personalities in South Lincs., passed to the rest which he had for some time sought, at 6 o'clock on Saturday morning, after as full a life as any man could wish to have. He played his part in many chapters; and now the book is closed.

The serious fall he had over the rail of the Sessions House stairs when going to a County Council meeting practically terminated his active public life; the shock would have been the death of most men. He recovered sufficiently to attend occasional meetings, but he never regained his old vigour, and a further fall at home brought the end nearer. For some months he has not been present at meetings and the end came in the inevitable course of Nature. As long as three years ago he was awaiting it with calmness and fortitude.

Having so largely passed out of public life, his death has not left the gap which it otherwise would have left, but it is nevertheless the snapping of a great link, between the old world and the new.

The Rugged Figure

Mr. Hall was, in his day and up to quite recently, much the most interesting and rugged figure in the life of the town and district. He has figured so largely in the public eye during the past forty years, has displayed so distinct and even unique a personality, and has so frequently come into collision with what he was wont to describe as "the classes", that probably the name of no man is better known throughout a wide district.

Before one can understand the late Mr. Hall aright - his Puritanism, his Radicalism, his Henry George turn of thought, it is necessary to remember that he comes from a race of old Scotch Covenanters. His grandfather, who was one, had a price on his head, which he nearly lost.

Though belonging to a Moulton family, he was born in Spalding, the son of a carpenter, and Mr. Hall himself became the last of six generations of carpenters.

In 1851 he completed his five years' apprenticeship to the historic trade, and was offered 8s a week as an improver. He contemptuously told his employer to give it to the poor, and turned his back on him.

He started to help in the building of a house near Fulney, but suddenly packed his tool-bag and left for Nottingham, there to make staircases with a partner he had picked up. Instead of 8s a week, he was making £3; they made staircases which carried the working-men to bed and cost 7s. 6d; they made staircases which ran to £40. He saw life in Birmingham, Sheffield, Manchester, and other centres.

The Romance of his Bride

Then, with the suddenness of tragedy, came an event of which he spoke in his later years with a lingering tenderness. A message arrived that his mother was dying from cancer. He reached home one sad Sunday; she died the following Tuesday. These last hours with the dying mother have stretched over half-a-century, and were real to the end. They will stretch into eternity. He made his mother's coffin; a piece of wood is now a sacred relic in his office. With that funeral deal in his knapsack as mascot, he set out afresh. He returned to Nottingham, and it was while he was at work on the mansion of an alderman and sheriff that he met his wife in romantic circumstances. She was Miss Dalrymple, a grand-daughter of Admiral Parker, and her mother was a cousin of the then Vice Chancellor, Sir James Parker. She could have boasted, had she wished, of seven relatives in the House of Commons and four in the House of Lords. Miss Dalrymple was a relative of the Sheriff whose house Mr. Hall was repairing, and the acquaintance began when she modestly offered him a cup of tea while he was at work. Many difficulties were overcome, and they were married. Mr. Cornelius Dalrymple Hall is their only son.

After many journeyings, Mr. Hall found himself in London Town putting the roof on the Tower of London. Under his direction, £60,000 was spent on Westminster Abbey. He superintended the re-leading of the roof; he put in the present £5,000 reredos. He knew Dean Stanley and heard his famous sermon on Livingstone. He laid the Prince's ballroom floor for the '51 Exhibition. During the fifteen years of London life he was a voluntary martyr at the House of Commons debates three nights a week in the great days of Gladstone and Bright.

A New Use for The Hammer

Thirty-six years ago, on the death of his father, he came back to Spalding to take his seat in the Hall Place and retain the unbroken Hall line. Spalding had not been without a Hall as a carpenter for hundreds of years. A year or two after his home-coming, he found it more satisfactory to wield a lighter hammer and drive bargains instead of nails. His first sale as an auctioneer, took place at Peterborough in 1879.

He brought the political torch from Westminster and lighted the fire of Liberalism in Hall Place, where there were little private meetings in days when to be a Liberal was a social crime.

He romped into the select circle of Improvement Commissioners like a bull into a china shop. In five minutes there were crashings. Just over 30 years ago he stalked into the Guardians Board Room and into the School Board, and stirred things up wherever he went. Without education himself, he was one of the leading local educationalists.

Among his posts were those of:
- County Councillor
- Chairman of Council School Managers
- Chairman of Willesby School Managers
- Grammar School Governor
- Guardian of the Poor
- Town Husband
- Member of the Standing Joint Committee
- Member of the Small Holdings Committee
- Member of the Eastern Sea Fisheries Committee
- Member of the Old Age Pensions Committee

Where They Bless Him

His greatest constructive work was in the interests of the small holder. In the 'eighties he rented land in the Gosberton Risegate district and set up there a successful colony of labourers on the land. The acre men soon became fifty-acre men, and there they call the name of George Hall blessed.......

His religion was the simple austere creed of the Society of Friends. He worked with a Bible in his drawer. It was his final court of appeal.

Mr. Hall played a great part in our social life, and we are the poorer for his passing hence.

Public Appreciation

A moving tribute was paid to the late Mr. Hall on Tuesday at the meeting of the Holland Small Holdings Committee, of which he was so long a member. The chairman (Mr. T.W. Banks, J.P.), with all the members standing, moved that a vote of condolence be sent to Mr. Hall's family in the sad bereavement they had sustained. Mr. Hall had been a member of that Committee ever since it was formed, and he had done a lot of hard, useful work. He (the Chairman) had been associated with him for over 20 years, and there was no old gentleman he respected more. They should all miss him (hear, hear.)"

Special Constables, 1914

Photographed below are the Special Constables enrolled at the Sessions House, August 1914.

Front Row: J. Harrod; A. Blyton; A.V. Greenall; B. Harris; Supt. Burton; A.L. Seymour; J.H. Lunn; J.C. Rayner; - Pearson.

Middle Row: J. Spikins; A.C. Nainby; W.R. Murrell; R. King; Sgt. T. Lorraine; H. Fall; V.E. Hancock; unknown; H.C.M. Dixon; D. Morgan; unknown; W. Simson; unknown; C. King; E.T. Waring; W. White; J. Belfitt; M. Kempston; - Venters; F. Bales; A. Bean; L. Massey.

Back Row: G.S. Kingston; H.W. White; T.A. White; E. Dalton; W.B. Massey; J.H. Longstaff; W.M. Tomblin; F. George; A. Hancock; A. Shepherd; R.D. Wellband; - Pratley; R. Sutterby.

Right: Advertisement from 1921.

Established 1873.

Telephone—17 Spalding.
Telegrams—Massey, Engineer, Spalding.

WILLIAM B. MASSEY
ENGINEER,
Excelsior Engineering Works, SPALDING, LINCOLNSHIRE.

THE SPALDING AND DISTRICT AGENT FOR

The "International Junior" Tractors
AND
The Famous "Glasgow" Tractors.

The "Trusty Titan" Tractor, Cockshutt International Ploughs, Martin Cultivators and other makes.
Speciality Tractor Agencies. Overhauls and Repairs.
Speciality Car, Lorry and Motor Cycle Agencies. Overhauls and Repairs.

Up-to-date Car, Lorry and Tractor Garages. Fully equipped Workshops and Machine Shop for all classes of Repairs and Overhauls.
GENERAL ENGINEERS.

The Spalding Silver Prize Band

The photograph shows the band in 1904.

Back Row: L. Williamson; E. Royce; H. Elderkin; E.T. Waring, conductor; Chas. Burrell; E. Garwell; M. Tomline.
Centre Row: F. Brice; E. Seaton; - White; J. Mason; S. Fidler; J. Harrod; P.G. Burrell; W. Edwards.
Front Row: G. Arnold; C.M. White (baker, The Crescent); T. Edwards; F. Steer; S. Smith (The Crescent); R. Mundy.

Francis McLaren.
M.P. for the Spalding Division 1910-17.

The Honourable Francis Walter Stafford McLaren, was the second son of Charles Benjamin Bright McLaren, who was later to become the first Lord Aberconway. He was born on 6th June, 1886, and educated at Eton and Balliol College, Oxford. His father was actively interested in steel, shipbuilding and colliery undertakings, and sat for many years as a Liberal M.P. before being created a peer in 1911. Francis McLaren's great uncle, John Bright (1811-89), is remembered for his association with Richard Cobden in the campaign which led to the repeal of the Corn Laws in 1846, and for his denunciation of the policy which led to the Crimean War in 1854.

In April, 1909, Horace Mansfield, who had sat as Liberal M.P. for the Spalding Division since 1900, announced that he would not contest the next General Election, and in the following July Francis McLaren was adopted as prospective Liberal parliamentary candidate. He was 23.

Above: Welland Hall - the Central Committee Rooms of Francis McLaren the Liberal candidate for the Spalding Division.

The General Election took place in January, 1910. The Conservative candidate was William Stapleton Royce, of Pinchbeck Hall, and the result was:

F.W.S. McLaren (Lib.) 5,527
W.S. Royce (Con.) 5,148

Liberal Majority 379

When elected Francis McLaren was the youngest Liberal M.P. in the House of Commons. From 1910 to 1915 he was parliamentary private secretary to Lewis Harcourt, Secretary of State for the Colonies.

Another General Election was held within a year - in December, 1910. W.S. Royce was again the Conservative candidate, the result being:

F.W.S. McLaren (Lib.) 5,335
W.S. Royce (Con.) 5,070

Liberal Majority 265

He married, on 20th July, 1911, Barbara, daughter of Sir Herbert and Lady Jekyll. A few days before the wedding a presentation was made to the M.P. and his bride by more than 2000 of his constituents. This took place at the home of his parents, at Bodnant, near Conway, and was attended by 2100 persons from all parts of the Spalding division. They travelled in five trains, leaving Spalding at 1.30 a.m. on Thursday 6th July, 1911, and getting home at 3.30 a.m. the next morning. The presents consisted of a silver tea tray, weighing 150 ounces, and a silver tea and coffee service and hot water jug of 100 ounces, subscribed for by the Liberals of the Division, and a case of solid silver dessert knives and forks, the gift of the Spalding Women's Liberal Association. This occasion was long remembered by many of those who took part in it particularly during the darker days that were soon to follow.

Soon after the outbreak of the First World War he took a commission in the Royal Naval

Above: The Honourable Francis Walter Stafford McLaren (1886-1917); Member of Parliament (Liberal) for the Spalding Division, 1910-17. In the uniform of the Royal Naval Volunteer Reserve.

Volunteer Reserve, and proceeded in 1915 to Gallipoli with the Royal Naval Armoured Car Squadron. He was wounded and invalided home. After recovering he transferred to the Royal Flying Corps, and was killed as a result of an accident whilst flying at Montrose in Scotland on 30th August, 1917. He was 31.

His widow, subsequently married Lieut. General Sir Bernard Freyberg, V.C., later Lord Freyberg, who was Governor General of New Zealand from 1946 to 1952.

Spalding Gentlemen's Society - The Museum, Broad Street

The Spalding Gentlemen's Society, one of the oldest learned Societies in the kingdom, and the earliest provincial association for the encouragement of archaeology, was founded by Maurice Johnson, F.S.A. (1688-1755), of Ayscoughfee Hall, Spalding, barrister-at-law,"the Antiquary".

It began with a series of informal meetings of a few local gentlemen at a coffee-house in the Abbey Yard, Spalding in 1709, to discuss local antiquities and to read "The Tatler", a newly published London periodical. In 1712, it was decided to place these meetings upon a permanent footing, and proposals were issued for the establishing of "a Society of Gentlemen, for the supporting of mutual benevolence, and their improvement in the liberal sciences and in polite learning". In that year formal meetings began with the appointment of officers and the keeping of minutes. The founder, Maurice Johnson, also played a leading part in refounding the Society of Antiquaries of London, and for some years an exchange of minutes took place. Francis, Duke of Buccleuch (1695-1751), Lord of the Manor of Spalding-cum-Membris, became Patron of the Society in 1732.

Early members included a number of notable eighteenth century figures, among them Sir Isaac Newton; Sir Hans Sloane, President of the Royal Society, whose Museum and library formed the nucleus of the British Museum; Alexander Pope, whose "Windsor Forest" was read in manuscript to the Society; George Vertue, the engraver; Dr. William Stukeley; John Anstis, F.R.S. Garter King of Arms; John Gay, the poet; the Rev. Richard Bentley, D.D.; Captain John Perry, the engineer; Samuel Wesley; Sir Edward Bellamy, Lord Mayor of London, 1735; and Lord Coleraine, President of the Society of Antiquaries. Later, long after the founder's death, other members included Sir Joseph Banks; Sir G. Gilbert Scott; Alfred, Lord Tennyson; Pishey Thompson, the historian of Boston; Lord Curzon; Lord Peckover; and the late Lord Ancaster, Patron of the Society from 1960 to 1983.

The Museum is, with the exception of the Ashmolean at Oxford, the oldest in the kingdom. The present museum in Broad Street was opened in 1911. The erection of this building was rendered possible by the generosity of certain well known members and a special bi-centenary appeal. The architect was Joseph Boothroyd Corby, of Stamford. Additions were made in 1925, and again in 1960.

Opposite page: Old cottages in Broad Street demolished to make way for the present museum.
Above: 9th July, 1910. The Foundation stone laying ceremony of the museum of the Spalding Gentlemen's Society.   Left to Right:
The Rev. P.L. Hooson,Vicar of Pinchbeck West, 1896-1909; Vicar of Weston 1909-1912, Rector of Easton-on-the-Hill, 1912;
G.L. Nussey of Algarkirk, woad grower and farmer;
J.B. Corby, F.S.A., of Stamford, the architect;
E.W. Bell of Spalding, chemist;
Dr. F. Husband, of Crowland;
Dr. S.H. Perry (1867-1952), of Spalding;
Dr. Marten Perry (1826-1918), of Spalding. President of the Society;
Edward Gentle (1823-1910), of Spalding;
Ashley K. Maples (1868-1950), of Spalding, solicitor, Hon. Secretary of the Society;
W.F. Howard, of Spalding, solicitor;
Everard Green, F.S.A., (1844-1926), Rouge Dragon (1893), Somerset Herald (1911),descendant of the Founder;
Mrs. W.S. Royce, of Pinchbeck Hall;
Major J.M. Wingfield, of Tickencote (representing the Johnson Family);
H. Stanley Maples (1851-1917), of Spalding, solicitor; Hon. Treasurer of the Society;
The Rev. Canon H. J. Palmer, Vicar of Cowbit, 1909-17;
E. C. Griffith of Hacconby Hall;
Dr. E.C. Chappell, Headmaster of Spalding Grammar School,1909-20;
Fitzalan Howard (1844-1930), of Holyrood House, High Sheriff of Lincolnshire, 1910;
W.S. Royce (1858-1924), of Pinchbeck Hall, Spalding; (later M.P. for the Holland-with-Boston Division, 1918-24);
George Goodwin (1851-1915), printer and stationer (exors. of Robert Appleby, Market Place);
The Rev. Samuel Yates, Pastor of the Spalding Congregational Church, 1877-1922;
J.H. Diggle, of Moulton, land surveyor and valuer.

Edward Gentle (1823-1910)

The life story of Edward Gentle is not comprehended within the memory of the present generation, and so the following extract from "The Spalding Guardian", of 31st December, 1910, will be of interest:-

Passing of another Spalding Standard.
Death of Mr. Edward Gentle at Eighty-Seven.
How he was hauled before the Pasha.

One of the best known and most interesting personalities in Spalding has been removed by the death of Mr. Edward Gentle, of Pinchbeck Street......... The late Mr. Gentle was born on August 31, 1823, at a little shop on the site where the Spalding Corn Exchange now stands. His father was a butcher and auctioneer.

Mr. Gentle went to school at the Spalding Academy, which was just beyond where the Central Schools (in Westlode Street), are now situated, and upon leaving he went as an apprentice to Mr. Samuel Elsdale Albin, who was a printer, on the premises now occupied by Messrs. Calthrop and Harvey, solicitors, in the Market Place.

There he learned Caxton's art, but after three years at this he went to sea. His many adventures included an appearance before the Pasha at Alexandria for tapping a eunuch on the head with an oar, and for which he suffered one day's imprisonment.

At the age of eighteen Mr. Gentle returned to Spalding, and again became a printer, carrying on a business of his own in the Sheep market. In the year 1853 he proceeded to London, and eventually became a traveller for the firm of Ullmer and Co., and subsequently to Messrs. Stephenson, Blake, and Co.

About a dozen years ago, shortly after the death of his wife, a Spalding lady, Mr. Gentle settled in Spalding, to enjoy a well-earned retirement and a pension from Messrs. Stephenson, Blake and Co.

He had a multitude of hobbies, which he was then able to indulge to his heart's content. An artist of considerable ability, his home, and the homes of his friends, have many evidences of his skill with the brush......He was once offered - and refused - £100 by a famous General for a perfect copy of Stanfiels's "Zuyder Zee."

Photography, too, interested him greatly, and he turned out some excellent local pictures, which he often exhibited, with magic lantern assistance.

He loved his garden, and especially his roses - throughout the summer and autumn he was rarely seen without a fine specimen of his own culture in his button-hole.

In later years the gramophone claimed him, and almost to the end he was in the habit of sitting for hours listening to music......

In short, Mr. Gentle thoroughly enjoyed life, and got the utmost out of it, to the last. It had no staleness for him; there was no ennui.

His Great Gift

Mr. Gentle was one of those who has from time to time done so much for the Gentlemen's Society of Spalding, which was founded in 1710. It was only two years ago that he gave the handsome sum of £650 to the Society towards the cost of the erection of a home of its own, in celebration of the bi-centenary of the Institution, and as a memorial to its founder, Maurice Johnson. As is well-known, this building is situated in Broad Street, and at the recent stone-laying ceremony a stone was laid by Mr. Gentle.

In spite of his weight of years, Mr. Gentle was hale and hearty, erect and energetic, with sight and hearing but very little impaired.

Edward Gentle died on 26th December, 1910, aged 87. Although present at the foundation stone-laying ceremony in July, 1910, sadly, he did not live to witness the opening of the museum in October, 1911.

Below: The exterior of the museum. The carved panels on the exterior represent the work of Jules Tuerlinckx, of Malines, a Belgian refugee, resident in Spalding during the First World War. The carvings are from designs made by E.M.M. Smith (1843-1920), the Society's Honorary (Operator) Curator. These panels consist of the arms of the founder over the library window, and above the entrance door a very elaborate carving based on the Society's book plate. On either side of this are two small panels bearing the monograms "S.G.S.". The three remaining panels bear the words Art, Literature, Science, indicative of the objects for which the Society was founded. The head carved in the roundel over the front door is that of Edward Gentle (1823-1910), a member who contributed largely towards the cost of the building.

Sundial at the Museum

Left: This was formerly on the street wall of the 'Crane Inn', named thus because of the crane on the near-by wharf, evidence of which can still be seen today (now the 'Saxon King'), in Double Street, and was moved from there and erected on the museum in 1913. It was given to the Spalding Gentlemen's Society by Walter Shirley Davy, brewer, of Newark-on-Trent, and owner of the 'Crane' Inn. The letters R.S.P. are the initials of Richard and Peregrina Slater. The date 1702. At that time Richard Slater, a merchant, resided at the 'Crane', which was then a private house. He was churchwarden in 1707, and died 12th September, 1716, aged 80. His wife predeceased him on the 7th of May of the same year.

The Maples Family, of Elmsford House, High Street

Right: Early 1870's. Ashley and Harriet (Stanley) Maples and family at home. (The house, now demolished, together with the grounds covered the site of the present Holland Road car park). Ashley and Harriet Maples are seated in the middle row. On the back row the Revd. William Maples, and on the extreme right Ashley Maples, junior.

Ashley Maples (1806-86), of Spalding, solicitor, was for more than half a century one of the most prominent figures in the public life of the town and district. He served as Clerk of the Spalding Board of Guardians, Superintendent Registrar, member of the Spalding Improvement Board, Town Husband, Feoffee of the Spalding Living, Governor of Moulton Endowed Schools, and Treasurer of the Spalding Gentlemen's Society.

In 1841, with William Crosskill, of Beverley, he purchased the Spalding Gas Works, on the bankruptcy of George Malam, who erected them in 1832. They were sold to the Spalding Improvement Board (the predecessor of the Spalding Urban District Council and the South Holland District Council) in 1863, for £13,700.

He was a staunch churchman of evangelical sympathies. In politics a Conservative - it was said he 'had a great knowledge of the politics of the county, and especially as regards the Southern Division of Lincolnshire, he having led the van in the Tory interest in many a hard-won victory'.

Below: On horseback, Ashley Maples (1837 - 76), of Spalding, solicitor. In partnership with his father. Resided at Stonegate House, Love Lane.

J. Laming & Son,

(ESTABLISHED 1870)

Auctioneers, Valuers,

AND

Estate Agents,

SPALDING.

Members of the Lincolnshire Land Agents' and Tenants' Right Valuers' Association.

Agents for

Lawes' Chemical Manures

AND THE

Imperial Fire and Life Offices, London.

Offices: **SHEEP MARKET, Spalding.**

H. Mitchell & Co.,
6, SHEEP MARKET, SPALDING. . . .

Dealers in

Pianofortes, Organs, Harmoniums,

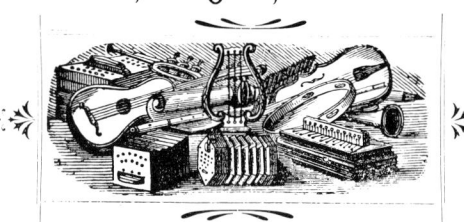

AND ALL OTHER KINDS OF

MUSICAL INSTRUMENTS,

And FITTINGS.

Instruments Let Out on Hire at Moderate Terms, and Tuned in Town and Country.

Bands Supplied for Quadrille and Garden Parties.

MISS MITCHELL, TEACHER OF MUSIC AND SINGING.

. . ESTABLISHED 1857. . .

J. White and Sons, Bakers,

DEALERS IN

Bran, Sharps, Barley Meal, Beans, Peas, Maize, &c.

Holders of the Royalty for the Manufacture and Sale (for Spalding and District) of

Oliver's Patent Brown Bread

The BEST BROWN BREAD in the Town or Neighbourhood. Many Imitations, but No Equals.

HOT TEA CAKES EVERY FRIDAY, or made to order when required.

FANCY CAKES, DOUGH and SEED CAKES, &c.

5 & 6, THE CRESCENT, SPALDING.

BUY

Elsom's Seeds.

Farm Seeds, Vegetable Seeds, and Flower Seeds, Made up in all-sized Packets.

A Large Stock of Peas & Beans.

SPECIAL QUOTATIONS TO MARKET GARDENERS.

Ropes, Sacks, Covers, Lines, Twines, Bags.

SPECIALITIES:

Corn, Meal, Flint, Grit, &c., for Poultry. Mixed Seeds, Sand, &c., for Cage Birds.

Porcelain In-Memoriam Wreaths. Gardeners' Sundries.

Elsom's, 9, Market Place, Spalding.

Transport, Rail and Road

The Opening of the Spalding Railway Station

Random Notes by "Spaldonian", - Joseph Wilson, editor of The Spalding Free Press, 1882-1909.

"It was on the 17th October, 1848, that the first passenger was able to book from Spalding to Peterborough or Boston, on the loop line. The 26th of the same month was observed as a general holiday at Boston and Spalding in honour of the event. Five hundred persons sat down to a grand banquet at Boston; and at a public dinner held at the Spalding Red Lion, Mr. B.A. Mossop (a well-known merchant of that day),occupied the chair, and Mr. G.H. Tatam the vice-chair. There were other festivities, including a balloon which refused to ascend; and there was great excitement in the town and district. How many people are aware of the fact that the line from Peterborough to Lincoln (via Spalding and Boston), was opened some two years before the line from Peterborough to London? It was not until August, 1850, that a passenger could book from Spalding to King's Cross; and then there was only one Parliamentary (third class) train a day, and the journey occupied about five hours....."

Below: Illustration taken from an engraving in "The Illustrated London News", of 11th November, 1848. The station was designed by John Taylor, of Parliament Street, London.

In those early days, the engines were small, the permanent way indifferent, the carriages uncomfortable, the pace rarely exceeding thirty miles an hour, and time tables were by no means an infallible guide....

The first railway station at Spalding was a very modest affair.... House, goods shed, offices and platform were of a very primitive order, and the Spalding residents speedily lodged a complaint with the G.N.R. Company, that the importance of the district demanded something much more imposing. It was some years, however - I believe not until the March line was opened in 1867 - before their appeal received any practical response.

.....Some of my earliest recollections are of the ruddy-faced, good-tempered, and kindly William Glenn, who for so many years and with such single fidelity discharged the duties of signalman and pointsman at the Winsover Road crossing.....He had sole charge of the Winsover Road crossing - gates and signals alike. There was no automatic locking of handgates; and what a "tottering time", the official referred to, had of it in watching trains and working signals on the one hand, whilst on the other he had to open and close gates by hand and give a keen eye to pedestrians, who would persist in crossing the line at dangerous moments.....The point and signal levers were fixed on a platform outside the hut, and in all weathers the hut had to be left to work these levers. Trains were not telegraphed on from box to box, as they are now. The whistle in the distance was the only intimation to the home officials that a train was approaching. Then came the rush to open the big gates by hand, and the scamper back to the cabin platform, to switch the points and lower the signal. It says much for Mr. Glenn's constant vigilance and persistent expostulations that during all his long years' supervision of the notoriously dangerous crossing, never a life was lost there.

The other principal crossing was on the Pinchbeck Road, near the Cemetery,and here our old friend Plowright had charge. The haste with which he frequently had to leave his house to secure his gates from demolition by ordinary or special trains of whose approach he had no intimation except the whistle, told somewhat heavily on a man of such a portly character as he was, but there is no recorded instance of any fatality occurring at this point.

The old Stepping Stone Lane crossing was a somewhat dangerous one, even in those times, and precautions for the safety of the pedestrians were of a primitive order. A gatehouse existed on the town side, but the good lady in charge (Mrs. Paul), was too fully occupied with her household duties to devote any time to looking after the foot-passengers. However, on the great extension of the goods yard, the crossing was superseded by the present bridge, and the house pulled down.....

The first stationmaster I remember at Spalding - and I believe the first who came - was Mr. Fellowes, who vacated that office in order to establish himself as a coal-merchant in the station yard. Then followed, I fancy in the order named, Messrs. Innes, Cooter, Blunt, Marsden, Rayner, Redford, and Mouncey. As Inspectors I recollect Mr. Johnson (who also retired from the railway service to become a coal merchant in the station yard). Mr. Shepherd (who succeeeded his father-in-law as landlord of the Railway Tavern), Mr. Joyce, Mr. Reckitt, and Mr. Spriggs. It was during Mr. Cooter's reign at Spalding station, that a lady, who was a dancing mistress, alleged that she tripped up on a torn carpet in the waiting room and sustained a severe nervous shock, for which she claimed heavy damages against the Railway Company......."

In 1900,Spalding (opposite above) was an important railway junction, the facilities being amongst the best in the county. Omnibuses from the "Red Lion" and the "White Hart" met every train. George William Redford was the stationmaster.

The situation of Spalding in relation to the railway network is described in 'Kelly's Directory of Lincolnshire' for 1900:-

"The Great Northern railway has branch lines from here to Peterborough, Bourne and Stamford, Holbeach and Lynn, and also to March, the East Lincolnshire line giving access to Boston, Louth, Grimsby and Hull. The Great Eastern and Great Northern joint line hence to Doncaster, passes through Sleaford, Lincoln and Gainsborough, giving direct communication between the Eastern Counties and the North. A branch line of the Midland and Great Northern joint railways from Bourne to Spalding, constructed in 1893, connects the existing lines with the Eastern counties, including the ports of Lynn and Sutton Bridge, thus opening up direct communication with the Midlands".

Above: Photograph of the Station c.1900.

Below: Spalding Station Employees and Others. 1901.
Back Row: Tunnard; S. Brighton; Jackson; E. Walker; Palmer; Billiald (W.H. Smith & Son).
Second Row: Shipman; G. Ingham; H. Bosley; T.N. Lewin; R. Brantlett; H. Foreman; Dan Slaughter; W. Cheavins; F. Colam.
Third Row: (seated) H.W. Tippler; George Barnett; George (Dad) Cook; Inspector Rickett; J. Harris (Manager W.H. Smith & Son bookstall).
Front Row: R. Tippler; Syd Swain.

Above: Spalding Station Ambulance Teams. 1906.
Back Row: A. Scupham; R. Dawson; G. Wells; F. Charity; J. Barr; Tom Taylor; J. Clarricoates.
Middle Row: H. Foreman; W. Carr; E. Elliott,jnr; J. Westmoreland; F.H. Impey; George (Dad) Cook; George Barnett; Harry Peck; E. Dolby; Griggs; J.H. Clayton; H.W. Tippler; R. Tippler.
Front Row: J. Avery; W.J. Mouncy (stationmaster); Dr. Douglas; Dr. G.L. Barritt; A. Burgess; F. Bourne; F. Chambers.

Opposite below and above: Sending bloom away from Spalding Station. Pre 1914.

Below: 23rd March, 1916. during the First World War.

    A 77mm. German Field Gun brought to Spalding for exhibition. It had been captured by the 15th Division at Loos on September 25, 1915. Large crowds assembled at the railway station and in the Market Place to see it arrive. The gun - weighing one ton - draped with a Union Jack, and red, white and blue wrappers, was drawn by members of the Spalding Fire Brigade, under the command of Captain J. Bailey, from the station to the centre of the town in front of the Corn Exchange, the procession being headed by the Spalding Silver Prize Band. The gun remained on display in Spalding for a month before being taken to Leek in Staffordshire.

    Below: Some of the members of the staff at Spalding Railway Station with the gun on its arrival at Spalding.

Above and below: Spalding Flower Specials. About 1930. "Flower Specials", left Spalding nightly by both the London and North Eastern and the London, Midland, and Scottish Railways for London, the Midlands, and the North, including Scotland. Tulips and daffodils being sent away in large quantities. The weekly total dispatched during the peak period being about 40,000 boxes.

Motor Meet at the White Hart Hotel

Early 1900's. A motor meet outside the White Hart Hotel. At the time this event took place the present portico over the hotel entrance had not been built. It was erected in 1916.

The landlord, S.R. Harper, is thought to be the bearded figure, wearing a cap, standing between DO 13 and DO 28.

Samuel Robinson Harper (1829 - 1910), was the landlord and proprietor of the White Hart Hotel, from 1875, when he purchased the property from the trustees of George North, until his death.

He was born in the village of Steeton, near Keighley, Yorkshire, on 29th January, 1829, the son of a farmer, and was educated at Keighley. In 1845 he went to Halifax, where he was apprenticed to a grocer, and later conducted a tobacconists business for some 15 years. He was Landlord of the White Hart Hotel, Wisbech, in 1865, and came to Spalding ten years later.

From 1894 to 1902 he represented the Central Ward as a member of the Spalding Urban District Council. He was for many years president of the Spalding and District Licensed Victuallers Association, an institution he was instrumental in establishing. A member of the Hundred of Elloe Lodge of Freemasons, he took an active interest in the Spalding Coursing Club, and the Lincolnshire Skating Association.

He married, in 1853, Elizabeth Woods, of Walpole St. Peters, and they had a family of four sons and four daughters. He died, 2nd February, 1910, aged 81. He left estate of the gross value of £7,037. 17s. 1d.; net personalty, £2,668. 16s. 7d.

Spalding's First Motor Car and First Lady Motorist.

Mrs. Emily Kate Parkinson, wife of Mr. Frank Parkinson, of 3 Havelock Street, at the wheel of her Benz motor car. This was Spalding's first motor car, and arrived in Spalding, on Sunday, 24th February, 1901, being driven from Nottingham by Mrs. Parkinson, who was accompanied by Mr. J. T. Andrews, of the Mill Lane cycle and engineering works, through whom the car was purchased.

She was granted a licence on 16th December, 1903, under the Motor Car Act of that year, for a $3\frac{1}{2}$ h.p. International B Dog Cart, seating four people. It was painted dark blue and picked out in red. The index number being DO 10. This registration was cancelled on 22nd July, 1909.

Frank Parkinson was a gifted amateur photographer. He was born in 1873, the son of William Parkinson, of Spalding, builder. He started work as a bricklayer in his father's business, and when he was first married lived at 3 Havelock Street. In 1910 he moved to Cherry Holt House, Pinchbeck, and became a market gardener and bulb grower. He died in 1956. Frank and Kate Parkinson had two children, Alice, who was born in 1896, and a son, Lennox, who died in infancy.

Motor Cars and Motor Cycles

On 31st January, 1899, "The Spalding Free Press", reported that:

'A motor car passed through Spalding on Friday, on its way from London to Skegness. It had been purchased by a syndicate at Skegness, at a cost of about £400, for the purpose of running trips for visitors and excursionists at that seaside resort. The car stopped for a short time at the Red Lion Hotel, and was quite an object of interest'.

Mr. Arthur Beales, of New Road, built the first motor-cycle in Spalding, in 1901, and rode one of the earliest motor cars seen in the town during Easter of the same year.

On 28th June, 1902, "The Spalding Guardian", noted that:

'Motor cycles are becoming very common in the district, and their "Teuf-Teuf", may frequently be heard in the town. The latest convert to this method of locomotion is Mr. G. W. Plowman, corn-merchant, who is much pleased with his "Excelsior". Mr. R. Cooke, of Decoy Farm, has for some time had a "Werner", and Mr. W. Pollin, clothier, carries large parcels into otherwise inaccessible districts on a "Minerva". Considering that this class of machine has not been really on the market much more than a year, they are marvellously simple, and the only real trouble seems to be with the driving belt, which is greatly affected by changes of weather, and is sometimes liable to slip'.

On 19th August of the same year "The Spalding Free Press" reported that:

'Motor cars in considerable number have passed through Spalding during the past fortnight. Some of the vehicles were of a very expensive type'.

In December, 1903, regulations under the Motor Car Act of that year were issued to the various County and County Borough Councils. For the County of Holland, Boston was to be the place of registration, and for Kesteven, Stamford. The index marks issued for Lincolnshire, were, for Lindsey the letters B.E., for Kesteven, C.T., Holland, D.O., for Lincoln, F.E., and Grimsby, E.C.

Mrs. Parkinson was thought to be the only lady in this district to whom a motor licence was granted under the new Act. Her licence was issued at Boston on 16th December, 1903.

Epilogue

Underneath the stairs
On the top shelf of the cupboard in the spare bedroom
Or in the cupboard beside the fireplace
Is that old shoebox.
This very often holds photographs and information of our past.
If the contents of this box are destroyed, our past is destroyed.
During the making of this book the search for some pictures and information has been unsuccessful.
Take care in what you destroy or people in the future could well lose touch with the past.
We owe it to the generations to come.

Michael Elsden
August 1986

Bibliography

Ambler R. W., ed.	"Lincolnshire Returns of the Census of Religious Worship 1851". Lincoln Record Society. vol. 72. Lincoln. 1979.
Boyes J., and Russel R.	"The Canals of Eastern England". Newton Abbott. 1977
Diggle J. H.	MSS. Spalding Gentlemen's Society.
Free Press Printing & Publishing Co.	"The Free Churches of Spalding &c" Spalding 1902. "Spalding and its Churches". Spalding. 1902.
Gooch E. H.	"A History of Spalding". Spalding. 1940.
Harmstone R.	"Notices of Remarkable Events and Curious Facts, with various and entertaining scraps, connected with the History and Antiquities of Spalding, in the County of Lincoln, and places adjacent. Collected and treasured in memory By "Old Robin Harmstone". Spalding. 1846. 2nd. edn. 1848.
Kelly's Directory of Lincolnshire.	London. 1st edn. 1885; 4th edn. 1896.
Lincolnshire, Boston and Spalding Free Press	
Lincolnshire Magazine and the Provincial Literary Repository.	-2 vols. Spalding. 1801 - 1802. The second volume issued under the title of 'The Provincial Literary Repository' only.
Lincolnshire Magazine.	4 vols. 1932 - 1939.
Lincolnshire Notes and Queries.	
Lincolnshire, Rutland and Stamford Mercury.	
Owen D. M. ed.	"The Minute Books of the Spalding Gentlemen's Society 1712 - 1755". Lincoln Record Society. vol. 73. Lincoln. 1981.
Pevsner N. and Harris J.	"The Buildings of England - Lincolnshire". London. 1964
Post Office Directory of Lincolnshire.	London 3rd edn. 1861; 4th edn. 1868; 5th edn. 1876.
South Holland Magazine.	vols 1 - 3. Spalding. 1869 - 71
Spalding Monthly Magazine.	Spalding 1866 - 67.
Spalding Guardian	
Watkinson A. J.	"A Short History of the Spalding Baptist Church 1646 - 1946". Spalding. 2nd edn. 1972.
White W.	Directory of Lincolnshire. Sheffield. 1st edn. 1842; 2nd edn. 1856; 3rd edn. 1872; 5th edn. 1892.
Wright N.	"Spalding - An Industrial History". Lincoln. 1973. 2nd edn. 1975.

Index

Abbey Buildings	46-7
Agricultural Show	109
Air Raids	70
Albion Brewery	21
American House	25
Ash Rev.R.G.	127-8
Ayscoughfee	35-8, 69
Baptists	17, 45, 131-5
Belvedere	45
Birch G.F.	26, 37, 110
Booth General William	143, 148-9, 150
Brick Making	107
Bulb Industry	98-9, 185-6
Burn Rev.H.	153-4
Burrell P.G. & Son	97
Butter Market	90-1
Catholics	128-9, 130
Cattle Market	16, 83-6
Chain Bridge	16, 22
Charinton Miss C.	118, 126-7
Charnwood	134-5
Christadelphians	154
Cinemas	41, 63
Constitutional Club	86
Corn Exchange	67, 75, 78, 90
Coronation Celebrations	160-2
Donington J.	140
Donington R.	140
Drill Hall	61-2, 64, 167
Fairs	87, 89
Fletcher W.	37, 102-3, 162
Folley The	17
Fountain The	68-9, 70
Free Church of England	130-1
Free Press	92-6, 134
Gas Works	26-7
Gentle Edward	175-7
Gentlemen's Society	174-8
Goodfellows School	32, 118
Grammar School	48, 50-6
Hall George	37, 85, 135-6, 168-9
Hall Place	67-9, 70-4, 109
Hallam & Blackbourn	104-5
Haverfield House	40-1
Hawley John	136-7
High Bridge	18-9, 20-1
Hobson Alfred	40-1, 68
Hobson's Fire	79, 80
Holyrood House	39, 40
Horse Fair	87
Jackson Capt.S	17
Johnson's Bakehouse	107
Jones Rev.J.C.	16, 93, 99, 131-5
Kingston's Corner	74, 85, 161
Kingston S.	29, 37, 107

Leverton H. & Co.	61-2
Library	37
Lincolnshire Regiment	163-6
Little London Bridge	28-9, 30-1
Locks Mill	32-3
Longbottom George	141
Lutyens Sir Edwin	36
Maples Family	16, 26, 175, 178-9
Markets	89, 90-1
Market Place	75-9, 80-1, 109
May Hirings	82
McLaren F.W.S.	36, 171-3
Memorial Service King Edward VII	161
Moore Rev.A.W.G.	124-5
Moore Rev. Can. E.	50-1, 64, 92, 115, 118-9, 123-4, 126-7
Motor Vehicles	62, 187-9
Mowbray Joseph	100
Myers F.	62
Methodists	138-9, 140-5, 148, 150
National Provincial Bank	105
New Road	83-6
Owl Tower	36
Pannell's Boat Yard	15, 22-3
Parish Church	113-9, 120
Particular Baptists	137-8
Patriotic Concert	146-7
Penningtons	70, 72
Pinchbeck Road	87
Prior's Oven	65-6
Prison	59, 60, 138
Quakers	16-7, 43, 135-7
Railways	16, 23, 112, 181-6
Roadmen	49
Royal Oak Inn	45
St. John Baptist Church	124-5
St. Paul's Church, Fulney	127-8
St. Peter's Church	126
Sessions House	64-5
Shadford Major	144, 150
Sheep Market	64
Silver Prize Band	171
Skinner T.J.	141
Special Constables	170
Spread Eagle Inn	151
Star Public House	48
Stead Rev.J.T.	142
Sunday School Festivals	155-9
Thatching	46-7
Town Hall	67
Townsend T.W.	39
Tradesmens' Excursion	112
United Reformed Church	152-4
Victoria Bridge	34

Volunteers	167
Walden & Son	100-1
War First World	36, 146-7, 170, 172-3, 185
War Memorials	36, 53
Watkinson Henry	92-3
Welland Hall	43-5
White Hart Hotel	81, 187

White Horse Inn	42-3
White J.T.	37, 45, 98-9, 135, 160
Willesby School	43, 57-8
Wilson J.	37, 93, 144, 148-9, 150, 181-2
Wykeham Chapel	120-4
Yates Rev.S.	86, 153
Young T.A.	128-9

Below: The Parish Church, Holyrood House, and Ayscoughfee Hall, as they would have appeared for most of the period that this book covers.

M. DALTON & SON,
Furniture Dealers,

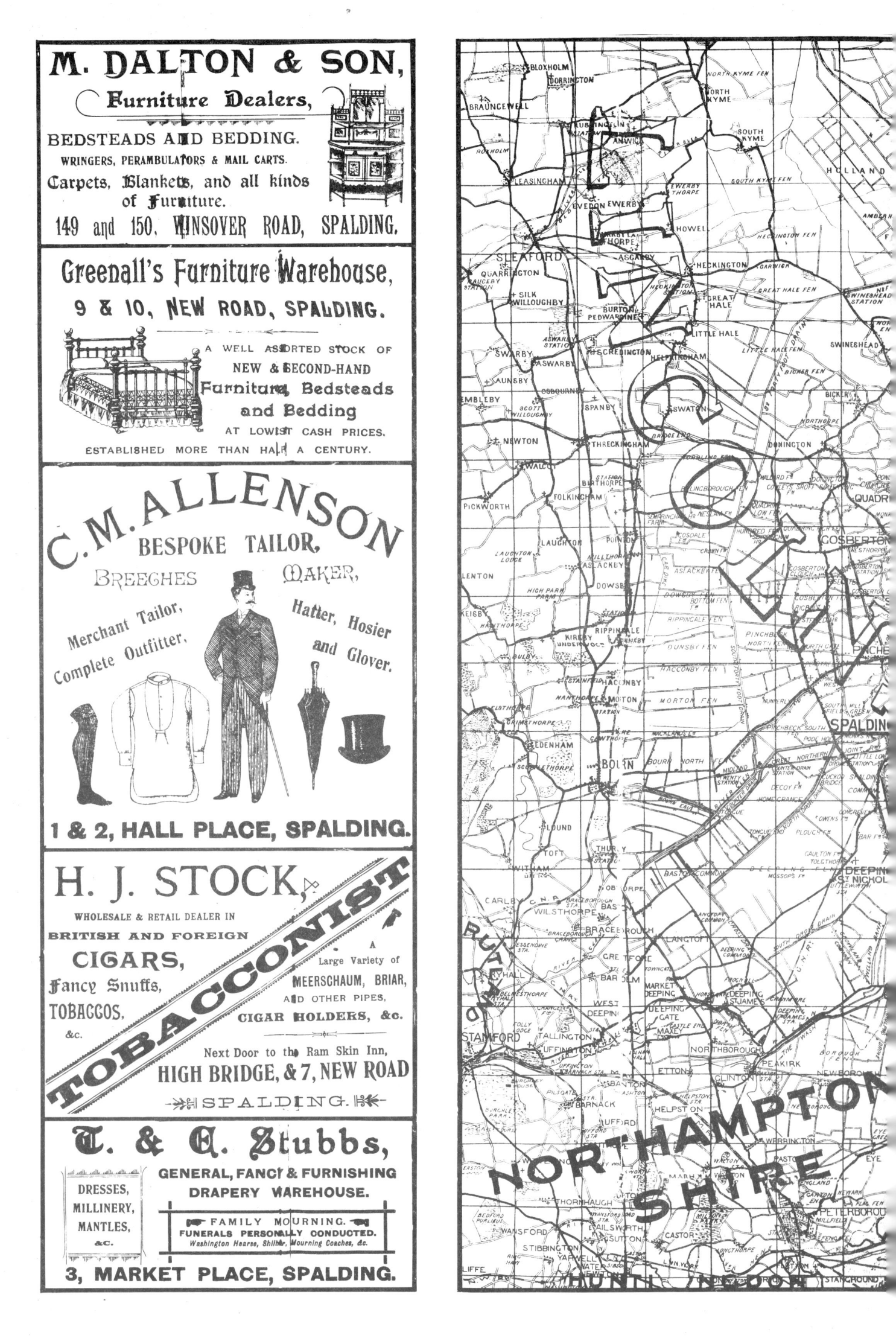

BEDSTEADS AND BEDDING.

WRINGERS, PERAMBULATORS & MAIL CARTS.

Carpets, Blankets, and all kinds of Furniture.

149 and 150, WINSOVER ROAD, SPALDING.

Greenall's Furniture Warehouse,
9 & 10, NEW ROAD, SPALDING.

A WELL ASSORTED STOCK OF NEW & SECOND-HAND

Furniture, Bedsteads and Bedding

AT LOWEST CASH PRICES.

ESTABLISHED MORE THAN HALF A CENTURY.

C. M. ALLENSON
BESPOKE TAILOR, BREECHES MAKER,

Merchant Tailor, Complete Outfitter,

Hatter, Hosier and Glover.

1 & 2, HALL PLACE, SPALDING.

H. J. STOCK,
WHOLESALE & RETAIL DEALER IN
BRITISH AND FOREIGN
CIGARS,

Fancy Snuffs, TOBACCOS, &c.

A Large Variety of MEERSCHAUM, BRIAR, AND OTHER PIPES, CIGAR HOLDERS, &c.

TOBACCONIST

Next Door to the Ram Skin Inn,

HIGH BRIDGE, & 7, NEW ROAD

SPALDING.

T. & E. Stubbs,

DRESSES, MILLINERY, MANTLES, &c.

GENERAL, FANCY & FURNISHING DRAPERY WAREHOUSE.

FAMILY MOURNING.
FUNERALS PERSONALLY CONDUCTED.
Washington Hearse, Shillibeer, Mourning Coaches, &c.

3, MARKET PLACE, SPALDING.